Myths at Work

Myths at Work

Harriet Bradley, Mark Erickson,
Carol Stephenson and
Steve Williams

Polity

First published in 2000 by Polity Press in association with Blackwell Publishers Ltd

Editorial office:
Polity Press
65 Bridge Street
Cambridge CB2 1UR, UK

Marketing and production:
Blackwell Publishers Ltd
108 Cowley Road
Oxford OX4 1JF, UK

Published in the USA by
Blackwell Publishers Inc.
350 Main Street
Malden, MA 02148, USA

ISBN 0-7456-2270-4
ISBN 0-7456-2271-2 (pbk)

A catalogue record for this book is available from the British Library.

Library of Congress Cataloging-in-Publication Data

Myths at work / by Harriet Bradley . . . [et al.].
p. cm.
Includes bibliographical references.
ISBN 0-7456-2270-4 (alk. paper) – ISBN 0-7456-2271-2 (pbk. : alk. paper)
1. Industrial sociology. 2. Organizational change. 3. Working class.
I. Bradley, Harriet.

HD6955.M98 2000
306.3′6 – dc21

00-032662

Typeset in 10½ on 12 pt Times
by Best-set Typesetter Ltd., Hong Kong
Printed in Great Britain by MPG Books Ltd, Bodmin, Cornwall

This book is printed on acid-free paper.

Contents

Acknowledgements

In *Myths at Work* we argue that a number of myths have developed about the changing workplace. To a large extent this has happened because some researchers have sought to ignore the complexities of the work environment, its context and, crucially, the people involved in work. By contrast, *Myths at Work* draws upon a number of pieces of research, which would not have been possible but for the co-operation, time and commitment of many workers, managers, trade unionists, researchers and policy-makers. We cannot mention all these people by name, but we wish to express our gratitude to all those who have assisted us in this venture. In particular we should like to thank Paul Stewart, Steven Tait and Derek Winter for their support and advice.

In addition, we wish to acknowledge the support of bodies, which funded the research, which is presented here. Part of the material presented in chapter 6 is based on research which was funded by the Open University's centre for Education Policy and Management and the Economic and Social Research Council (grant no. 000237007). Harriet Bradley's research on gender differentiation in trade unions, reported in chapters 4 and 7, was also supported by an ESRC grant (R000234124) and a term's research leave from Sunderland University.

Our respective institutions also deserve thanks, as they provided research leave and/or provided financial support, and in doing so facilitated the editing and preparation of the manuscript. These are the Department of Business and Management, University of Portsmouth, the School of Humanities and Social Sciences at the University of Sunderland, the Department of Sociology at the

University of Bristol and the Department of Cultural Studies and Sociology at the University of Birmingham.

Last, but certainly not least, we wish to thank our friends and families who have supported us throughout this endeavour and put up patiently with the demands it made on our time.

Abbreviations

A Level	Advanced Level
AEEU	Amalgamated Engineering and Electrical Union
AFL–CIO	American Federation of Labor–Congress of Industrial Organizations
ATL	Association of Teachers and Lecturers
AUT	Association of University Teachers
BAe	British Aerospace
BBC	British Broadcasting Corporation
BIFU	Banking Insurance and Finance Union
BPR	British Process Re-engineering
BTEC	Business and Technical Education Council
CBI	Confederation of British Industry
CCTV	closed-circuit television
CEF	College Employers Forum
CNC	Computerized Numerical Control
DE	Department of Employment
DES	Department of Education and Science
DfE	Department for Education
DfEE	Department for Education and Employment
DTI	Department of Trade and Industry
EETPU	Electrical Electronic Telecommunications and Plumbing Union
ELS	Education Lecturing Services
FDI	foreign direct investment
FE	further education
GCSE	General Certificate of Secondary Education
GHS	General Household Survey

GNP	gross national product
GNVQ	General National Vocational Qualification
HE	higher education
HEFCE	Higher Education Funding Council
HR	Human Resources
HRM	Human Resource Management
ILO	International Labour Organization
IIP	Investors in People
IT	Information Technology
JIC	just in case
JIT	just in time
LFS	Labour Force Survey
LPH	Landing Platform Helicopter
LRD	Labour Research Department
MBA	Masters in Business Administration
MBS	management by stress
MIT	Massachusetts Institute of Technology
MNC	multinational corporation
MoD	Ministry of Defence
MP	Member of Parliament
MSC	Manpower Services Commission
MSF	Manufacturing Science and Finance
NAO	National Audit Office
NATFHE	National Association of Teachers in Further and Higher Education
NCVQ	National Council for Vocational Qualifications
NEDC	National Economic Development Council
NETTs	National Education and Training Targets
NHS	National Health Service
NIDL	new international division of labour
NSM	new social movement
NUMMI	New United Motor Manufacturers Incorporated
NVQ	National Vocational Qualification
OECD	Organization for Economic Co-operation and Development
ORF	output-related funding
PRP	performance-related pay
QCA	Qualifications and Curriculum Authority
QUANGO	quasi-autonomous non-governmental organization
RO	Royal Ordnance
RSA	Royal Society of Arts
RSI	repetitive strain injury
SCELI	Social Change and Economic Life Initiative

SCOTVEC	Scottish Vocational Education Council
SEC	social economic categories
SEIU	Service Employees' International Union
SVQ	Scottish Vocational Qualification
TEC	Training and Enterprise Council
TGWU	Transport and General Workers Union
TNC	transnational corporation
TQM	Total Quality Management
TUC	Trades Union Congress
UAW	United Auto Workers
UN	United Nations
WERS	Workplace Employment Relations Survey
WIRS	Workplace Industrial Relations Survey
WTD	Working Time Directive
WTO	World Trade Organization
WYHU	West Yorkshire Homeworking Unit
YTS	Youth Training Scheme

Introduction: Myths at Work

This book is about change at work and the frameworks that are being used to explain it. Some of these frameworks which are promoted by influential people and are widespread in popular belief we label 'myths'. The purpose of the book is to explore critically and to challenge some of these core myths.

There is a general agreement that during the last two decades there have been profound changes in the organization of work. Processes of economic restructuring, occurring on a global scale, have brought about changes for all of us in the jobs we do, our labour market opportunities and the shape of our individual career paths. Such changes may be analysed in terms of globalization; of the change to a post-industrial society; a shift from Fordist to post-Fordist production methods; or a move in Western societies to a new consumer-based form of capitalism. A new international division of labour (NIDL) is discerned in which manufacturing processes are characteristically sited in developing countries where unskilled labour is plentiful and cheap, while the more developed societies of the West become specialists in services, research and design, requiring a highly skilled technical and professional workforce. These developments are changing the way we work and the way we live.

In this book we offer a critical account of these changes. In developing this critique we use the concept of 'myth' in two senses. First, by 'myths' we refer to widely believed bodies of ideas about the way work is changing. These ideas are held by entrepreneurs, managers, politicians and policy-makers; they have been explored and developed by many academics, especially in management and business studies and in economics. They are spread and popularized by the mass media, and are taken up by many members of the public. For example, a matter of particular current concern in Britain is the notion of the *feminization* of work, the replacement of male workers by women, and the adverse consequences of that change for men. Stories about boys' relatively poor performance in schools and men's labour market disadvantage are common in the British press, while politicians and educationists are already devising policies to set things right. Feminization is one of the myths explored critically in our book.

But the word 'myth' in its standard usage has a deeper meaning: it goes beyond mere description to explanation; not just *how* things are changing but *why* they are changing. Myths by this definition are ways that people in specific cultural contexts make sense of the worlds they inhabit and account for prevailing patterns of social interaction. Thus the notion of *globalization*, one of the central myths discussed in this book, is used to explain many aspects of change at work: the rise of part-time jobs, the decline of manufacturing in Western societies, and, indeed, feminization.

From what has been said so far it should be grasped that the notion of myth, as we employ it in this book, is not quite the same as the commonly used distinction between 'rhetoric' and 'reality' as employed, for example, by Noon and Blyton (1997) in their very useful book on workplace relations, *The Realities of Work*, or in other texts critical of managerialism. This implies a difference between *what is really happening* and what managers and politicians *say is happening*. Although we make similar criticisms of management rhetoric at points in the book, we are using the idea of myth in a rather different way. We do not use myth as synonymous with 'false', nor do we necessarily imply a hard distinction between 'truth' and 'falsehood'. Instead in the chapters that follow we are concerned to 'unpick' and deconstruct the myths to show which aspects of them have credibility and which do not. To do this we draw on our own research fieldwork, which was carried out in the North East of England, and on other evidence from international research studies which probes beneath the surface of workplace change. Our argument is not so much that myths are deliberately used to mask reality, as that particular versions of reality have more 'sticking-power' than others and so become popularly accepted. Such explanations of social change are often one-sided and misleading. Our aim is to air alternative versions about what is happening at work.

Indeed, our title *Myths at Work* involves another set of double meanings. The phrase indicates that we are exploring myths about work which are developed and used *within work organizations*. But the myths are also actively 'at work' in that *they influence future devel-*

opments within the organization. This is because they are so widely believed that people use them as the basis for actions and decision-making. In particular, a wide range of professionals are involved in developing policies based on these myths: management consultants, businessmen and their representatives, individual managers, personnel departments, educators, training agencies, local councillors, civil servants, government ministers, even trade union officials; the list could be extended. Myths inform strategic choices made within workplaces, which then affect the lives of all within them. American commentators Nelson and Smith describe the process as follows: 'Whether they have options or not, employers *believe* that they need to move towards flexible employment structures to meet the exigencies of globalization and deregulation. Employees . . . are subjected to the strategies (e.g. downsizing, subcontracting) that result from these beliefs of employers' (1999: 17, our italics).

Our analysis here bears some resemblance to Michel Foucault's accounts of strategies of power and governmentality; ideas (or discourses) promoted by various interested professional groupings are the basis of 'regimes of power' or 'technologies of the self'. These constitute an array of disciplinary practices and procedures designed to turn society's members into 'docile bodies', to make them conform. Where we depart from common Foucaultian arguments is that we do not see the myths or 'discourses' as necessarily forming the base of 'subject positions' (ways of constructing social identities) for those who are their targets. On the contrary, we shall aim to show that working people have their own agendas and often construct selves in ways quite different from the intentions of their superordinates. One major concern in this book is to counterpose the voices of those at the receiving end of processes of change to those who initiate the changes. Another concern is to suggest what sociological approaches are most useful in understanding processes of change.

Management and the Study of Work

Two developments have contributed significantly to the formation of the body of myths about work explored in this book. The first of these is the increasing tendency for the study of work relationships to be framed by concepts employed by managers (such as flexibility, empowerment, performance management). Nigel Thrift (1999) shows how what he sees as a new culture of management has been strongly influenced by the work of academics. He describes an increasingly close alliance developing between academics in business and management schools and those responsible for running organizations: note, for example, the increasing numbers of MBAs (Masters in Business Administration) on offer.[1] Such courses are of growing popularity among undergraduate students as well. This tendency has favoured the promotion of accounts of work which are 'top-down', or based on management views. As a result the rich heritage of workplace studies from both Britain and America is in danger of being marginalized.[2]

Such a link between business interests and the development of the study of work and industry is not new. There is a strong tradition of industrial sociologists and psychologists working as 'Servants of Power' in Baritz's evocative phrase (1965). This is hardly surprising, given that academics and researchers are frequently paid by the state, its agencies or business-financed corporations (such as Nuffield and Leverhulme in Britain, Carnegie and Rockefeller in the USA, Volkswagen in Germany). Inevitably, there is pressure to be 'accountable' to the paymasters and to produce work that is 'relevant' and 'useful' in their terms. But this has coexisted with a long-standing tradition of critical study of work relations, which has its roots in classical sociology and is enabled by the countervailing ethos of 'academic freedom' and the ideal of social science as 'objective' and 'interest-free'. This radical strand was fostered by Marxism in Britain and in the USA by the 'Chicago school', which endorsed the study of 'outsider' groups. Peter Berger (1963) saw the function of sociology as revealing the true social relationships beneath the conventional surface, while Howard Becker (1970) announced that there never was a good sociological study which failed to upset somebody. This tension between the functions of serving the status quo and of radical critique, which is present in all social science, reaches its height in the sociology of work, whose core topic is the social relations of capitalism. Should its aim be to help capitalists to make the system work better or to challenge the parameters of that system?

Analysis of work organization and relationships was central to the evolution of sociology as an academic discipline: it was a key concern of the initiator social theorists (Auguste Comte, Adam Smith, J. S. Mill, Karl Marx, Emile Durkheim, Max Weber). Marx in particular brought to social thought the tradition of critical analysis of capitalist work relations, including the key concepts of 'class conflict' and 'alienation'. Even those who disagreed with Marx tended to consider work relations in the light of his critique. For example, Weber focused on competition and conflict *within* the non-propertied class, rather than the central conflict of interests between capital and wage labour which Marx saw as the driving force of history, while Durkheim's concept of anomie can be seen as a reworking of the notion of alienation, but focusing on moral integration rather than power. So the legacy of classical theory was to consider work as a locus of conflict and disharmony, and this view can be seen as a contribution to the radical tradition.[3]

When the distinct sub-discipline of industrial sociology developed in the early twentieth century, conflict was still a key theme. But as Michael Rose (1975) shows in his excellent account of the history of industrial sociology, the impetus here was to help management to find ways of handling discontent and conflict. Drawing on some of Durkheim's ideas in particular, industrial sociologists and psychologists such as Elton Mayo, Alan Fox, A. H. Maslow and Chris Argyris explored the roots of workers' attitudes and behaviour and suggested ways in which managers could integrate employees into the organization and secure their consent and loyalty. This kind of approach is still typical of the disciplines of management studies and organizational behaviour, their key concerns being conflict management, increasing efficiency and performance, and effective leadership styles. The current school of 'Human Resource Management' (HRM) is the direct inheritor of the earlier approaches such as 'Human Relations' which developed in the 1920s, 1930s and 1940s.[4]

As we indicated above, a counter to this approach came from other sociologists of work who picked up themes from the classic theories. For example, the *Affluent Worker* studies carried out by Goldthorpe et al. (1969) drew on Weberian theory in an exploration of the meanings of work in employees' lives, using it to challenge the work of management-orientated industrial sociologists: a concern with workers' orientations replaced an interest in management policies. But perhaps the prime spur to radical analysis of work was Harry Braverman's *Labor and Monopoly Capital* (1974), which reinstated Marx's theories of capitalist development and alienation as central to the study of work. Braverman believed that change in the technical and social organization of work, the capitalist 'labour process', was driven by the attempts of managers to tighten control over their employees' labour. The 'labour process debate' generated by Braverman's book involved critical responses to his arguments about employer strategies of degradation of jobs, consequent decay of craft skills and the loss of control and autonomy among working people. It also inspired a wealth of studies of specific industries and organizations, exploring different modes of labour process development. These Marx-influenced workplace studies supplemented earlier research which had explored processes of class conflict and accommodation (such as Beynon 1984; Gouldner 1965; Nichols and Beynon 1977). In addition, the second-wave feminist movement in academia in the late 1970s and 1980s inspired a number of classic studies of women workers. Feminist sociologists were concerned to investigate the relation between capitalism and patriarchy, class and gender consciousness within the workplace (for example, Cavendish 1982; Pollert 1981; Westwood 1984).

However, the collapse of Western academic Marxism after the break-up of the Soviet empire, together with a shift of emphasis in feminism away from economic aspects of gender disadvantage to cultural issues, such as sexuality, the body and representation, have led to a gradual drying-up of these workplace studies in the radical tradition.[5] This created a vacuum which was increasingly filled by work from HRM practitioners and management studies. For example, the research of Womack et al. (1990) triggered academic and managerial interest in the idea of 'lean production'; Peter Wickens (1987) extolled the virtues of Japanization, while Atkinson and Meager's (1986b) account of the 'flexible firm' generated an immense discussion on the virtues of flexibility. While academics continue to reflect critically on all these issues, nevertheless the agenda is increasingly set by management concerns. Interviews with managers, together with analysis of management documents and of management policies and procedures, have become the prevalent methods of investigation, while studies involving interviews with workers are becoming few and far between (Thompson and Ackroyd 1995). Even in the critical feminist tradition, workplace studies of women at the top of the hierarchy have largely taken the place of the old studies of female factory workers, for example Judi Marshall's (1995) and Judy Wajcman's (1998) studies of women managers or Linda McDowell's work on women in the finance sector (1997).

Poststructural Tendencies

A second factor involved in this tendency to offer 'top-down' accounts has been the growing influence of postmodern and poststructural theory within the study of work and organizations. Postmodernists dismiss the work of modernist theorists, such as Marx or Durkheim, who have offered 'grand narratives' of the historical developments of work organization and social arrangements. Viewing such theories as fictive impositions on a disorderly and random reality, they call for small-scale studies of specific situations. Theories of class and conflict in particular are viewed with scepticism by many postmodernists, who have announced 'the death of class' which we discuss as an important myth in chapter 7. Poststructuralists also reject modernist thinking and substitute for a classic sociological interest in material inequalities a concern with language, which they see as constitutive of social relations, and with the 'deconstruction' of linguistic categories they consider oppressive. Poststructuralist adoption of the ideas of Michel Foucault, in particular, has encouraged the use of discourse analysis. This fosters an interest in managerialism and its characteristic linguistic practices.

Two influential texts which exemplify these latter tendencies are Paul du Gay's *Consumption and Identity at Work* (1996) and Catherine Casey's *Work, Self and Society* (1995). Although in these excellent and interesting studies both Du Gay and Casey interviewed working people, they did so in the context of managerial discourses which they see as operating to reconstruct the self-identities of working people. Du Gay looked at the retail industry and the promotion of entrepreneurial values among its employees; and also discusses the way that public-sector organizations have been 'reimagined as enterprises' (p. 181). As a result, he suggests, public-sector employees, too, are being refashioned as entrepreneurial selves. Casey uses a similar approach in her study of Hephaestus, a large American corporation: tactics of marginalizing trade unions and inducing a sense of commitment to the corporation by employing discourses about team-work and the corporate family are designed to reconstruct the selves of the employees, causing them to abandon their old collective affiliations in favour of a new individualism. While many of Du Gay and Casey's arguments are interesting and convincing, there is an assumption that work identities are formed by people's adopting 'subject positions' within managerial discourses. Thus the managerialist agenda is seen to frame workplace arrangements and workers' behaviour and attitudes. Such sophisticated poststructural accounts serve to reinforce the 'top-down' approach which commences analysis by listening to managerial voices. Curiously, considering the stress put by both poststructuralists and postmodernists on diversity and the plurality of voices, the views of workers – especially those at the very bottom of the hierarchy – tend to be absent from these kind of accounts.[6]

As Skeggs (1997) argues, this tendency to focus on the accounts offered by the more powerful and privileged elements in society, and to use them as the basis for construction of sociological theorizing and generalization, has led to a gradual silencing of less powerful groups. Nelson and Smith, in their exploration of how working-class people in America are 'making do' in a climate of increasing job insecurity, note that one 'hears little from workers themselves' (1999: 180). Class, thus, plays a generally diminishing role in the sociological agenda. Thompson and Ackroyd (1995) show more specifically how within the sociology of work and organization such processes have led to a misleading sense that 'all is quiet on the workplace front': with a consequent neglect of worker resistance and a false assumption of compliance with managerial objectives; they state: 'As industrial sociologists, we have to put labour back in, by doing theory and research in such a way that it is possible to "see" resistance and misbehaviour and recognize that innovatory employee practices and informal organization will continue to subvert managerial regimes' (1995: 629).

Unpicking the Myths

Redressing the balance and recapturing the alternative views of those with less powerful voices is one of the key objectives of this book. This is accomplished through examination of some influential myths, unpicking them and revealing what is one-sided and misleading within them. Our objective is to present a more rounded and convincing picture of workplace change.

Each of the next nine chapters deal with one of nine selected myths. We start by setting out the myth and the work of some of its key proponents. Then we offer a critical slant on the myth by examining research evidence which challenges some key aspects. In doing this, we want to emphasize the importance of the case study as a method of exploring processes of change. While survey research which generates large data sets, such as WIRS (Workplace Industrial Relations Surveys) and SCELI (Social Change and Economic Life Initiative), is extremely important and useful, aggregated data often gloss over the intricacies and complexities of change; while the snapshot nature of such survey work has limitations for revealing exactly how processes of change operate over time.

We illustrate our arguments by drawing on our own research, which was carried out in the North East region of Britain around the towns of Newcastle and Sunderland. It took the form of case study research and interviews. Harriet Bradley conducted 198 interviews with employees, and others with managers and trade union representatives, in five different organizations: a superstore, a bank, a chemicals factory, a Civil Service agency and a hospital trust. The focus of the interviews was workplace change, gender and union membership. Mark Erickson conducted research into the defence industries, focusing on Swan Hunter Shipbuilders, Wallsend – a naval shipyard where the core business was construction and refitting of Royal Navy warships – and the Royal Ordnance factory, Birtley, an ammunition components plant. At both sites he interviewed staff at all grades: management, shop floor and ancillary. Carol Stephenson worked with Phil Garrahan and Paul Stewart on their study of Nissan UK as an example of the methods of 'lean production' in the context of regional decline and unemployment. Subsequently she researched relationships between Nissan and their suppliers, such as Ikeda Hoover, exploring strategies designed to promote flexibility and uncovering workers' resistance to change. Steve Williams studied the fortunes of the trade unions in the region; he interviewed national and local union officers, shop stewards and members in an attempt to show how unions were responding to the threat of membership decline, and in the face of a posited decay of collective values.

Our research helped us to place current changes in a longer perspective of regional development; it revealed how changes are experienced and perceived by the less powerful. We draw on our interview material throughout the book; but since our research was confined to one very distinctive region of the United Kingdom we also refer to other workplace studies from Britain, America, Europe and elsewhere in our investigations of 'myths at work'. While some developments are specific to nation and region, the processes we explore are common to all advanced industrial economies.

The Myths at Work

Some of the myths we discuss in the book could be described as 'meta-myths', by analogy with the poststructuralist term 'meta-narratives'.[7] A meta-myth is a grand and overarching notion used to explain broad processes of historical change. Globalization, discussed in chapter 1, is one such meta-myth. The change to a global economy is used to account for many changes in production and work organization. In Richard Rorty's words, 'what industrialization was to America at the end of the nineteenth century, globalization is at the end of the twentieth' (1998: 84). As we shall argue, globalization is often used as excuse by managers for imposing cuts and changes on their employees.

One of these changes is what Americans call 'downsizing', the dismissing of workers who are seen to consitute 'slack' in the production system, in order to make the organization 'leaner and meaner'. Lean production is one of a number of economic processes explicitly linked by managers to globalization which are discussed in chapters 2 to 4. Chapter 2 considers the view of lean production as the 'one best way' to achieve profitability in the global economy. Lean production is often linked to 'flexibility', which is seen as a necessity if firms are to compete and survive in the current climate. One way of achieving flexibility is by the deployment of various forms of 'non-standard labour', such as the use of part-time and temporary workers. In chapter 3 we consider the proposition that non-standard work is advantageous to many workers, especially married women. This in turn is linked to the feminization of work, the topic of chapter 4.

Chapter 5 introduces another important and influential meta-myth: the notion of the triumph of science and technology. Economic progress has long been viewed in terms of the increasingly systematic application of 'rational scientific methods' to production. Such a notion of scientific rationality was central to Weber's account of the development of capitalism. In recent decades, the focus has especially been on the application of microtechnology and computers within workplaces. These innovations are seen as steadily and irresistibly transforming our working lives. We challenge the idea that such developments are inevitable and always beneficial. Closely linked to this idea of the 'technological fix' is the prevalent notion that some Western societies suffer from a 'skills shortage', a lack of suitably trained technical workers; this is investigated in chapter 6.

Our last package of myths does not deal with the techniques and organization of production but the social relations which surround them. A controversial meta-myth is the notion of the 'death of class', which is the subject of chapter 7. There are various strands to this myth, all of which are important in terms of understanding how current societies operate. One is the idea that work is no longer central to people's lives. Another is the claim that we live in a 'classless society'; an alternative view is that class no longer means much in people's lives and so is not the base of political attitudes and action. This leads us to explore in chapter 8 the related issue of trade union decline: unions have traditionally been seen as vehicles of class consciousness and class interests which are now seen by some as outmoded. Is there no longer a need for trade unions in the 'flexible future'? Finally, chapter 9 deals with a myth that is far from new but remains extremely influential: the idea that people work only out of economic motivations. This myth legitimates the award of mammoth salaries to top managers and professionals, who, it is said, will leave their firms if they are not adequately recompensed for their talents; it was a powerful part of the 'fat cat culture' of the 'New Right' years in North America and Europe. Our exploration of the myth does not dispute the importance of economic rewards, but suggests that work plays a much more complex part in our life than the mere receipt of a weekly or monthly pay packet.

Chapter 9 is also used to introduce some of the critical perspectives on work currently on offer, drawing on ideas derived from Marx, Habermas and Foucault. Theory is discussed again in our concluding chapter, which sketches out what we see as the necessities for a better-informed sociology of work: a return to detailed exploration of workplace relations, involving case studies and interviews with employees as well as with employers; an awareness that economic choices are not made in a vacuum but in specific political contexts; a critical attitude to deterministic accounts; and the development of a radical framework for analysing the workplace which still draws on some of Marx's insights but can also grapple with the complexities of social relations as they evolve in the twenty-first century.

Conclusion

In this chapter we have set out our argument that current changes in the workplace are apprehended and explained in terms of a widely believed set of ideas, which we have called 'myths'. Our view is that these myths emanate largely from a managerial perspective on change, which has also been endorsed by successive governments, Conservative and Labour. Although we are not claiming that these myths are entirely 'false', we *have* suggested that they misrepresent processes of change because the perspective they offer is one-sided and partial. Specifically, change is viewed from a 'top-down' perspective. We have discerned two important influences on the formation of these myths: first, the growing dominance in the sociology of work and organizations of practitioners of HRM and business studies and an accompanying neglect of radical workplace case studies, partly as a result of the crisis of Marxist theory, partly because of the practical difficulties of carrying out research involving interviews with employees.[8] Secondly the more general influence of post-structuralist thinking in social science diverts attention from material inequalities and analysis of structural divisions in society.

In subsequent chapters we explore the selected myths, employing a critical perspective which offers a more balanced and nuanced picture of how change is occurring. Finally, in the Conclusion we offer our own theoretical perspective on change. To develop a complete and adequate explanation of developments at work in all their complexity is, we believe, a crucial task for social scientists. For our own lives, and those of our children, will be vitally affected by these changes.

1

The Myth of Globalization

> In practice, companies of all shapes and sizes throughout the world accept the globalization of business and economics as a fact of life. They are not debating its existence; they are responding to its effects.
>
> (Fitzgerald 1997: 739)

Introduction

The above quotation, extracted from an article written by Niall Fitzgerald, a senior executive with the Unilever corporation, highlights the degree to which 'globalization' has recently come to attract popular attention. For Waters (1995) it 'may be *the* concept of the 1990s, a key idea by which we understand the transition of human society into the third millennium' (p. 1). Some idea of the extent to which the notion of 'globalization' has captured the interest of the academic community is evident in the growth in the number of books being published about the subject. On 29 June 1999 a search of the catalogue of Internet booksellers Amazon revealed the existence of 290 books in print with 'globalization' somewhere in their titles, including such diverse works as *The Development of West Indian Cricket*, vol. 2: *The Age of Globalization*, *The Globalization of News* and *Korean Enterprise: the quest for globalization*.

The increasing prominence of 'globalization' is identifiable elsewhere. For example, in the spring of 1999 the prestigious Reith lectures on BBC Radio were delivered by the British sociologist Anthony Giddens. His talks illuminated aspects of what he called 'the runaway world', a trend that not only incorporates globalization, but also changes in the way in which risk, tradition, democracy and the family are conceptualized and experienced. According to Giddens, we 'live in world of transformations, affecting almost every part of what we do. For better or worse, we are being propelled into a global order that no one fully understands, but which is making its effects felt on all of us' (Giddens 1999). Not only has 'globalization', then, become a major component of attempts to describe social, political and economic trends on a world-wide scale, but it has also increasingly been seen as a way of theorizing them. This is why we refer to globalization as a 'meta-myth'.

Although we will explore, necessarily briefly, the concept of globalization and assess the evidence for its existence, our purpose here is not to deny that it is occurring. Others have already taken the opportunity to do this at far greater length than we have available here (Hirst and Thompson 1996). Rather, we contend that the emphasis frequently placed on 'globalization', as opposed to capitalist economic restructuring, of which it is but the latest manifestation, diverts attention from the context within which economic and social relations, in particular the experience of work and employment, are constructed and reconstructed. This occurs largely in localities which are typified by distinctive place-related characteristics. The myth we wish to criticize, then, is not that capitalist economic restructuring is relatively insignificant on a global scale – on the contrary, it is clearly broader and more powerful in its reach than ever before – but that individual places are confronted by a similar range of problems and that they are affected in a broadly equivalent manner. In order to unpack this part of the 'globalization' myth we will examine certain developments in respect of work and employment in one distinctive, atypical place – the North East of England – and show that while a considerable amount of flux is clearly evident, it cannot be divorced from the effects of continuity.

Globalization: Definitions, Theories and Evidence

Although the concept of 'globalization' has recently attracted increasing attention among politicians, business executives and academics, it is important to bear in mind that the significance of economic, social and cultural intercourse across and beyond the boundaries of individual states has long been recognized. For one thing, economic activity has been conducted on a distinctively international scale for centuries now (Hobsbawm 1979). For example, the Atlantic slave trade, profits from which were crucial to the way in which industrial capitalism originated in Western Europe during the late eighteenth and early nineteenth centuries, operated outside the boundaries of individual states (Blackburn 1997). Indeed, the notion of a 'modern world system' was elaborated by Immanuel Wallerstein in order to conceptualize the historical expansion of economic activity on an international basis from the fifteenth century onwards (Wallerstein 1979).[1] In the cultural arena, the transformation in the power and reach of communications technologies during the post-Second World War period, in particular the increasing diffusion of television, led the Canadian social theorist Marshall McLuhan to identify a growing 'global village' (McLuhan 1964).

Thus, the extent to which aspects of economic, social and cultural activity have long been international in their nature must be acknowledged. What, then, is held to be special about 'globalization'? To identify its defining characteristics it is helpful to draw on definitions which have been offered by other writers. For example:

> The multiplicity of linkages and interconnections that transcend the nation states (and by implication the societies) which make up the modern world system. It defines a process through which events, decisions, and activities in one part of the world can come to have significant consequences for individuals in quite distant parts of the globe. (McGrew 1992: 65–6)

> . . . an historical process which engenders a shift in the spatial reach of networks and systems of social relations to transcontinental (or interregional) patterns of human organization, activity and the exercise of social power. (Perraton et al. 1997: 258)

> Behind . . . globalization is a single underlying idea, which can be called *de-localization*: the uprooting of activities from local origins and cultures. (Gray 1998: 57, original emphasis)

From these definitions it can be seen, then, that the concept of 'globalization' appears to have two important and related features which distinguish it *qualitatively* from earlier international processes of economic, social and cultural interaction. First of all, globalization is seen to involve greater interdependence or interconnectedness on a planetary scale. In the economic sphere this might mean, for example, that corporate decisions made in, say, Japan, have an immediate and profound impact on investment decisions and employment levels in plants in Britain. In respect of the environment, ecological disasters, such as the 1986 explosion of the Chernobyl nuclear plant in the

Ukraine or the increasing extent of acid rain, are seen to have rapid and significant consequences, not just for the states where the problems arose, or even their immediate neighbours, but for the world as a whole.

Secondly, there is the process which John Gray (1998) has referred to as 'de-localization'. This refers to the growing extent to which greater interdependence and interconnectedness in the world lessens the scope for economic, social, political and cultural institutions and processes to be locally determined. In shaping and influencing such activities, then, the importance of place, of discrete geographical spaces, apparently dwindles significantly in a world characterized by increased globalization.

At this stage it would be helpful to introduce some theoretical perspectives. If we can get a purchase on why globalization came about, we shall be in a better position to consider its significance. Writers have broadly considered globalization as a distinctive feature of contemporary modernity; as a characteristic of postmodernity; and as a key component of a new stage of 'informational' capitalism.

His 1999 Reith lectures notwithstanding, perhaps the most distinctive contribution made by Anthony Giddens to the debate on globalization has been to present it as a major feature of 'high modernity' (Giddens 1990). For Giddens, a key aspect of modernity has been the significance of what he calls 'time–space distanciation'. By this Giddens is referring to the way in which, during the modern period, developments in transport and communications technologies have meant that local events and institutions have come to be increasingly influenced by distant developments. Thus there is a process of 'stretching' between the local and the distant. For Giddens, then, 'modernity is inherently globalizing' (1990: 177).

The most emphatic attempt to understand globalization, not as an expression of modernity, but as a fundamental departure from it, has been offered by Martin Albrow in his 1996 book *The Global Age*. Albrow contends that the expansion of the 'Modern Project' has reached its limits, given the declining authority of the nation-state, and that an emerging 'global age' is replacing the modern one. Globalization constitutes 'the arrest of what was taken for granted' and is not 'the latest stage of a long process of development' (Albrow 1996: 101). Although Albrow's effort to theorize globalization as a rupture with modernity is undeniably ambitious, his reluctance to consider empirical evidence substantially weakens his argument.

Thus Albrow does not dislodge David Harvey's 1989 book *The Condition of Postmodernity* as the most significant attempt to go beyond modernity in understanding globalization. In a way this is surprising since nowhere in this work does Harvey (1989) refer expressly to the concept of globalization. Nevertheless, one of his principal arguments – that the rise of flexible, post-Fordist patterns of capital accumulation since the 1970s and 1980s (see chapter 2 of this volume) and technological innovation have accelerated a process of 'time–space' compression and given rise to 'postmodernity' – can be seen as an important, if largely implicit, contribution to explaining globalization.[2]

Underpinning the analyses of both Giddens and Harvey, though understated by both of them, is the recent transformation of technology and communication facilities. For a number of writers the intensity of recent technological change and improved transport and communications have been critical in providing the impetus behind globalization (Cairncross 1997; Dicken 1998; Leyshon 1995). However, only Manuel Castells – in his 1996 book *The Rise of the Network Society* – has satisfactorily incorporated the importance of technological change within an overarching conceptual framework which can be used to understand globalization. Central to Castells's thesis are two trends, the emergence of which can be traced to the 1970s. First, Castells highlights the significance of the 'information technology revolution', including the development of microelectronics, the exponential growth in computing power and the rapid diffusion of optical cable networks. Second, like Harvey (1989), Castells focuses on the process of capitalist restructuring since the 1970s, in particular the growth of more flexible patterns of accumulation.

Although the emergence of these two trends in the 1970s was a 'historical coincidence', their relationship is somewhat complex. The nature of technological innovation was profoundly affected by the institutional context within which it arose, principally the United States in the 1960s, but then came to shape and influence subsequent capitalist restructuring on a much larger scale during the 1970s and 1980s – so much so that a new mode of 'informational capitalism', based on the application of advanced information technology, has come to characterize the world economy. According to Castells (1996), it is 'informational' because economic well-being is increasingly dependent upon the ability 'to generate, process, and apply efficiently knowledge-based information' (p. 66). But, importantly, it is not only 'informational', it is also 'global'. Castells argues that 'under the new historical conditions, productivity is generated through and competition is played out in a global network of interaction. And it has emerged in the last quarter of the twentieth century because the

Information Technology Revolution provides the indispensable, material basis for such a new economy' (p. 66). Castells goes on to make two further important points about globalization. Not only does he conceptualize it as a process, and not an end-state, but he also highlights its uneven, asymmetric character.

Having considered some theoretical explanations for globalization, what, then, is the evidence for it? For some (for example, Waters 1995) developments in the cultural sphere are the best indicators. The recent acceleration of technological change, the transformation of communications and the more informational character of contemporary economic and social activity have combined to produce increasingly globalized consumer markets. Well-known corporations like Coca-Cola, McDonalds and Microsoft now operate on a global scale, developing and marketing their products accordingly. For one commentator this is resulting in a 'globalization of consumer tastes' (Ohmae 1994: 172). Consumers have enhanced opportunities to seek out and procure goods and services which satisfy them since they have access to a greater number of markets. According to the business writer Frances Cairncross: 'Commerce, including many kinds of retailing, will become increasingly international. Armed with a credit card, the nearest thing we have to a world currency, people will eventually shop around the world' (1997: 23–4).

It is not just the expansion and increased interconnectedness of consumer markets which appear to provide evidence of globalization. Cultural forms such as Hollywood films (Giddens 1999) and popular music (Webster 1995) now attract audiences across a wide range of territories, and not just in the advanced capitalist societies. In Malaysia, people are preoccupied with English Premier League football, with matches being constantly replayed on the television. Moreover, receding transport costs and greater provision mean that people enjoy far more scope than ever before to travel to different parts of the planet, including those that have hitherto been largely unaffected by tourism (Waters 1995).

The growing interconnectedness apparent within the global economy has frequently been cited as evidence of globalization. Perraton et al. (1997), for example, have observed 'a rise in economic activity that is world-wide in scope and a growing intensification of economic flows and activities across societies and between people, a process of both growing extent and intensity'(p. 274). The principal stimulus to economic globalization has clearly been the transformation of communications and the rapid diffusion of information technology. These have allowed corporations and financial institutions to enhance their cross-border economic activities and have rendered distance increasingly unimportant. Developments in four areas in particular have attracted the attention of writers.

First, there has been the huge growth recently in international trade as a proportion of output in services and manufacturing. As Held et al. (1999) have observed, it 'is not simply that a greater proportion of domestic output is traded than ever before, but is also the case that a rising proportion of private domestic output is potentially tradeable and therefore subject to international competition' (p. 171). Although the pattern of global trade remains distinctly uneven, with the advanced Western economies continuing to dominate, the growing participation of newly industrialized countries is held to be indicative of a greater degree of world-wide interconnectedness. For example, in 1963 the countries of East and South East Asia were jointly responsible for 1.51 per cent of overall manufacturing exports. By 1995 their share of this trade had risen to 19.9 per cent (Dicken 1998: 36).

Second, writers have drawn attention to the transformation of world financial markets: developments in communications and information technology have not only allowed them to operate on a world-wide scale twenty-four hours a day, but have also made possible the instantaneous transmission of huge amounts of financial data between different centres. One oft-cited statistic is that in the mid-1990s about a trillion (a million million) dollars were exchanged on global financial markets every day, some ten times more than in 1979 (Perraton et al. 1997). According to one commentator there are 'nowadays facilities for the continuous and real-time flow of monetary information, for round-the-clock trading in stocks, bonds and currencies. These developments have enormously increased both the volume and velocity of international financial transactions, bringing with them a heightened vulnerability of any national economy to the money markets' (Webster 1995: 143).

Third, the increasing amount of foreign direct investment (FDI) in the world economy has also been presented as evidence of globalization.[3] Dicken (1998) shows that although the growth of FDI has been a characteristic of the world economy for some decades now – in the 1960s it outstripped both the rise in global gross national product (GNP) and that of world exports – following some retrenchment during the 1970s and early 1980s, it accelerated again from 1985 onwards relative to production and exports, although the recession of the early 1990s did cause a temporary slowdown (p. 42). Much of this acceleration has been ascribed to the more prominent role played by Japan. At $306 billion in 1995 outward direct investment from Japan had increased by nearly seven times over the 1985 figure of $44 billion. There has also been an increasing amount of FDI generated by the newly industrialized countries of East and South East Asia. Between 1985 and 1995 their share rose from about 3 per cent to 8 per cent of global FDI (Dicken 1998: 44).

Fourth, multinational corporations (MNCs) play a key role in generating and directing FDI. According to data from the United Nations, by 1998 there were appoximately 53,000 MNCs operating in the global economy, responsible for some 450,000 affiliates (Held et al. 1999: 236), although the official statistics may by no means capture all of them (Dicken 1998).[4] The ability of MNCs to operate beyond the boundaries of individual countries has led some writers to identify them as a growing source of power in the world, at the expense of nation-states (Strange 1996). Using a rather ugly term, Ohmae (1994) has referred to the increasing 'nationalitylessness' of MNCs (p. 182), while Cairncross (1997) argues that in their capacity to establish and sustain operations throughout the world, 'more companies will become footloose' (p. 25). John Gray is worth quoting at length on the growing power of the MNCs:

> They are able to divide the process of production into discrete operations and locate them in different countries throughout the world. They are less dependent than ever before on national conditions. They can choose the countries whose labour markets, tax and regulatory regimes and infrastructures they find most congenial. The promise of direct inward investment, and the threat of withdrawal, have significant leverage on the policy options of national governments. Companies can now limit the politics of states. (Gray 1998: 62–3)

Robert Reich has pointed to the way in which something as seemingly uncomplicated as a television advertising campaign for a single product might involve operations in several parts of the globe. The strategy may have been originated in Britain, the filming of the advertisement undertaken in Canada, its sound added back in Britain again and the final version edited and prepared for transmission in the United States. Examples like this indicate that in 'such global webs, products are international composites' (Reich 1991: 113).

The enormous growth of such economic interconnectedness on a global scale has prompted an interesting discussion about its impact on the policy-making and regulatory capacities of individual nation-states. For some the sheer magnitude of change in communications and information technology, and the associated rise in global economic activity, has meant that not only are nation-states no longer the force they once were in influencing and shaping the direction of social and economic processes, but they are becoming increasingly irrelevant, given the permeability of national boundaries and the 'death of distance' (Cairncross 1997; Ohmae 1994; Strange 1996). Reich has highlighted the incapacity of governments to regulate much international economic activity. He writes:

> [by] the last decade of the twentieth century, governments could successfully block at their national borders few things other than tangible objects weighing more than three hundred pounds. Much of the knowledge and money, and many of the products and services, that people in different nations wish to exchange with one another are now easily transferred into electronic blips that move through the atmosphere at the speed of light. (Reich 1991: 111)

Even a sober analyst like McGrew (1992) has suggested that globalization is inevitably diminishing the sovereignty of national states.

In particular, it is held that governments now enjoy much reduced, if any, scope to manipulate their economies in order to maintain the quantity and quality of employment (Gray 1998). Countries which propose inflating their economies in order to create jobs risk provoking the displeasure of the financial markets and prompting the withdrawal of funds. Moreover, the ability of 'footloose' firms to switch operations to lower-cost areas of the globe places restrictions on the capacity of countries to improve the quality of employment, through greater labour market regulation in particular. For example, look at the ease with which new technology has allowed certain airlines, such as British Airways and Swissair, to relocate part of their ticketing and accounting operations to sites on the Indian subcontinent (Cairncross 1997).

The growth of low-cost imports from newly developing countries (especially those in East and South East Asia, where production and labour costs are generally much lower than in the advanced Western economies) has also been identified as a threat to employment levels in the West. Economists have expended a considerable amount of effort exploring the degree to which rising inequality in labour market rewards and high levels of unemployment in the West have been caused by the growth of global economic interconnectedness. Richard Freeman (1997) has observed that the overall effect is difficult to ascertain but that it is probably significant and likely to increase. More forcefully, Adrian Wood (1994) argues that the rise in the amount of trade between countries of the 'north' and the 'south' has had a major impact on the labour markets of the former, the diminution of job opportunities in areas of manufacturing for example. For Gray (1998), 'the overall effect of global free trade is still to drive down the wages of workers – most particularly unskilled manufacturing workers – in advanced countries', and, moreover, to make 'mass unemployment a problem without a simple solution' (pp. 85, 89); and Rorty (1998) has argued that increased job insecurity has been a notable effect of globalization.[5]

The Limits of Globalization: Some Critiques

Clearly, then, the evidence for globalization would appear to be strong, particularly given labour market trends in advanced Western economies; however, some notable reservations about the salience of the concept have been raised.

In the first place, the novelty of the magnitude of the openness and interconnectedness of the international economy has been questioned (Weiss 1997). Some have suggested that the world was economically more integrated in the half-century prior to the outbreak of the First World War in 1914 (Kozul-Wright 1995). Writers in this vein tend to argue that while there has been a notable recent increase in the degree of 'internationalization' in the global economy, there is a question mark over whether this really is sufficient to constitute 'globalization' (Kozul-Wright 1995; Hirst and Thompson 1996; Vandenbroucke 1998).

Second, the extent to which there has been a diminution in the power and authority of states has also been questioned. Weiss (1997) shows that the increased participation in the world economy of the newly industrialized countries in East and South East Asia – Singapore, for example – can be ascribed largely to the influence of strong, developmental state forms. Held et al. (1999) criticize the view that economic globalization has invariably led to reduced state power; rather, it is being rearticulated and reconstituted under different conditions. Panitch (1994) makes a convincing argument for the continued viability of nation-states as sources of power in the world economy, suggesting that international developments in economics and politics are still largely determined by social processes within states. Furthermore, the alleged 'footloose' character of MNCs notwithstanding, genuine rootlessness is exceptionally rare. Not only do the overwhelming majority of MNCs have an important home-base, but they also remain embedded, institutionally and culturally, in national economies (Allen 1995; Dicken 1998; Hirst 1997).

Third, although there has been substantial recent growth in the volume of international trade and other economic activity, it is evident that this has been confined to certain parts of the world. Three regions – North America, Western Europe and parts of East and South East Asia – commonly known as the 'triad', dominate the world economy. Even the pattern of FDI, frequently held to be a key indicator of globalization, remains largely restricted to the advanced capitalist societies and the newly industrialized countries of East and South East Asia (Dicken 1998). As Castells (1996) has observed, much of the planet remains excluded from the networks of informational capitalism: sub-Saharan Africa, for example.

Finally, it has been argued that the effects of increased international economic activity on employment have been somewhat overstated by many of the proponents of the globalization thesis (ILO 1996). For one thing, there are various other factors which have exerted downward pressure on the quantity and quality of employment, including overall demand deficiencies in Western economies and political factors, especially the pressure to reduce union power and deregulate the labour market. Dicken (1998) notes the sharp decrease in employment in automobile manufacturing in Western countries during the past twenty years. However, very little of it can be ascribed to increased competition and import penetration from developing countries. Given these critiques, why has the concept of globalization attracted so much attention?

This question is addressed in Paul Hirst and Grahame Thompson's substantial critique of economic globalization: *Globalization in Question* (1996). Hirst and Thompson begin by contrasting an 'international' economy with a 'globalized' one, and suggest that while the former may exist, the latter is a long way off. They then argue that although the scale of the international economy has grown in recent years, it is no more open than it was between 1870 and 1914; that international trade and financial flows are largely confined to the developed economies; that multinational corporations continue to be rooted in home states; and that, despite increasing international economic turbulence, regulatory institutions, such as the World Trade Organization, established in 1995, have the capacity to provide robust governance in an international order. Hirst and Thompson (1996) consider that the current fetishization of 'globalization' is a largely political development; it is promoted as a device to absolve states of the responsibility for securing and improving life chances for their citizens.

In an earlier piece they suggested that the concept of globalization is attractive to those on the political left because it shows global capitalism in its true colours and the 'illusory nature of reformist strategies', and also to those on the political right, since it can be used as a pretext for the deregulation of labour markets and the diminution of welfare provision (Hirst and Thompson 1995: 414). The rhetoric of globalization is often deployed by governments as an excuse for inaction and for excising policy initiatives which may have a progressive character. It is held that in a world dominated by the growth of rampant, uncontrollable capitalism, states can do little to protect their citizens from the play of market forces; to secure their standard of living employees must moderate their demands, give up the protection offered by trade unions, embrace more flexible working practices and resign themselves to the need for constant change. Thus globalization is 'a myth which exaggerates the degree of our helplessness in the face of contemporary economic forces' (Hirst and Thompson 1996: 6).

Putting Globalization in Its Place

We have already emphasized that our main purpose in writing this chapter is not simply to expose globalization itself as a 'myth', despite the level of support for such a view. For one thing, as we have already noted, this has already been effectively done. Moreover, sophisticated studies of global change, in particular those of Dicken (1998), Held et al. (1999) and Castells (1996), do attempt to highlight the paradoxes, nuances and countervailing tendencies inherent within globalization, while at the same time retaining it as a useful device for conceptualizing the growth of world-wide interconnectedness. McGrew (1992), for example, views globalization as a 'contingent' and 'dialectical' process. Thus, among other things, not only does it involve 'universalization' but also 'particularization'; and at the same time as there is a trend towards 'homogenization', there is also an increase in 'differentiation' (p. 74). Approaches such as this one, then, reveal globalization to be a distinctly uneven process, but one which is none the less becoming ever more important in so far as it shapes political, social and cultural developments across the planet.

Bearing these points in mind, in respect of the impact on work and employment we wish to highlight the mythical nature of globalization in two interrelated respects. First, the emphasis which has often been placed on the novelty of recent globalizing trends misrepresents the extent to which they are based on what has gone before. We wish to emphasize that globalization, while clearly representing a more advanced state of capitalist development and expansion, is less of a rupture with the past than has often been supposed. The significance we attach to continuity, then, brings us on to our second point. It has been argued that increased global interconnectedness diminishes the importance of place as a factor in defining and shaping social relations, for example the way in which people experience change at work. Both Gray (1998) and Waters (1995) point to the way in which 'de-localization' has been an effect of globalization; that in influencing and shaping how people live their lives the geographical characteristics of individual places matter less and less.

In so far as sociologists have tended to focus on globalization as an abstract and overarching formulation,[6] they tacitly reinforce the view that it has reduced the importance of locality in shaping social identity and activity. Writers in the field of economic geography, however, have recently highlighted the large extent to which discrete geographical places mediate the impact of globalizing trends (Allen and Hammett 1995; Dicken et al. 1997). Amin and Thrift (1997), for example, emphasize that despite its increased global reach, much of the basis of economic activity remains the preserve of particular places: 'habits, customs, informal learning environments, industrial cultures and economic expectations are not the characteristics of distanciated global networks, but the essence of *entrenched* institutional and social arrangements within different local contexts' (p. 153, original emphasis). These considerations imply that in order to capture the nature and significance of globalizing trends, and their impact on work and employment in particular, it is important to explore the mediating influence of place. The prevailing social and economic characteristics of a particular area may have profound effects.

The Impact of Global Change in an 'Old' Region: the North East of England

We have therefore chosen to examine the experience of a deliberately atypical region: the North East of England, an area where we have all undertaken research into various aspects pertaining to work and employment.[7] The region's economic, social and cultural distinctiveness can be largely attributed to its relatively early industrialization, hence its designation as an 'old' region. During the nineteenth century certain staple industries came to dominate the regional economy: coal-mining, iron and steel production, shipbuilding and engineering in particular. In 1913 there were over 200,000 coalminers employed in North East pits (Sawbridge et al. 1984). The nature of the region's industrialization helped give rise to a style of trade union organization which, while solidaristic, was also characterized by a distinctively reformist outlook (Beynon and Austrin 1994).

Recent economic change, however, of the kind many have associated with the globalization process, has profoundly affected the industrial structure of the North East. There has been enormous decline in employment in hitherto staple industries. The last working deep coal-mine in the Durham coalfield, Wearmouth in Sunderland, closed in 1994 and the site is now home to the city's football club. The level of manufacturing employment in the region fell from 410,000 in 1979 to 181,000 in 1998 (Robinson 1988; *Labour Market Trends* May 1999). An increasing proportion of employment in manufacturing can now be found in plants established by new inward investors, particularly companies from overseas, since the North East is perceived to be characterized by willing and relatively cheap skilled labour. Peck and Stone (1992) noted that two-thirds originated from outside the UK. High profile examples in the 1980s included the Nissan car plant established at Washington, near Sunderland, and in the 1990s, a Samsung electronics plant at Billingham in Cleveland.

The often transient character of this inward investment might perhaps be held up as evidence for the increased power of 'footloose' companies in a globalized world. For example, in 1998 the German conglomerate Siemens announced it would not be going ahead with its proposed plant on North Tyneside; and in the same year Fujitsu closed its electronic assembly plant near Darlington. Employment opportunities and job security in key parts of the regional economy are therefore frequently subject to the investment whims of powerful multinational companies. Further, the extent to which MNCs are able to establish global patterns of production and work organization throughout their operations – the universal elaboration of 'lean' production techniques by companies like Nissan for example (see chapter 2) – can be seen as an example of the way in which 'cultural differences are tending to be subsumed within a single idealization of appropriate organizational behaviour' (Waters 1995: 81).

The insecure character of work and employment in the region is not only an expression of the seemingly 'footloose' nature of inward investment, but is also a function of the growth in importance of service-sector employment. Not only has there been an increase in the proportion of employees working in the public sector – in education, health and local and central government – but employment in private services has also risen significantly, a trend which has led some commentators to refer to it as the 'new engine of growth in the north' (Darnell and Evans 1995: 13).[8] For one thing much new employment in sectors such as retailing, leisure, finance and education is characterized by more 'flexible' patterns of working – non-standard jobs which are increasingly held by women. In her research into five organizations in the North East, Harriet Bradley (1999) found that a considerable degree of insecurity prevailed in both private and public sector workplaces and was even evident among 'hitherto more protected groups of employees, such as office staff and public sector professionals, as organizations restructure their employment hierarchies and "downsize" to get rid of slack' (p. 217). Such a condition would appear to lend weight to John Gray's (1998) contention that globalization and the rise of 'anarchic capitalism' have brought many deleterious effects for employees. The result has been the decimation of many hitherto stable occupations, a rise in job insecurity, a process of 're-proletarianization' among working-class jobs and a tendency towards the 'de-bourgeoisification' of middle-class ones (pp. 71–2).

One of the most significant features of globalization is held to be its destructive effect on collective labour organization among employees (Castells 1996). The decline of the trade unions in the North East can be held up as a further indication of how the enhanced power of capital, and its increased ability to eke out opportunities for accumulation on a global scale, has greatly affected the experience of employment. Not only have unions in the North East witnessed considerable membership decline – the regional membership of the Transport and General Workers' Union (TGWU), for a long time the largest union in the UK, fell from 90,000 in 1978 to 44,000 in 1992 (Sawbridge et al. 1984; TGWU 1993) – but employers, particularly those setting up new plants, have become much more reluctant to recognize them (Beynon et al. 1994; Peck and Stone 1992).

Many of the distinctive employment trends of the North East region would appear, then, to be driven by the forces of global economic change which we discussed earlier in this chapter. However, as we will now see, the experience of the North East also highlights the significance of other factors, most notably political interventions and the continued importance of place-related characteristics. This indicates that, despite the impact of more globalized economic forces – and their presence is clearly significant – change is none the less built on continuity.

For one thing, industrial decline has been a long-term phenomenon in the North East and long pre-dates the recent alleged wave of globalization. Indeed, the recent growth in the number of overseas plants notwithstanding, in an attempt to ameliorate the effects of de-industrialization, successive governments have long tried to encourage firms to invest in the North East through various regional policies. In the 1930s, for example, the government established a new industrial estate in the Team Valley in order to encourage firms to move to the region. Similarly, in the 1960s Courtaulds was attracted by incentives to Spennymoor and it established a plant there (Hudson 1989). The region became known, then, as a 'branch-plant' economy, in that while many companies relocated premises to the North East, their headquarters and principal operations remained elsewhere. Thus work and employment in the region has long been adversely affected by 'footloose' capital.

The defence industry in the North East is a particularly good example of a sector with a 'branch-plant' character; moreover, it has been largely shaped and defined not by globalizing economic forces, but by national government intervention. With the ending of the Cold War, and the resulting contraction of defence spending, the UK defence industry faced a considerable crisis in the early 1990s. The Royal Ordnance factory (RO) at Birtley was privatized in 1987 and purchased by British Aerospace (BAe); the headquarters of the Royal Ordnance division remained in Chorley, Lancashire, and it was here that all corporate and overall production decisions were made. BAe used the branch-plant model to restructure Royal Ordnance through the crisis caused by the end of the Cold War and closed a number of sites. Employment at Birtley fell from 1,400 before privatization to a current figure of about 300, ostensibly because of a decline in government orders for ammunition. This pattern of downsizing was repeated at other defence industry sites in the North East. Swan Hunter Shipbuilders in Wallsend, the UK's last large naval surface vessel manufacturer, shed over 3,000 jobs in the 1990s; it remains open, but only as a ship refitter and it is no longer involved in production.

It is possible to interpret these developments as effects of globalization, particularly since increased foreign competition, notably from the Far East, has led to a decline in orders for civilian ships. It has been interventions by national government, however, which have had the most critical impact on the North East's defence industry. In respect of ammunition, most recent defence procurement orders made by the UK government have been placed abroad, ostensibly on cost grounds. In the case of shipbuilding, the UK Royal Navy remains a major customer; Swan Hunter Shipbuilders had a global reputation for quality and was the Navy's shipyard of choice for the purchase of large surface vessels. The decision of the UK government, on cost grounds, to award the contract for the Landing Platform Helicopter to a consortium led by VSEL in Cumbria was directly responsible for the collapse and near closure of the Swan Hunter shipyard, which left the Wallsend community in ruins with no further prospects of employment for shipyard workers. Furthermore, the Royal Navy must now source its large surface vessels from abroad.

The North East's defence industry has been reliant on government orders for decades and the end of the Cold War was no major surprise. In respect of ammunition and ships the UK government took strategic decisions to withdraw from defence manufacturing in the region under the guise of making cost-based decisions. Conversion to civilian production was not considered; moreover, it is unlikely that the reduction of indigenous capacity will result in long-term financial benefits. It must also be remembered that while some parts of the UK's defence industry were being sacrificed in the 1990s – Swan Hunter and Royal Ordnance in the North East, for example – others were the beneficiaries of major investment.

Given that the North East has been the site of considerable recent inward investment, it might be assumed that newly established plants would be characterized by global patterns of work organization and structure (see Waters 1995): the 'lean-production' approach, for example. However, the degree to which MNCs adapt to prevailing local social and economic conditions has been highlighted (Dicken 1998), and in chapter 2 we will explore at some length the way in which companies adapt the 'lean' model depending on the context within which they are operating. This has been particularly the case in the North East, where companies have taken considerable steps to try and ensure that trade union influence is minimized for example.

Although we have noted the increasing importance of service-sector employment in the North East, the major growth in employment has come in the public services. According to official data, 29 per cent of employees work in the education, social work, health, public administration and defence sectors (*Regional Trends* 1998). This has little to do with globalizing forces and is largely an expression of policies of national government. One trend has been the expansion of further and higher education (there are five universities in the region). Another has been the relocation of central government functions away from London; for example, in order to cope with labour shortage and to promote regional development, parts of the Inland Revenue were moved to Gateshead in the 1960s and a massive complex was established at Long Benton to deal with social security matters. The NHS (National Health Service) is a major employer in the area, which reflects the growth of the health service as people's expectations and demands have risen. Thus a significant part of recent economic change in the North East has been driven not by processes of globalization, but by national policy interventions. Indeed, government agencies have also played a crucial role in attracting inward investment to the region in recent years.

Finally, while trade unionism in the North East of England, like elsewhere in the UK (see chapter 8), experienced many set-backs during the 1980s and 1990s, it is evident that it retains a considerable regional resilience. For one thing, union membership remains higher in the region than elsewhere in England. In 1996 union density (the proportion of employees who are union members) was about 30 per cent for England as a whole; in the North it was 42 per cent. Interestingly, there is a marked difference in density among public-sector employees: nationally it was 60 per cent, in the North it was 72 per cent. Moreover, regional union leaders continue to exert influence in local state structures and, despite their preference for non-union arrangements, employers often discover that they cannot entirely exclude a union presence from their plants (Shaw 1994; Wray 1996). Clearly, it is still possible to discern the presence of a distinctive union 'culture' in the North East (Martin et al. 1995). Bradley (1999) described how young employees had been told by their parents to join a union when they got their first job.

From this discussion, then, it should be clear that, despite the significance that many attach to global economic forces in shaping the structure and nature of work and employment, political factors, derived at national level, none the less retain a strong influence. Moreover, change, whether it is driven by economic factors or political interventions, manifests itself in places which are characterized by their own distinctive social and cultural heritage. As Nelson and Smith have pointed out:

> Over the long run, there certainly are trends that influence all regions – there is a world or 'global' economy. These trends, however, are always worked out in conjunction with the unique characteristics of specific locales as well as with vast disparities between regions. . . . Different locales have quite different cultures when it comes to how their labour forces will be deployed. . . . In fact, there is good reason to believe that far from long-term, widespread trends producing a convergence across the regions of the nation (or indeed the world), the specificities of different locales are becoming more rather than less important. (Nelson and Smith 1999: 4)

Conclusion: Globalization and Polarization

Underpinned by significant technological change, the character of contemporary societies, particularly the advanced capitalist ones, has come to be strongly influenced by the deepening intensity of global economic and cultural interconnectedness. Increasingly powerful MNCs, the rapid growth of international trade, the accelerating rate of FDI and the volatility of international financial exchanges all highlight the extent to which capitalism is being restructured on an increasingly global scale. At the same time, this is triggering the evolution of distinctive new forms of social action, such as the 'Zapatista' rebellion in Mexico, for example (Castells 1997). However, despite the apparent novelty of such developments it is evident that they constitute an evolutionary trend; contemporary 'globalization' must be placed in its historical context (Held et al. 1999). The emphasis on newness has, as some have argued, offered governments a pretext for the renewed pursuit of neo-liberal economic policies, in particular the promotion of labour market 'flexibility', since this is deemed essential for sustaining international competitiveness. In this sense, then, globalization can be judged a 'myth' (Bourdieu 1998; Hirst and Thompson 1996), since it is more of a fashionable political discourse than a substantive development.

In our formulation we have been careful to argue that, given its increasing scope and intensity, contemporary capitalism is qualitatively different from what has gone before. However, the emphasis placed on 'globalization' diverts attention from the way in which more intensive capitalist relations of production are played out in localities, particularly their impact on jobs, and the extent to which they are shaped by contextual factors. Thus in the case of the North East of England we have identified a number of factors – the region's social, cultural and political heritage, and the nature of national government intervention in particular – which have mediated the impact of global economic imperatives. The quantity and quality of employment in the North East have long been more adversely affected by economic forces than other regions; current globalizing trends represent an intensification of this process. One of the major effects of globalization, then, is to increase the degree of polarization between regions which are economically relatively successful and those which are not.

2

The Myth of Lean Production

> In short, lean thinking is lean because it provides a way to do more and more with less and less – less human effort, less equipment, less time, and less space – while coming closer and closer to providing customers with exactly what they want. Lean thinking also provides a way to make work more satisfying by providing immediate feedback on efforts to convert muda [waste] into value . . . it provides a way to create work rather than simply destroying jobs in the name of efficiency.
>
> (Womack and Jones 1996: 15)

> It's a worry anywhere now; no job is for life. I think people realize that. I mean there are some jobs that are a bit more secure than others. I think Nissan is, I mean recently they got voted the most productive car plant in Europe. That is down to the workers, it starts at the bottom and works its way up. If we weren't all working together they wouldn't be at the top, would they? I think the more they [the workers] put into it, the more they are going to get out. I think I will be there until retirement.
>
> (Nissan worker)

The future of work is lean and flexible. It is a future of mutual dependence and prosperity for workers and employers, or so we have been told. Lean production has been touted by some management theorists as a method of achieving flexibility and therefore reducing waste within the workplace (Womack et al. 1990). Flexibility has become the driving concept behind the restructuring of work in recent years. Four basic types have been identified. Flexibility can refer to an employer's ability to vary the number of workers involved in a given part of the work process at a given time in order to meet fluctuations in demand for a given function or product; this is numerical flexibility. Second, flexibility can relate to the suppleness of the organization of a corporation; that is, organizational flexibility. A third form of flexibility – functional flexibility – requires workers to be multi-skilled and to perform a variety of tasks in the production process. In this way tasks performed by workers can be adjusted to meet changing business demands. Managers must ensure that such skills are utilized when the market, or new forms of technology, demand it (Atkinson 1984). A fourth type, financial flexibility, supports numerical and functional flexibility (Piore 1986).

The work of Womack et al. (1990) has become influential in management circles, not only because it identified a strategy for maximum flexibility and low waste, but also because it offered both a prescription and a threat: go lean or die. The potency of the message was heightened as the traditional foundations of work organization, Fordism and Taylorism, were beginning to present challenges to profitability. At the same time, increasing global economic competitiveness encouraged employers to take advantage of labour weakness to restructure their workplaces.

Many governments have welcomed the introduction of lean production to their economies. British governments in particular have made clear their faith in the ideal of lean production.[1] Indeed, as this chapter will reveal, the Conservative governments took a pro-active role in preparing the ground for incoming investment, and actively promoted the strategy of lean production. More recently the failure of the public sector to embrace the logic of flexibility brought an angry outburst from Labour Prime Minister Tony Blair:

> People in the public sector are more rooted in the concept that 'if it's always been done this way, it must always be done this way' than any group of people that I've ever come across. You try getting change in the public sector and public services – I bear the scars on my back after two years in government.[2]

The aim of this chapter is to expose a series of myths concerning lean production. The most influential is that the late twentieth-century period can be defined as post-Fordist with a coherent package of 'lean-production' practices prevailing in workplaces; however, lean-production strategies are not widely available to employers, nor do they occur in any uniform way that might suggest that a new era of production has emerged. But since some employers have adopted some of the components of the lean-production strategy, this chapter will examine the implications of these changes. This examination in turn uncovers further myths associated with lean-production techniques, which weaken the claim that lean production is beneficial for both workers and employers. It will be argued that lean-production techniques are best understood as part of a capitalist initiative to intensify work and increase control over workers. However, contrary to the claims made by proponents of lean production, this is far from a 'win-all' situation for employers. Many lean-production strategies are high risk. They are heavily dependent upon the active co-operation of workers, many of whom are employed by supplier companies, over whom employers have little influence. Furthermore, the ideology of goal hegemony that 'we' (workers and employers) are all 'in it together', is difficult to maintain, especially when workers realize that the new work strategies increase the pace of work and reduce the amount of control they have over jobs.

Finally, we argue that many of the myths about lean production arise from the failure of management theorists fully to research the experience of workers and to appreciate how important worker co-operation is to the success of lean production. Advocates of lean production tend either to ignore workers, or wrongly to assume that they benefit from the emergence of lean-production strategies.

The Decline of Fordism and Taylorism

During the 1980s, it was claimed that Fordism was in crisis and was being replaced by a new era of post-Fordism, based on the flexible organization of production and the minimization of waste. The term 'Fordism' is derived from Henry Ford, the American auto manufacturer who pioneered mass production in the early decades of the twentieth century. Ford did not invent Fordism, but combined a number of established principles which gave rise to a characteristic set of industrial relationships.

One of these was scientific management (often known as Taylorism). Frederick Taylor devised a system of scientific measurement to monitor or maximize output, such as 'time and motion studies'. He believed that workers were motivated by economic need only, and recommended the adoption of piece rates to ensure worker productivity. Taylor proposed an increase in the division of labour as a way of separating conceptual activities from the actual execution of work. Henry Ford intensified Taylorist principles in reorganizing his production lines on a large scale (Elger 1979).

Ford's enormous success stemmed from economies of scale and also from the increased control of labour. This was achieved through tight organization of the labour process and also through the introduction of new wage policies. In 1914 Ford paid his workers five dollars a day, a previously unheard-of sum, which ensured he was able to recruit and maintain a pliable, non-unionized workforce (Beynon 1984). The result was a system capable of the mass production of standardized goods, which enabled Ford to undercut dramatically craft production, and which came to be mirrored by many mass production industries.

During the course of the twentieth century, Fordism had become the organizing principle behind mass production in general. In the 1970s and 1980s, however, a number of critics argued that Fordism had begun to present a challenge to profitability in manufacturing. Employers were unable to match their products or services to volatile market demands and tastes. The employment conditions of Fordism led to worker disaffection with adverse consequences for quality control. Furthermore, restrictive practices on the part of many workers and trade unions made reform of the workplace difficult for employers; Fordism was increasingly seen as wasteful and overly rigid.

While Henry Ford's dream was to keep the unions out, trade unionism and collective bargaining became the linchpin of the Fordist era. Holloway describes the relatively high wages paid to industrial mass production workers under collective bargaining as compensation for the 'death' that resulted from alienation within work, which was 'cashed' in the 'life outside' of work. Fordist wage payments formed part of the bargaining process of what has been called a Fordist contract; high wages in return for management control and alienation. After the Second World War, with relative economic prosperity in the advanced capitalist countries, collective bargaining became a tool in the struggle for shop floor control. Workers sought 'payment for change': that is, financial incentives in order to ensure their compliance when capital sought to reorganize the workplace (Holloway 1987).

Payment for change was just one of the problems employers experienced as a result of the Fordist strategy. Under this regime, alienated, deskilled and bored workers commonly adopted a hostile stance towards their employers. Demarcation strategies (the principle of doing only one's own job, as tightly defined in the job description) were adopted in order to preserve employment security. The result was that many employers came to see their workplaces as overstaffed and inflexible. Workers were unwilling to share their considerable knowledge about how the product or the labour process could be improved, and during periods of economic prosperity employers faced high levels of labour turnover and absenteeism as a result of worker discontent.

Fordism utilized a form of production organization subsequently termed JIC (just in case). Under JIC, if there was no restricted market, the capitalist manufacturer opted for high volume production of standard products in order to achieve economies of scale. These long production runs offset losses which occurred during the time required for setting up machinery designed to produce a single or limited product type. In case of disruption, buffer stocks of inventories were held so that the system could continue to function. Such stockpiling was the origin of the 'just in case' designation; spares were needed just in case a supplier failed to deliver or just in case of quality defects or emergencies. But this system was wasteful; it involved reliance on unnecessary 'extras' – labour, parts, storage space and even time. A further problem of wastefulness was that this high-volume system was not flexible in response to peaks and troughs of market demand, nor to changes in market tastes (Sayer 1986).

These challenges to profitability were largely manageable until the onslaught of economic depression in the 1970s. The search for solutions to the problems of Fordism drew attention to the relative success of Japanese industry. The result was the emergence of a body of work which linked the work organization associated with Japanese success to post-Fordist and lean production.

Proponents claimed that post-Fordist, lean-production work strategies eliminated the need for adversarial industrial relations. The old battlefields of demarcation and struggles over the frontier of control would disappear with the development of a system of production, which was based on flexibility, continual change and the recognition by labour and capital of their mutual interdependency. Post-Fordism represented a reversal of Taylorism, where employers simply 'dictated' what should occur, when and where. Under the new system, the key to success was the development of a co-operative and knowledgeable workforce, which was involved in continual innovation and was able to influence the development of the work process and product. (Atkinson and Meager 1986a; Kenney and Florida 1988; Oliver and Wilkinson, 1988, 1990; Piore and Sabel 1984; Wickens 1987.)

Before moving on to examine lean production in greater detail, we note several problems with the accounts discussed above. To term an era 'Fordist' assumes the universal application of Fordist principles, ignoring variations in the way it was implemented. Indeed, in many workplaces it was not adopted at all.[3] In addition, the initial success and eventual 'failure' of Fordism can be better understood through reference to the changes in the economic and political context within which the system operated (Clarke 1990). Nevertheless, as the quotation from the Nissan worker that opens this chapter testifies, the notion of a wasteful organizational past has caught the public imagination.

The Promises of Lean Production

The term 'lean production' was first coined in a Massachusetts Institute of Technology (MIT) study of the world's major car manufacturers, which claimed that in order to ensure survival, employers must eliminate waste from the production process and become lean. The success of Japanese car manufacturers was seen to exemplify the benefits of lean production. Furthermore, the study argued that lean production was the only way to ensure success and that it was available to employers in a range of contexts (Womack et al. 1990; Womack and Jones 1996).

The problems raised by Fordist mass production and JIC are overcome through the adoption of a more flexible system known as 'just in time' (JIT). This derives its name from the fact that parts, supplies and workers are delivered to the production process at the very point at which they are needed, just in time. Buffer stocks are small and are augmented only to replace parts removed 'downstream' in the production line. Workers at the end of the line are given output instruction and instruct the workers immediately upstream to produce the parts needed (Sayer 1986). This ensures that employers can shift to produce differing goods very quickly in response to market demand.

At each step of the lean-production process, quality is built in rather than 'tested in' at the end by the elimination of faulty goods. The smaller the buffer stock, the more sensitive the system to error and the greater the incentive to prevent or reduce the occurrence of defects. Effective error elimination requires management, process engineers and workers to be highly knowledgeable about the details of production, and for that knowledge to be shared. This is facilitated by the organization of workers into teams, which improves the experience of work and allows workers to achieve more as a result of group co-operation.

The team concept underpins 'quality circles' and other continual improvement strategies such as *kaizen* (continual improvement), which allow workers to work together to identify problems and suggest solutions. Another option for employers is the introduction of suggestion boxes, providing workers with an extra route to communication with their supervisors. In this way workers can help effect change in their workplace. According to Wickens (1993), motivated and confident workers, such as those employed by Nissan UK, ceased to be afraid of change and began to participate in it.

JIT enables firms to meet the demands of changing markets, since goods are produced for a customer and not for stock. Under JIT, the establishment of a new production facility is not seen as a matter of setting up a standardized line and 'chasing volume', it is a matter of building up production slowly, making piecemeal improvements to the work process. This again demands the involvement and co-operation of a flexible workforce. Demarcation norms are swept away as workers are more fully involved in all stages of the planning, inception and execution of production. Workers may be expected to do regular preventative maintenance on technology and to take responsibility for remedial work.

It is claimed that under the lean-regime workers are seen as assets with useful insights into the problems of work; employers become 'investors in people'. Success is dependent upon a skilled workforce, which is committed to the long-term goals of the organization. Under lean production, motivated workers take responsibility for the working environment and thereby accept that their security is bound up with the success of their employers; formerly 'blue-collar' workers take on a 'white-collar' persona and responsibilities (Wickens 1987). In Japanese companies, this produces relationships of mutual respect and regard, enshrined in the employment for life (*nenko*) system, which is said to illustrate the advantages won by non-adversarial industrial relations and 'company' unionism (Hinvers 1988).

Employers and employees, so the claim goes, share the benefits of these strategies. Workers win job security through their commitment to lean production, and this secures the long-term viability of the company. Workers are less alienated and bored because the quality of their working lives improves. Consequently, hostile industrial relations are replaced by co-operation. Therefore, trade union representation may not be necessary, and employers and workers may wish to replace independent unions with company-specific arrangements. The MIT report claimed that contemporary Ford workers in the United States were pleased to break the United Auto Workers' (UAW) contract with their employer – which involved narrow job descriptions – in order to do the jobs required of them under the newly introduced lean-production system. Womack et al. (1990)

claimed that these workers no longer fought with management over the introduction of change because new work practices allowed them genuine participation.

Lean Production for Everyone?

At this stage two critical points can be made about the claims put forward by Womack et al. (1990). First, the post-Second World War success of Japanese corporations stemmed not solely from the organization of the work process, but also from the structure and nature of the domestic Japanese economy. Haslam et al. (1996) argue that the absence of independent trade unions and the restrictions inherent in the *nenko* system provided domestically based Japanese corporations with benefits not enjoyed overseas. Japanese workers typically worked longer hours and for less than their counterparts elsewhere. Furthermore, while the focus of attention has been on large, 'core' Japanese corporations, the relative success of these companies has been won at the expense of 'non-standard' workers, typically employed in 'peripheral' small-scale companies, who do do not enjoy job security and the benefits and disciplines of *nenko* (Coyne and Williamson 1991). Japanese transplants, which have adopted the same work organization strategies as their 'mother' plant in Japan, have fared relatively poorly. This suggests that the lean approach is not as significant in creating Japanese success as has been supposed.

The view that lean work organization is a long-term panacea for declining profitability is further challenged by reference to the current condition of the Japanese economy. When recession hit Asian economies in the 1990s, neither the advantages of the domestic economic and political structure nor lean work practices were sufficient to protect the Japanese economy (Haslam et al. 1996).

Second, relatively few companies have opted for a 'full package' of lean strategies. Only powerful MNCs, embarking on a greenfield venture, have been able to develop a comprehensive JIT system, by gathering around them compliant suppliers. A number of commentators have argued that it is very difficult to identify a common lean-production model at work (Williams et al. 1992) and that the predicted Japanization of British industry has not occurred (Procter and Ackroyd 1998). Where the strategy has influenced the workplace, employers take a 'pick and mix' approach, choosing particular elements of the strategy which are right for them; wholesale adoption of the strategy is relatively rare.

Despite the threat 'go lean or die', many employers eschew the lean option and have sought other methods through which to win advantages over labour. Even some Japanese-owned transplants have chosen not to pursue the 'Japanese way'. Companies outside Japan, which have been able to mimic elements of the Japanese context, such as the selection of vulnerable workforces, have prospered irrespective of the fact that they did not adopt lean-production strategies (Wood 1989b).

This suggests that new management techniques do not have transcendental virtues, which can be easily applied to any context (Haslam et al. 1996). It also suggests that many employers – even those powerful enough to employ the full lean package, if they wish to – are not convinced that lean production is the only way and the best way to go.

Working Smarter, not Harder?

Since many employers have adopted some components of the lean-production package, we now need to explore some of the claims about its efficacy. The claim that workers work 'smarter, not harder' implies a more efficient work-place and enriched work conditions, but no notable increase in work-loads. However, a growing body of case study evidence refutes these claims and suggests that benefits are largely claimed by employers, while workers concede to reduced job security, work intensification and erosion of independent trade unionism (Garrahan and Stewart 1992; Graham 1995; Lewchuk and Robertson 1996; Stephenson 1994; Moody 1997).

Some critics claim that new work strategies must be seen as part of a capitalist response to declining profits and the need to tighten control over workers. For example, Beale (1994) and Garrahan and Stewart (1992) argue that in the UK Conservative governments 'prepared the ground' for a number of high profile Japanese inward investors. This involved the introduction of anti-union legislation, the provision of state resources for the defeat of powerful trade unions in the coal and print industries, the radical restructuring of nationalized industries and an attack on manufacturing which led to a dramatic increase in unemployment levels in the early 1980s. Lean inward investors were courted and coveted by the government and were provided with development grants to support their new enterprises. The availability of land, grants and economically vulnerable workforces offered major lean producers the right environment to ensure profitability and control over their workforces. First Nissan, then Toyota and Honda introduced transplants to the UK. The government considered its efforts to be worthwhile, since these companies sought to disseminate lean-production strategies to indigenous industries and hoped that this would promote a further shift in power away from organized labour in favour of capital.[4]

Case study evidence suggests that lean production increases both the pace of work and control over workers. For example, while functional flexibility is seen to be a key component of lean production, typically workers experience numerical flexibility. While the boundaries of demarcation are broken down and workers are moved between jobs, they are required to do the same job, in different parts of the plant or on different parts of the product. Lean production does not involve workers in multiskilling (the broadening of skills) or enskilling (the deepening of skills) as claimed by its proponents. Rather, horizontal enlargement of jobs is occurring: that is, workers are involved in multi-tasking, or 'job-loading', performing a range of semi or unskilled activities in addition to their core work (Garrahan and Stewart 1992; Stephenson 1994).

The erosion of demarcation and the introduction of multi-tasking facilitate the employment of fewer workers than would be necessary in the wasteful workplace. Consequently, rather than securing employment, as the opening comments from the Nissan worker suggested, lean-production strategies make it easy to dispose of workers who are now perceived as unnecessary because of multitasking. Many of the workers who make lean production possible are 'peripheral workers', employed on a non-standard basis, who do not enjoy the benefits of a long-term or full-time employment contract. These workers are used to reduce waste since they are introduced only when necessary, and can be fired with relative ease.

One of the additional tasks expected of workers is to monitor the quality of their own work and that of their colleagues. This reveals three key features of the lean-production strategy; first, that workers become individually accountable for their work; second, that they are open to the scrutiny of their peers; finally, where possible any unnecessary 'pores' – breathing or rest spaces – in the working day are filled (Moody 1997; Stephenson 1994). While the rhetoric of lean production states that team working is intrinsically good news for workers, some managers, when interviewed, are prepared to be explicit about the underlying nature of the system: 'Team working means that if a worker goes to the toilet before a designated break time, the others in the team will say, "Hey, you have to manage yourself better;

don't go to the toilet until the break"' (manager at Nissan Yamata Engineering).

This statement illustrates the realities of lean production: workers who are under pressure to do their work at the 'right quality', while carrying out a range of other tasks, are unlikely to be sympathetic to those who are 'letting the side down'. Where there is no coherent alternative analysis of lean production, such as might be provided by an effective trade union, it is likely that this type of peer conflict will arise (Delbridge 1998). If workers 'manage each other' in this type of 'pressure cooker' situation, the presence of intrusive middle management may be unnecessary and indeed counterproductive. Management's intention is that this horizontal conflict will replace vertical conflict, between workers and their managers.

While it is true that quality monitoring ensures that mistakes are dealt with early and waste is eliminated, case study research reveals that what is defined as a quality mistake by managers may not necessarily affect marketability (Garrahan and Stewart 1992). Perhaps the real importance of quality control is that it encourages self and peer management and competition between workers, thereby reducing the likelihood of worker collectivity. In some instances competition between teams is promoted by the award of 'quality scores', thus increasing team group pressure to conform (Stephenson 1994).

Most of the critical research drawn upon above stems from qualitative research methodologies. However, several large-scale surveys of workers support these findings. For example, Lewchuk and Robertson surveyed 1,670 workers employed in sixteen workplaces in the independent automotive components sector in Canada. Far from 'owning their own change', the majority of workers felt that they were not able to affect the negative aspects of their work and half of those questioned claimed they could train another worker to do their job in a few days. Contrary to the claim made by Womack and Jones (1996) in the quotation that opens the chapter, these workers are doing 'more and more with less and less'. Sixty-one per cent reported that their work was either too fast, too heavy, was done by too few people, or in too little time (Lewchuk and Robertson 1996). Graham's work (1995) suggests that lean production has frequently had an adverse effect on the health and well-being of workers: 'I asked Steve from team two how many people he thought were having [repetitive strain injury] wrist problems. He said he would guess that easily 25% are having problems, even if they haven't been put in splints' (Graham 1995: 88).[5]

A Rejection of Fordism and Taylorism?

Critics claim that lean production is not a rejection of Fordism. Mass production and standardization of products or services and processes remain. Indeed the Fordist pay bargain (high wages as compensation in return for compliance) is still a feature of the car industry. Neither is lean production a rejection of Taylorism; for example, time and motion study is still extensively used. Further, while workers are often asked to contribute, this is not strictly speaking a reversal of Frederick Taylor's original ideas. Moody reminds us that Taylor himself recommended that information should be gathered from all appropriate sources, and that workers held a wealth of 'know-how'. Whatever the method of gathering information, however, management alone hold the authority to decide what changes are to be made and when. For example, Toyota management used workers' ideas from quality team discussions to increase their hold over the workplace, but disregarded these teams when major changes were to be made in 1992. By 1994, once the teams had divulged what they knew, they were disbanded entirely (Moody 1997).

While critical commentators largely agree that there is no rejection of Taylorism, there is disagreement as to whether lean production represents a new hybrid or an intensification of the Taylorist approach. Berggren, looking at Swedish industry, sees lean production as a hybrid situation where the goals and some of the techniques of Taylorism remain alongside additional strategies, which strip workers of ideas. He terms this 'flexible Taylorism' (Berggren 1989). By contrast, Parker and Slaughter claim that an intensification of Taylorism is occurring. They conducted case study research into the joint US/Japanese auto manufacturer NUMMI (New United Motor Manufacturers Incorporated), based in Freemont, California, which employs a team-based, lean-production system[6]. NUMMI claim this represents a rejection of Taylorism, since workers' knowledge of the production process is recognized and utilized for improvements. However, Parker and Slaughter argue that this new system can best be described as 'management by stress' (MBS). Under MBS the entire production system, including the workforce, is placed under continual pressure in an attempt to identify weaknesses in the system, unproductive 'gaps' in the working day or 'unnecessary strengths'; that is overstaffing or an over-long time allocation. Workers work to standard operation guidelines, reminiscent of the Fordist situation. However, under MBS breakdowns and stoppages are considered useful since they allow management to identify areas where resources should be targeted or removed. Workers are encouraged to stop the line when they fall behind or need help. Alternatively, where breakdowns never occur, managers can identify 'over-resourcing' and workers will be given additional tasks to perform, or some workers will be removed. This system is based on the assumption that pressure is the most effective way to motivate workers and as a consequence they face intense scrutiny, while the speed and intensity of their work is at a constant productive maximum (Parker and Slaughter, 1988).

Most critical commentators agree on the negative impact of lean strategies such as quality circles and *kaizen*. Their function is twofold: they allow changes to be made – but only those sanctioned by management – and they cut across the trade union's traditional role of go-between and 'problem solver'. *Kaizen* and quality circles enable managers to hear workers' gripes at first hand, and if there is a need to act to avoid confrontation, they can do so, without the involvement of a 'third party'. Both practically and ideologically, these strategies legitimate the absence of trade unions and can be used to facilitate speed-up, multitasking and the intensification of work.

However, Milkman (1997) argues some American workers, particularly where there have been poor industrial relations and intensive Taylorist work strategies, have welcomed these innovations. To be listened to after years of being told 'what to do' is an intensely powerful experience. Furthermore, for keen workers, lean production provides an opportunity to 'shine'. These factors, together with the absence of alternative employment and alternative interpretations of the new workplace, explain why many workers are willing to co-operate with lean strategies, at least in the short term.

A central objective of lean work strategies is the promotion of 'goal hegemony': persuading the employees to share the company's aims. Lean working is as much a battle for hearts and minds as it is an exercise in eliminating waste. This can be seen as an attempt to incorporate workers, but research suggests that they can quickly become disappointed when the promises of lean production fail to materialize. If workers do become increasingly disillusioned, lean production may not herald an end to strife.

An End to Strife?

A key part of the myth of lean production is that it promises an end to workplace conflict. To that end employers attempt to marginalize or incorporate trade unions. The need for third-party involvement is negated and indeed could be detrimental to the new order (Oliver and Wilkinson 1990).

Attempts to undermine trade unions in the name of 'goal hegemony' stem from a desire on the part of lean employers to win control of the workplace. At the same time a sense of collectivity among workers is attacked through the introduction of performance-related pay and the encouragement of competition between work teams. These attempts at undermining worker collectivity are evidence of continued and even renewed conflict, rather than an end to it.

Greenfield lean corporations have attempted to negotiate highly restrictive trade union agreements, as was the case at Nissan UK. Alternatively, where circumstances allow it, they avoid union recognition altogether. This is exemplified by Milkman's research into Japanese direct investment in California. Of the sixty-six plants in her study only five allowed trade union recognition. At brownfield sites workers who had previously been associated with unions under the previous regime were not re-employed.[7] With the absence of a union, employers were able to pursue savings by keeping wages low, employing a vulnerable, typically migrant, work-force and frequently hiring workers on short-term contracts which were renewed but not made permanent (Milkman 1992).

In fact MNCs avoid industrial conflict by selecting economically vulnerable environments for lean developments. Typically, lean employers have chosen environments where labour is weak as a result of high levels of unemployment, thus ensuring a good supply of grateful applicants and the hope of compliance with new work practices. In such cases lean MNCs utilize green workforces which are industrially naïve and lacking experience of mass production.

These are common themes – research on Nissan UK by Garrahan and Stewart (1992) and Stephenson (1988; 1994) by Graham on Isuzu (1995) and Parker and Slaughter on NUMMI (1988) reveal similarly weak labour markets, compliant or absent trade unions and the careful scrutiny of hopeful applicants. Recruitment is used as a way of hiring workers with 'appropriate attitudes' to the work process, not necessarily those with the most appropriate skills, so that pro-union workers are excluded. Graham (1995) argues that the pre-employment recruitment stage is the beginning of a process of control whereby workers are inculcated into managerial ideology. This focuses on ensuring that workers understand the need for 'being a team worker', 'quality consciousness' and portrays unions as dangerous and undesirable.[8]

Parker and Slaughter (1988) claim that worker acceptance of MBS is most likely to be achieved where there are few alternative sources of employment and they, too, note the importance attached to the rigorous screening of applicants. Once employed by NUMMI, commitment was maintained through the use of penalties for failure; workers faced pressure from managers, reduced perks and undesirable assignments when they were viewed to have failed. Hence personal stress as well as system-stress supports MBS.

It would be wrong, however, to assume that in all situations unions have acquiesced to the demands of lean employers, that unions are obsolete or that they are always beaten during periods of high unemployment. These themes will be explored again in chapter 8. However, it is worth noting that unions in the UK have offered differing approaches to the introduction of lean-work practices into brownfield sites and have been successful in eliminating some of the more damaging aspects.[9] Similarly, while the absence of a trade union and alternative employment opportunities might restrict worker resistance, it would be mistaken to assume that lean production offers employers a 'win-all' situation.

Lean Production and the Problems Facing Employers

Lean production presents employers with many challenges. It is a high-risk system, with few 'buffers' or spare staff to cover unforeseen disruption, which relies heavily on workers' co-operation, particularly where layers of middle management have been discarded. As a consequence the strategy is prone to disruption. In failing to consider workers, proponents have underestimated the role workers might play in that disruption.

Where JIT is employed, disruption to the supply of goods or services, especially where these are single-sourced, can be catastrophic, bringing entire networks of production to a standstill in a very short period of time (Moody 1997). Typically, powerful corporations at the centre of the JIT 'web' (supply network) serve harsh financial penalties on 'failing' suppliers, even though the damage to corporate profits and image will have already been done. A 1988 strike by British workers brought the whole of Ford's European production to a standstill. Sierras assembled in Belgium ran on French transmissions, which were powered by British engines and components, supplied on a JIT basis. The dispute was resolved within nine days; none the less it cost Ford $927.5 million in lost production and $34.1 million in retail sales (Parker and Slaughter 1988: 45).

Rather than being an asset, workers are often the lean employers' biggest headache. While management gurus and business theorists declare that the impact on workers is positive, a consensus between workers and employers is assumed rather than fully explored (Thompson and Ackroyd 1995). For example, the MIT study was substantial in its scope, yet failed to investigate the concerns of workers in any of the workplaces studied. Analysts of this genre display an almost ideological commitment to lean production, ignoring the potential impact on workers and the possible disruption workers might inflict. For example, Roper et al. (1997) conducted a case study of two plants where JIT was failing. The authors focus exclusively on the technical elements of the strategy's implementation in order to locate the fault, while ignoring the role of workers. They hint at worker manipulation of the JIT system – '*Received customer order, leave in desk till last minute, hand to team leader, not enough time, yahoo! More overtime!*' – but fail to explore workers' activities and perspectives more fully (p. 34).

The high incidence of injury, often the outcome of RSI (repetitive strain injury), which was common with the traditional Fordist set-up, continues to be a problem for employers and workers alike. For example, Nissan UK wish to maintain their image as a paternalistic and successful employer, and therefore avoid making injured workers redundant. As this worker explains, the solution identified allows Nissan to maintain their image, but was not beneficial to injured workers in the long run:

> I got a neck injury 'cos I had done the same job for like three and a half years, erm. . . . So they took me off there and put me on another landing, so it was border line whether . . . I would have to leave the company, with me neck you know, erm. . . . But they are running out of options [where to move workers] . . . and like Nissan always say that they never make anybody redundant but they have a separation by agreement deal. . . . I mean they [the workers] were getting like six months' wages, which is a canny whack, but once you haven't got a job, you haven't got a job! (Nissan worker)

A related problem is what to do with an 'ageing' workforce? Nissan workers in their thirties express anxiety about how long they can continue with a punishing pace of work. Nissan have the added problem of dealing with this issue sensitively, in line with the rhetoric of industrial harmony and goal hegemony. Characteristically, it has shared its problems with its workers, calling it, 'The Ageing Worker Problem', and has asked for suggestions from the shop floor. The situation has yet to be resolved!

Maintaining the appropriate image is an ever-present problem for lean employers. Various eventualities can dent the hegemonic ideology: redundancies, the failure of the JIT system, the use of 'macho management' tactics, or the breaking of promises. Workers at Ikeda Hoover, a JIT supplier to Nissan UK, have developed an active trade union base, which has led to occasional stoppages. The union was developed by skilled women sewing-machinists, who enjoyed the security of knowing they had skills in scarce supply. Ikeda workers claim that these disputes induced Nissan's management to 'organize' electrical faults, pretending to their own workers that a technical fault had caused the stoppage. Thus Nissan employees were sheltered from the knowledge that all was not well with their unionized neighbour. Under JIT, the lean producer is only as good as their suppliers. As the Nissan case study illustrates, the context chosen by the parent company may offer excellent conditions for success, but the suppliers who follow their part-owner to provide JIT deliveries may struggle in the very same environment, since their needs are not necessarily those of the main plant (Stephenson 1994). The consequences of such failure are not just financial. At Valley Co. in South Wales, Delbridge (1998) found that disruption in the JIT system undermined workers' confidence in their managers and in the system as a whole.

Delbridge notes a number of forms of worker resistance, ranging from overt activities such as stoppages to symbolic acts, which display dissatisfaction and 'distance' the worker from the goals of the employer. Delbridge (1998), Graham (1995) and Stephenson (1994) each provide accounts of stoppages in lean-production plants which arose when the visage of 'all for one' slipped. Symbolic acts of resistance appear to be quite common and range from refusing to sit down at team meetings or failure to wear the company uniforms to more significant acts, where workers withdraw discretionary effort.

Even where harmony appears to prevail, in-depth interviews reveal that appearances can be deceptive. Interviews with apparently committed Nissan UK workers, who arrive early, leave late and present the right emotional response to work, reveal that they were engaged in what Knights et al. (1985) call 'cynical compliance'. They 'cheat' by going 'through the motions' of what is expected by their employers, but eschew genuine goal hegemony. As one worker explained, the appearance of commitment, irrespective of true feelings, can secure both continued employment and freedom from intense scrutiny:

> There was this one lad who left the other week. He was told off for coming at five to, that is five minutes before he was due to start. Good practice is being about ten to fifteen minutes before hand. He was told it was not good practice coming in at that time . . . that was not the

> Nissan way of doing things . . . they are given a pretty good general idea that they are expected to be there early and leave late type of thing, that way you avoid the hassle . . . appearance is very important, more than anything else, more than what is really going on. (Nissan worker)

Going through the motions while remaining cynical may be a relatively futile exercise for workers, in terms of securing radical change. Nevertheless, it illustrates that for many, commitment to lean working is 'paper-thin' (Stephenson 1994). Given the absence of alternative jobs, alternative perspectives on lean production and lack of effective trade unions, these are the only 'safe' responses available. Rather like the air hostesses in Hochschild's study (1983), who, when asked to smile by their managers, fixed a permanent lurid grin on their face, these acts remind us that workers employ whatever means possible, no matter how limited, to secure dignity at work. We are reminded that the workplace is not necessarily a place of out-and-out consent or combat; rather co-operation and resistance are combined in everyday working lives (Delbridge 1998).

Conclusion: People, Politics and Power

The myth of lean production springs from a basically flawed position. Proponents offer a 'top-down' approach to understanding and researching the workplace. They see employers as the sole 'movers and shakers' who make workplaces failures or successes; their ideas are paramount. Within this genre is an inherent faith in capitalism, which, it is believed, can work for everyone, if only employers, managers and consultant gurus get the details right. The role of workers is either ignored or assumed. Where they do feature, the concern of proponents of lean production is to get them to adopt the 'right' attitudes and 'motivation' in order to 'function' effectively (Womack et al. 1990; Peters 1992).

Not all management writers fall into the trap of ignoring workers in order to promote the next big thing. Indeed some useful accounts of the changing experience of work, such as Delbridge 1998, emanate from Management Schools. We can also distinguish between critical accounts, which provide useful insights into the new workplace (Graham 1995), and those that go further, by viewing industrial restructuring as part of a strategy of capitalist regeneration. These studies are concerned with issues of power and political change, and are driven by a critical understanding of the dynamics of capitalism.

From this more radical perspective, lean production is viewed as a strategy for redressing the balance of power, away from workers towards capital. Beale (1994), Garrahan and Stewart (1992) and Moody (1997) make this point most forcefully, tracing the development of these new work strategies to the recession of the 1970s and 1980s and the actions of right-wing governments concerned to undermine the power of organized labour.

Lean production has been presented as symptomatic of the emergence of a new era of post-Fordism. This position is flawed in two ways. First, lean production does not exist in any uniform, comprehensive or universal manifestation. A few powerful MNCs have been able to adopt most of the lean-production package. However, each corporation approaches lean production in its own way. A range of factors and decisions influence the shape of the new workplace. It is therefore difficult to identify a single entity which we may designate 'lean production'.

Second, even where the strategy is attempted or where some component parts are adopted, there is no radical departure from the past. The foundations of Fordism and Taylorism remain, with some adjustments. The mass delivery of largely standard services or products continues, but workers are now expected to break demarcation boundaries and perform a range of semi-skilled or unskilled tasks in addition to their core task. The Taylorist search for the 'one best way' continues, but in a variable form. Workers are encouraged to share their knowledge and contribute to goal hegemony in return for job security and participation in the change process. However, the power to determine which ideas are implemented and who shall benefit remains firmly in the hands of employers. A further variant on Taylorism is that workers are made individually accountable and are scrutinized by managers and in some cases by their peers. The lean worker is visible and vulnerable, no longer part of the collective, and often no longer part of an effective and independent trade union.

Perhaps the most valuable insight offered in this chapter is that lean production presents employers with few easy solutions to the problem of sustaining profitability and competitiveness. It is a highly vulnerable system, which is dependent upon the co-operation of workers, not only those employed by the parent company, but also those in supplier plants where wages and conditions tend to be inferior. This core–periphery split creates enough problems, but in addition lean producers must maintain their image of efficiency and paternalism even though lean practices are likely to bring about deterioration in working conditions. Lean production is full of contradictions, and it is that gap between the rhetoric and the reality of the strategy which may force many employers to steer away from adopting the full package.

One of the greatest threats to the myth of goal hegemony is the inability of lean production strategies to ensure long-term employment security. Economic vulnerability does a great deal to underpin workers' commitment to lean production. The Nissan worker quoted at the outset of this chapter has faith in the view that lean practices and hard work will ensure his job security. However, external forces in the global economy as much as work organization and the commitment of workers determine corporate profitability. The closure of Nissan's near neighbour, Fujitsu Microelectronics, following the global decline in the price of microchips, is evidence of this (Hetherington 1998). A further problem is that workers whose efforts sustain the lean system may find that the sheer pace of their work excludes them from job security as they grow older, particularly where there is no effective union to negotiate an equitable solution. In this respect, lean production is a high-waste strategy: it wastes the wealth of workers and in many instances shortens their working lives. When the myths are exposed, managers may be left with the problem of managing very disappointed workers.

3

The Myths of Non-Standard Employment

> More and more individuals are behaving as professionals always have, charging fees not wages. They find they are 'going portfolio' or 'going plural'. Going portfolio as I suggested earlier means exchanging full-time employment for independence.
>
> (Handy 1994: 175)

> Like everyone else, in the back of your mind, worries about the future, redundancies. At one time the Civil Service was considered the most secure job, once you were in you were in for life, but like everything else that's changing.
>
> (Female civil servant)

Introduction

Conventional wisdom dictates that while in the recent past workers enjoyed full-time 'jobs for life', there is a current trend towards non-standard forms of employment. Many writers perceive this shift to be profound, inevitable and irreversible. Although for workers such change frequently leads to a deterioration of employment security, it has been claimed that such wholesale restructuring brings numerous benefits. Workers are given greater choice in how they want to participate in paid employment, thus allowing their other commitments to be met with greater ease (Handy 1994; 1995; Hewitt 1993). The provision of non-standard employment, in so far as it increases labour market flexibility, allows employers to reduce waste and match output with product market demands more easily. The economic benefits are therefore enormous since, in a more globalized context (see chapter 1), organizations must constantly find new ways of satisfying customer needs.

In this chapter we will examine empirical evidence which shows that many of the positive claims made for the 'new era' of non-standard employment are unfounded and mythical. Not only has the extent of the shift to non-standard employment been exaggerated, but so too have the benefits to both employers and workers. Indeed, workers' ability to choose particular forms of employment is affected by a range of factors, most notably gender and class. Finally, we will argue that the growth of non-standard employment does not necessarily tally with the emergence of a vibrant, competitive and modern economy. Conditions of employment associated with non-standard employment are typically poor and hardly form the basis of a world-class economy.

The Age of Non-Standard Employment?

The term 'standard employment' is used to refer to situations where employers provide an employment contract, which sets out a long-term commitment to full-time employment. Typically, a number of conditions are attached to this contract: regular hours and pay, the provision of a designated workplace, with pension and sick pay arrangements and often the opportunity to join a trade union. As Fevre (1991) points out, such standard employment is exemplified in a number of classical sociological accounts of the workplace in the advanced capitalist economies, most notably in Beynon's *Working for Ford* (1984). Beynon's workers worked together in the Ford site on Merseyside: they had long-term contracts with a series of associated benefits, including holiday entitlement and sick pay. The work patterns of their lives were relatively straightforward, at least during the economic boom of the 1960s when Beynon carried out his research. These workers knew what they would be doing each week, when they would begin and end work, which people they would see at work and roughly how much they would be earning.

More recently, Beynon (1997) examined non-standard employment or what he calls 'hyphenated jobs': part-time,[1] temporary work, homework and self-employment. He attributes the purported increase in the non-standard workforce to a number of factors: employers' desire to increase numerical flexibility; the demise of manufacturing jobs; the increase in service-sector employment and the accompanying feminization of jobs. As we saw in chapter 2, the concept of numerical flexibility refers to the variation in the number of workers involved in a given part of the work process at a given time. Numerical flexibility enables employers to match production capacity with market demand; to employ workers only when necessary; and to let them go when convenient without incurring penalties, such as redundancy payments.

Management theorists have claimed that the utilization of non-standard employment is a clever corporate strategy capable of regenerating industries and therefore the economy in general. In the 1980s Atkinson and Meager (1986a) formulated the model of the 'flexible firm'. They argued that organizations were increasingly dividing their workforces into 'core' and 'periphery' groups. The core workforce would typically experience standard employment since they have the skills and competencies needed on a regular basis. If specialist skills are required, or if there is a need to raise production, then peripheral workers could be hired when necessary as non-standard workers. They may be employed directly by the flexible firm, on a temporary or part-time basis, they may be self-employed or they may be hired through agencies or subsidiaries. The benefits to the flexible firm are seemingly obvious. It has no need to train employees; it can buy in the appropriate skills when necessary in order to match market demands; and it can reduce waste by operating in a leaner way (see chapter 2). Once the need for peripheral workers ends, they can be shed with few penalties. Moreover, if agency workers are used, the agency selects, hires and fires workers and deals with other distractions such as National Insurance contributions.

Clearly, the flexible firm model is something of an 'ideal-type': a construct designed to show how organizations could maximize numerical flexibility. Nevertheless, a range of strategies for enhancing numerical flexibility can be seen to exist. Employers may rely entirely on non-standard workers to provide the necessary suppleness or they may opt to procure greater flexibility from 'core' employees. Beynon (1997) observes that employers may use both non-standard workers and 'non-standard hours', by increasing the use of shift work, night and weekend work, for example.

There is strong evidence of a trend towards greater non-standard employment in the UK. The number of jobs in manufacturing, where standard employment was for a long time commonplace, has declined dramatically, from seven million in 1979 to less than four million by 1995. During the same period the number of jobs in the service sector, traditionally associated with non-standard employment, increased by over a million (Beynon 1997). Citing evidence drawn from studies of employers' labour-use strategies in the 1980s and 1990s, Dex and McCulloch (1997) reported that part-time working was evident in 85 per cent of UK workplaces. Temporary workers were used in 20 per cent of establishments; subcontractors in three-quarters of establishments; and about 10 per cent of employers had made use of homeworkers. Drawing on these studies, as well as on official data, they concluded that in 1994 'at least one quarter of men and one half of women of working age held non-standard jobs' and that the 'structure of employment in the early 1990s looks very different from its appearance at the end of the 1970s, with the most change having taken place in the early 1980s' (p. 173).

The increased participation of women (particularly married women) in employment accounts for some of the increase in non-standard employment. Forty-five per cent of all women workers work part-time compared with 10 per cent of male workers. In the 1990s, the female part-time workforce increased by 28 per cent, while female employment as a whole grew by 22 per cent. However, increasing numbers of men also now work on a part-time basis. In the ten years up to 1998, the male part-time workforce grew by 138 per cent – from 556,000 to 1,320,000. Part-time employment is largely concentrated in clerical work, personal and protective services and sales. These occupational groups account for 60 per cent of the part-time workforce. Part-time employees earn just 70 per cent of the hourly earnings of full-time workers and very few – about 5 per cent – are employed in managerial positions (LRD 1999).

Some commentators view the increase in the number of part-time jobs as usefully fulfilling the needs of those who lack commitment to full-time, permanent employment. Catherine Hakim (1995) has famously argued that although career women choose standard employment, a more domestically minded group chooses non-standard forms of employment, allowing them to maintain their primary commitment to childcare and domestic work. Feminist claims that women take such work because the cost of childcare is prohibitive is disregarded by Hakim as a smokescreen, an attempt to divert attention away from the fact that many women do not wish to succeed in paid employment. This lack of commitment is evidenced by high labour turnover rates among non-standard women workers. Hakim argues that part-time work is not inherently exploitative; rather, such non-standard employment offers workers the choice to develop careers, but weak commitment to work leads women to refuse opportunities for betterment. Hakim also claims that even in 1995 most part-time workers had many of the same legal rights and protections as their full-time counterparts. Thus it is not non-standard employment that is poor; it is the attitude of workers.

Hakim's arguments have been heavily criticized as an attack on feminist demands for greater equality for women both in work and at home. Her claim that women are to blame for their own failures will be considered again in chapter 4. Nevertheless, the view that non-standard employment, such as part-time working, provides workers with positive choices has also been proposed by some on the political left. Patricia Hewitt (1993) argued that because of changes in the structure of society and in social relations, there needed to be a change in attitudes towards employment. She takes as given the increase in non-standard employment and argues that these changes offer valuable choices and opportunities. The flexible firm enables both men and women to fit paid employment more easily around the demands of family life. Hewitt commends innovative forms of part-time employment, such as those aligned with school terms, for example, but which allow wages to be spread out over the course of the year so that no 'hungry gap' occurs. Writing in Britain, in the middle of a long period of Conservative rule, Hewitt qualified her enthusiasm for non-standard employment by calling for state intervention to ensure 'fair flexibility'. In order to provide all employees with basic rights at work, she called for the introduction of a minimum wage, a maximum working hours directive, time off for parents and the adoption of the EU's (European Union's) Social Chapter, all of which have now been implemented – albeit in a diluted way – by the Labour government elected in 1997. Hewitt also argued that employers, too, must play their part in ensuring that non-standard employment is not used as an excuse for exploitation (Hewitt 1993).

The influential management theorist Charles Handy (1994) has also associated employment flexibility with personal choice and freedom. He sees the demise of the 'standard job' as a positive opportunity for personal regeneration. Handy writes of a new 'portfolio' approach to life, which involves the worker developing a package of different forms of employment; some would provide the necessary monetary security, while others would be more satisfying, or just for fun! Employment ceases to be the 'all and everything' of life; labour market flexibility would allow workers to 'dabble' in many types of experience. Since corporations no longer guarantee career structures for their employees, individuals must build their own personal career plan. Over time people would develop a dossier of employment experience, increasing their labour market appeal. They would work, as many professionals currently do, for 'customers, not wages', moving between different clients. Handy (1994) claims to envy his children who have the freedom to choose their own employment by 'going portfolio' (p. 73).

Positive notions of choice, freedom and opportunity are recurrent themes here. Handy and Hewitt are not entirely satisfied that non-standard workers are sufficiently supported by the state; nevertheless, each emphasizes the potential benefits of such employment. Moreover, the increase of certain forms of non-standard employment has been seen as an indication of the resurgence of the British economy. Under successive Conservative governments the numbers in self-employment rose from 1.76 million in 1979 to 3.27 million in 1994 (13 per cent of the workforce), and this was presented as evidence of the emergence of a new entrepreneurial culture. In the 1980s over 200 measures were enacted, at a total cost of over £1 billion, to encourage the growth of self-employment and small businesses (MacDonald 1997). This was seen as crucial to the development of a more competitive, dynamic and less rigid economy.

Interestingly, a degree of consensus now exists between the two main political parties in the UK on the question of labour market flexibility. While the Conservative government clearly possessed an ideological commitment to the promotion of non-standard employment, not least because it was inimical to trade unionism (see chapter 8), New Labour has generally followed suit. Individuals close to the present Labour government have celebrated the merits of non-standard employment. For example, John Stredwick, an adviser to British Prime Minister Tony Blair on employment and economic matters, provides positive examples of the portfolio worker in action, and outlines the key benefits for both employers and employees (Stredwick and Ellis 1998). Hewitt and Handy are also very close to New Labour, one as an MP (Member of Parliament), the other as an adviser. Furthermore, an emphasis on the importance of building flexible labour markets, while at the same time ensuring fairness, has characterized the Labour government's employment policies; it is seen to underpin the development of a dynamic, competitive and, above all, modern economy capable of thriving in a more globalized and knowledge-driven world (see DTI 1998c; Leadbeater 1999). Thus there is a consensus that a radical and irrevocable break with the past has occurred. There is no going back, non-standard employment and the flexible labour market are the future and workers must accommodate such a paradigm shift as best they can.

Non-Standard Employment: A Radical and Irrevocable Break with the Past?

Anna Pollert (1988a; 1988b) was among the first to argue that the term 'standard employment' is something of a misnomer. Calling a situation 'standard' assumes that all workers were fortunate enough to enjoy permanent full-time employment with its associated benefits. In reality only relatively privileged workers – typically white, male and skilled – benefited from these conditions. Women, immigrants, young and black workers and the semi-skilled or unskilled were generally excluded from standard employment. Pollert concluded that the recent interest in non-standard employment is an expression of its growth among previously privileged white, male and skilled workers. Yet Pollert was also sceptical about the notion of a dramatic increase in non-standard employment. She argued that proponents of the radical break thesis had misinterpreted the evidence. For example, employers' attempts to increase numerical flexibility had been mistakenly associated with the rise of non-standard forms of employment. In reality, many employers had increased numerical flexibility through the use of non-standard hours, such as weekend working or overtime (Pollert 1988b).

Pollert was particularly dismissive of the 'flexible firm' model, since there was little evidence for the emergence of 'core' and 'peripheral' groups (1988b). Wide-scale employment restructuring was largely confined to the public sector, suggesting that it resulted from an ideological commitment on the part of the British Conservative government.

Claims for an enormous swing toward non-standard employment hold no more water in the 1990s. Drawing on data from the influential and comprehensive Social Change and Economic Life Initiative (SCELI) survey and the later Employment in Britain survey, Gallie (1998) strongly argues that the shift towards non-standard employment has been more imaginary than real. He points out that the size of the temporary workforce remained stable through the 1980s and early 1990s at around 5 per cent of the total, with some expansion occurring in the mid-1990s. Although there was a significant rise in part-time employment between 1984 and 1995 – an increase of 25 per cent – Gallie's analysis of the Employment in Britain survey suggests that much of this employment is relatively permanent in nature and cannot be considered to represent an increase in employment insecurity.

The prevalence of some forms of non-standard employment – such as homework, for example, which will be discussed in greater detail in the following section – is almost impossible to calculate. Nevertheless, a wholesale abandonment of permanent and full-time work has not occurred and there is little evidence to suggest an increase in 'job hopping' as implied by Handy's notion of the portfolio worker. Meadows (1999) claims that in 1975 the average job lasted just over six years, and that by 1999 this period had been reduced by just six months. She concludes that despite rhetoric to the contrary, the UK labour market displays a remarkable degree of stability in the attachment of employees to a particular employer.

Given the scarcity of evidence for a radical change, how and why did this myth about non-standard work originate? Pollert (1988b) situates the debate within the political context of the mid-1980s. The Conservative government had launched bitter attacks on organized labour and on the nationalized industries. Against a backdrop of high levels of unemployment, the government published a White Paper in 1985 – *Employment, the Challenge for the Nation* – which set out to ditch the long-standing view that the state should prioritize and support full employment. Dominating the document was the message that future employment would be insecure and that people should adapt rapidly (Pollert 1988b). The notion of a radical and irrevocable break with the past, then, has an ideological and political dimension. Through the notion of a break with the past the Conservative government sought to re-educate the workforce into a new mindset, where the emphasis is on flexibility, individualism and entrepreneurialism, rather than collectivism and rigidity. Moreover, this message has penetrated, as many workers have come to see their employment as more precarious than that enjoyed by previous generations. As a result, many workers have lost confidence in the ability of trade unions to protect their best interests (a theme returned to in chapter 8) and have come to believe, like the Nissan worker quoted at the outset of chapter 2, that employment security can only be secured through 'good behaviour' as defined by their employer.

In the next section, attention moves to the claim that non-standard employment can be equated with economic rejuvenation. It will be argued that not only has the shift to non-standard employment been exaggerated, it is doubtful that there is an irrevocable trajectory towards this form of employment; employers recognize a number of limitations arising from the adoption of such a strategy and some have consequently avoided them. Moreover, we will argue that many forms of non-standard employment can best be described as poor and therefore do not provide the basis for a vibrant, world-class economy.

Non-Standard Employment and the Emergence of a Vibrant Economy'?

The push towards increased non-standard employment has been ideologically driven. Behind the rhetoric of enterprise, individualism and flexibility, the reality for many workers is employment that is casualized: characterized by low pay, insecurity and poor working conditions.

Successive governments have maintained that the growth in self-employment and small businesses shows an increase in the entrepreneurial spirit in Britain. However, the long-term survival rate of the self-employed and small businesses is very poor. In a follow-up to a survey of young entrepreneurs (MacDonald and Coffield 1991), MacDonald (1997) found that of the original sample of eighty-six businesses, of those that were traced, fifty-eight had failed, ten were 'plodding' and only four were genuinely succeeding (p. 107).

Ironically, many of these 'entrepreneurs' were pushed into self-employment by the absence of alternative employment in a context of high unemployment. At a qualitative level the experience of self-employment had been poor. Many of those who had failed in self-employment suffered psychological trauma and left their businesses with huge debts – one twenty-seven-year-old owed £200,000. Even when businesses did survive, very often the owner's take-home pay was low. The self-employed find themselves in a cut-throat world of kill or be killed – a 'risky business' indeed (MacDonald 1997: 108–10). Moreover, contrary to the rhetoric of Handy (1994), the majority of the self-employed do not work in creative or professional occupations, but in sectors such as construction, where they constitute 45 per cent of that workforce (Beynon 1997: 33).

Many self-employed workers have been 'cut loose' by their employers, and have been re-engaged on a self-employed basis. This practice is not just the preserve of small-scale or disreputable employers. To focus on the British case again, in further education (FE) and higher education (HE), student numbers have increased dramatically in recent years and much employment has been casualized in order to meet this demand and to ensure cost advantages for the employers. In evidence submitted to a select committee inquiry, the National Association of Teachers in Further and Higher Education (NATFHE) claims that of the 58,185 academic staff employed by HE colleges and 'new' universities (former polytechnics), 25,000 are employed on a part-time basis (House of Commons Education and Employment Committee 1999).[2] Breaking that figure down further, the 1999 Bett report stated that in 1998 38 per cent of academics were employed on an hourly-paid or casual basis (Bett 1999).[3] The Bett report and the trade unions both criticized institutions that have sought to win competitive advantage at the expense of relatively vulnerable workers.[4]

In FE, following the recommendations of the erstwhile College Employers' Forum (CEF), in 1995, a number of colleges have begun to employ non-standard workers through third party agencies, Education Lecturing Services (ELS) in particular. ELS has claimed that it is working, or has worked, with about 200 colleges, approaching half of the total number, and has some 40,000 lecturers registered with it (*Times Educational Supplement*, 27 March 1998). Some colleges in Britain – North Tyneside, for example – dismissed all their part-time staff and re-engaged them on a self-employed basis through the agency. Staff with many years of service returned with a lower hourly rate and with the added responsibility of funding their own professional indemnity insurance (House of Commons Employment Committee 1996). Contrary to the view that the growth of non-standard employment reflects economic buoyancy, the casualization of employment in HE and FE was born out of desperate attempts to cut costs – an indication of crisis rather than confidence. According to NATFHE's evidence 27 per cent of FE colleges are in weak financial health, a significant increase since 1994. This is crisis management and those worst affected by it are among the most vulnerable in our society.

Other forms of non-standard employment also appear to offer few rewards to workers. In particular homeworkers are likely to experience poor quality employment. In making this point, it is important to make a distinction between homeworkers and those who work from home. Many of the latter are skilled or professional workers using computer technology. By contrast, 'homeworkers' tend to be semi-skilled or unskilled workers and are generally paid on a piece-rate basis.

Homeworkers' wages tend to be very low. A 1997 survey of British homeworkers based in Yorkshire revealed an average pay rate of just £1.93 per hour (Conlock 1998: 2). Although many homeworkers will have been helped by the April 1999 introduction of the £3.60 national minimum wage, it is unlikely that many will earn more than this flat rate: 'Now that I've found a good homeworking employer I get £3.50 an hour; before that I got £9.20 a week for 40 hours' work [23p per hour]' (Worker quoted in Conlock 1998: 1).

Research suggests that health and safety is a particular problem for homeworkers. They are unlikely to be working in environments that are designed for labour. Often conditions are cramped, particularly since workers attempt to accommodate play areas for their children alongside machinery and parts needed for work. Workers, their families and visitors to the home are at risk of injury. For reasons to be discussed in greater detail below, homeworkers are less likely to be represented by a trade union and consequently may not be aware of the hazards associated with their work. An additional threat to health and safety results from working excessive hours. In line with other EU countries, the British government introduced a Working Time Directive in October 1998, which limits the average number of hours workers are legally entitled to work to forty-eight in a week. However homeworkers that are paid on a piece-rate basis are unlikely to heed these directives, particularly where rates of pay are very poor.

Although wages and conditions have been a focus of the debate about the quality of non-standard employment, the social and political experience of work is equally important. For many, homeworkers in particular, non-standard employment means social isolation, loneliness and loss of the enjoyment of labour. Sociological accounts of the workplace provide graphic insights into the sheer pleasure that workers frequently derive from social interaction at work. For many it is that social interaction which makes work tolerable. Women tobacco workers in Anna Pollert's study, *Girls, Wives, Factory Lives* (1981), hoot with laughter at anecdotes about home life, husbands and sex. In 'Banana Time' (1960), Donald Roy writes of workers creating social dramas around 'fruit breaks'; these enable them to punctuate the seemingly endless day and survive the monotony of their work. The workers encountered in these sociological accounts had a sense of identity, common purpose and, in some instances, such as the Ford motor plant studied by Beynon (1984), political power. For many non-standard employees, however, the opportunity to enjoy that element of work is gone. Many will not see their counterparts; some will see them only fleetingly. The social, emotional and political deprivations of non-standard employment are too often ignored.

A qualitative study commissioned by the West Yorkshire Homeworking Unit (Conlock 1998) found that respondents complained of anxiety, loss of confidence and of agoraphobia as a result of spending many years working at home, seeing little of the outside world. This can lead to stress, especially where wages are low, employment is insecure and employers demand that deadlines are met. As this worker testifies, the day can be punishing and lonely, with serious implications for both mental and physical health:

> I often suffered from backache due to lifting heavy rugs. My arms ached from pulling them through the machine. There was dust everywhere and it made my nose itch. I felt depressed every morning when the kids had gone to school. I knew I would be working until three, then again after tea. The same lonely routine every day. All this just to earn ten to fifteen pounds a day. (Quoted in Huws 1994: 28)

It is important not to conflate all forms of non-standard employment. The business executive who has made a free and informed choice to become self-employed is not in the same position as the home-worker who works in isolation for £40 a week. Yet even those who have made such an active choice will have been well advised to have calculated the costs of working alone, missing out on company pension schemes, paid holidays and sick leave, before taking the self-employment 'plunge'. They should also be aware that one of the primary problems they face is one of 'self-exploitation', as this worker found:

> The danger is of . . . 'self-exploitation'. It is very difficult for me to draw clear boundaries round what I'm doing . . . I can't at the end of a specific time say well, you know, I've done a day's work. When I was in paid employment . . . if you were having an off day, without too many pricks of conscience, you could sit there a bit slumped at your desk and just react to whatever happens . . . [now] it's not like that. Of course one can slump, but one is not being paid to slump. You have not achieved anything. (Quoted in Haddon and Silverstone 1993: 39)

This pressure to be self-motivating is a problem even for highly skilled and well-paid self-employed workers. There is little regulation of homeworkers' working time; nobody 'cracks the whip', so they must crack it themselves, either in pursuit of a deadline, a goal or much-needed cash. The main distinction between the relatively well-off groups and the homeworkers examined in the studies by Huws (1994) and Conlock (1998) is that the latter are 'self-exploiting' as a result of economic necessity and the very low wages paid to them, often through piece-rates. They are not building business or developing new computer programmes, but are paying the gas bill.

Non-standard workers are also often politically disadvantaged. Most non-standard workers lack bargaining power or 'leverage' for a number of reasons. In the main, they can be easily replaced and are less likely to be represented by a trade union than standard workers. Heery (1998a) notes that in the 1990s many unions appreciated that their survival depended on their ability to represent non-standard workers. However, locating these workers is difficult. Many non-standard workers are literally 'invisible' if they work from home and are unlikely to come into contact with union representatives. Similarly, part-time and temporary workers can be difficult to trace, particularly if they frequently move in and out of employment or between jobs. These workers may not even meet their colleagues, beginning and starting their work at different times; as a result the opportunity to identify common interests is limited. The short-term nature of employment may lead non-standard workers to question the logic of joining a union.

Where employers have been able to force a core–periphery split within their workforces, with peripheral workers hoping to gain core status, employers can take political advantage of the vulnerability which both sets of workers are likely to experience: one group (the periphery) wishing to gain secure permanent employment, the other (the core) hoping not to be 'ousted' by the reserve arm of labour waiting on the periphery. In Ikeda Hoover UK, when core workers refused to accept the introduction of new technologies, temporary workers were forced to adopt them, thereby undermining their permanent counterparts (Stephenson 1994).

While non-standard employment seems littered with potential dangers from the workers' point of view, employers too have found that an over-reliance on it may be hazardous. To return to the FE case, although some colleges sacked part-time lecturers and re-engaged them via agencies on a self-employed basis, many others, recognizing the potential dangers of such a strategy, resisted this approach. College principals expressed discomfort with the ethics of treating loyal staff in such a way, while others revealed a number of more pragmatic concerns. They were less than confident that employing workers on a self-employed basis constituted a watertight way of avoiding the provision of potentially costly employment legislation. Nor were they confident that agencies could satisfactorily supply the skilled personnel needed, especially when those skills were in relatively short supply. Some principals claimed that any savings resulting from such a strategy would have been relatively insignificant. Furthermore, given the weak financial situation of many colleges, it was felt that the money paid to agencies in return for the supply of lecturers could be better spent improving conditions within the college itself and on supporting core staff (Williams 1998). This brings us to their final objection: that the forced introduction of non-standard employment may cut across the notion of goal hegemony outlined in chapter 2. As Beynon (1997) noted, you cannot 'downsize' or 'force self-employment' on workers and then ask for 'togetherness' (pp. 29–30). Purcell et al. (1999) notes employers' need to balance carefully the financial gains accrued through flexible work methods against the danger of damaging the good will and reciprocity that exists between employers and employees: for example, workers' staying late at short notice to complete an order, in return for flexibility around childcare (p. 36). A forced increase in numerical flexibility, especially where workers see a deterioration in their own working conditions, shatters the illusion that 'we all work together' and may increase workplace antagonism. We have seen how peripheral workers in Ikeda Hoover were used to threaten the position of core workers. However, this tactic backfired on the employer since, rather than blaming their peripheral colleagues, core workers sought to develop the trade union further so that temporary workers could be made permanent (Stephenson 1994).

Non-Standard Employment as Life-Enhancing Choice?

The view that non-standard employment enables workers to make choices suggests a number of things: that non-standard employment is of sufficient quality to merit people taking it as a positive choice; that as a result of choosing non-standard employment, workers can improve their lives in some way; that a number of realistic alternatives are available; and that workers have sufficient power to make such decisions about their employment.

We would argue that good quality employment comprises relatively good wages, which can be achieved without the need for excessively long working hours or overtime. The presence of employment security, a high standard of health and safety and access to union representation are further indicators of such a state. Associated benefits might reasonably include paid sick leave and holiday entitlement, maternity and paternity leave and possibly access to a pension scheme. On the basis of the discussion in the previous section, it would be reasonable to argue that many forms of non-standard employment constitute 'poor work' (Brown and Scase 1995) and that workers who 'choose' them are unlikely to enjoy improvements to the quality of their lives.

Nevertheless, we must not homogenize non-standard forms of employment. Some offer good opportunities, are genuinely chosen by workers and enrich their lives. The crucial factor is power. If workers have skills that are sought after, but are not readily available in the labour market, they may have the power to engineer a positive outcome from the non-standard situation. Similarly, where people are free from financial or ideological constraints they are more likely to be able to make positive choices about their work, on their own terms. It is this crucial question of power – or rather, the absence of it – which eludes those who seek to claim that non-standard employment is a life enhancing choice.

For example, Hakim (1995) makes much of the 'choices' women enjoy about their paid employment. However, her work has been heavily criticized, primarily by feminist writers, not least because it is based primarily on statistical data, from which participant intent is assumed, rather than fully explored (Bruegel 1996; Ginn et al. 1996). When the pressures facing women are fully understood, the question of whether real choices are available to the majority is called into question.

Women continue to carry the bulk of responsibility for domestic work and childcare, a point that will be explored further in chapter 4. Nevertheless, Hakim claims that their decision to opt for non-standard employment is not affected by the availability of reasonably priced childcare. This point has been heavily contested, and serves to illustrate that Hakim focuses almost entirely on the financial–rational decisions she assumes all women are capable of making.[5] She neglects the emotional and health costs associated with carrying the 'double burden' of employment and unpaid work in the home. In a survey of social services staff Ginn and Sandall (1997) claim that women with caring responsibilities were choosing part-time employment because the stress placed upon them when working full-time led to emotional and physical exhaustion.

The choice for women not to pursue paid work is perhaps a luxury in the modern era. Ginn and Sandall (1997) note that women's wages are increasingly important in keeping households out of poverty. Given the frequency of marriage breakdown and the inherent disadvantages of the pension system, women are well advised to seek their own income in order to qualify for state or private pensions.

Moreover, the ideology of domesticity continues to affect the lives of women. There is much social pressure placed on women to meet high standards as housewives and mothers. While some women face relatively subtle pressure to conform to 'the norm' of giving up employment or taking non-standard employment on becoming a mother, others face hostility if they break social codes. Sandra Jones's fascinating account of gender discrimination in the police force reveals women coming under great pressure to leave employment once they married or had children. The assumption of male officers was that women's 'new careers' as housewives and mothers would take precedence over paid employment and as a result they would cease to be effective and reliable colleagues, especially when faced with dangerous work situations (Jones 1986).

Another major rationale for workers of both sexes 'choosing' non-standard employment is to avoid unemployment, something we highlighted earlier in respect of self-employment. Many workers in depressed labour markets take non-standard employment out of necessity rather than choice. Women and ethnic minority members may be pressured into it because of discrimination and racism. A survey of female domestic and catering workers in the North East of England by the trade union UNISON (1993) reveals that many carried two or even three part-time jobs. Not only does this illustrate the problems associated with measuring the growth of these work forms, it also indicates that workers frequently do not choose this situation with much enthusiasm, but because they are 'underemployed': that is, they want more employment than one non-standard job offers.

Some commentators have claimed that remaining on the unemployment register long-term has ceased to be an option in Britain; Allen (1997) calls this the loss of the right to be idle. New Labour's employment policies have increasingly placed the unemployed under scrutiny. They are required to account for their job-seeking activities in order to prove themselves 'worthy' of state assistance. This is not a meaningless exercise in surveillance as there are real consequences to providing the wrong answer, such as the loss of benefits.

From her examination of homeworking in Europe, Sheila Rowbotham (1998) argues that the majority of those embarking upon this form of employment are pursuing the only option available to them in order to avoid long-term unemployment and the scrutiny associated with this. For Rowbotham, these homeworkers tend to be vulnerable women, often from ethnic minorities, attempting to juggle domestic and paid employment. Many experience language problems and fear workplace racism, and some have disabilities. The majority of published material on homeworking concurs and argues that to have the 'choice' between homeworking and unemployment is to find oneself 'between a rock and a hard place'. In a qualitative study, homeworkers demonstrated a desperate need for income and none were homeworking purely out of interest or boredom. One of the many problems these desperate workers face is in securing genuine work rather than scams, which require them to pay in advance for training or materials 'kits', after which the work mysteriously disappears (Conlock 1998).

Homeworking does allow workers who might otherwise be excluded from the labour market to participate in paid employment. In Conlock's (1998) survey, 90 per cent of respondents reported that, given the choice between equal pay and conditions at home or in the workplace, they would continue to opt to work at home. However, these workers were quick to point out that they would prefer not to experience the penalties associated with this form of work, such as low wages, social isolation and reduced political power (p. 3).

Some workers are undoubtedly in a position to make real decisions regarding their working arrangements. In Britain, the Labour Research Department claims that the majority of people working part-time do so out of choice. Nevertheless, the proportion who do so involuntarily, because they cannot find full-time work, has risen by 50 per cent in the last ten years, from 8 per cent to 12 per cent

(LRD 1999). Certainly, many women happily choose part-time work following childbirth, and not as a result of social pressure or the demands of the 'double burden'. Likewise many workers have freely decided to become self-employed, particularly those who are relatively well placed in the occupational hierarchy. The difficulty is that it is almost impossible to determine the proportion of women working part-time who would have made a different decision had their ideological, domestic or financial situation been different. Nor is it possible to calculate how many of the self-employed in Britain are in fact refugees from redundancy and unemployment, and who would rather return to paid holiday and sick leave, rather than relish the 'freedom' of being 'your own boss'.

The notion of an active choice implies that a series of realistic options are available, but also that people are in a suitably powerful position to make decisions, rather than to have them made on their behalf. This suggests the importance of freedom from crippling financial pressures, the scrutiny of the state and from dominating ideologies.

Is there a Radical Future for Non-Standard Employment?

A word of caution: to suggest that all forms of non-standard employment constitute poor work and that all workers aspire to standard employment would be to create two more myths. Standard employment may be ideal for some, but not for all. Radical writers have argued that, given appropriate political circumstances, non-standard employment could provide the basis for a more egalitarian society.

As we face a new millennium, most nation-states face the problem of a growing divide between the rich and the poor.[6] Some writers, most notably Hutton (1995) in Britain, perceive this trend to be potentially serious. Many in employment work long hours and experience increased work intensity, often as a result of the introduction of the lean approaches discussed in the chapter 2. At the same time others are under-employed or are in peripheral, vulnerable employment. Some are outside the sphere of employment altogether. Hutton argues that Britain is characterized by a '30–30–40' society: 30 per cent of workers are in peripheral, non-standard employment with few associated benefits; an additional 30 per cent are without employment and depend on benefits; and the remaining 40 per cent are in relatively secure employment. The division between the 'work rich' and 'work poor' creates deep divisions in our society. Hutton asserts that the result is an iniquitous and unstable society, which affects everyone in a detrimental way since it leads to increased crime and places intolerable pressure on public services (1995).

Radical commentators such as Gorz (1980; 1982), Mellor (1992) and Robertson (1985) have argued that non-standard employment could provide the basis for a more egalitarian society. If many are unemployed or under-employed, while others work long hours and face stress and in some cases ill health, the rational solution could be to apportion work more equitably. In some countries flexible work practices have already begun to be used to enhance social equality and opportunity. It is instructive to compare Britain, where the New Labour government has watered down the already timid Working Time Directive (WTD), with the situation in France, where pressure from the unions has initiated more of a concerted effort to share work around, working towards a thirty-five-hour working week for all. In Holland all new public-sector jobs are reduced time. Certainly, political and welfare context plays an important role in influencing the forms of flexible employment embarked upon by employers and the likely outcomes for workers. Building on Esping-Anderson's (1990) categorization of social welfare systems, Huws et al. (1999) note that in Nordic countries social welfare is based on 'social democratic' principles, typified by universal benefits which are funded by taxation and are not conditional on head-of-household status or labour market participation. As a consequence, unlike in 'corporatist' regimes (Germany, France, Belgium, Italy) and 'liberal' regimes (Britain, Canada, Australia and the USA), flexible work practices are likely to be more benign in nature as they are 'internal' in nature. That is, flexibility is likely to be achieved by workers who remain part of an internal core rather than as a result of their banishment to the periphery. Furthermore the welfare system enables workers to take advantage of opportunities arising because of flexible work practices as it allows them to move between jobs without jeopardizing pension rights etc. (Huws et al. 1999: 30–2).

Mellor, Gorz and Robertson share concerns for the long-term environmental sustainability as well as the promotion of social and gender equality. Robertson calls these 'SHE' thinkers (sane, humane and ecological). However, such writers generally argue that only in a post-capitalist society could non-standard employment provide the basis for new and more equitable patterns of social and economic life. There is therefore an important distinction between these radical ideas about how working time could be rearranged for the benefit of all and those put forward by Handy (1994). Handy's ideas appeal to the educated middle classes and for good reason. They do not challenge the social order, but leave inequality intact. Critics have rightly claimed that in the present circumstances, particularly where social welfare regimes are punitive rather than genuinely supportive, the ability to opt for less employment or to pick and choose when and how to work is a luxury available only to the relatively powerful and wealthy.

Conclusion: People, Power and Politics (again)

In the previous chapter we concluded that when seeking to understand social change, people, politics and power should never be removed from the frame. This discussion of non-standard employment supports such a contention. The myths we have examined are based on the assumed intent of those taking non-standard work, rather than on proper investigation; writers tend to ignore the political and power inequalities which many workers experience.

We argue that the shift to non-standard employment has not been as profound as has frequently been suggested, nor does it provide easy answers for employers seeking to make savings or increase control over the workplace. Moreover, this myth obscures a political agenda: Pollert's (1988b) argument that the myth of a secure past and an insecure future emerged as part of a process of re-education of the British people by the Conservative Party is compelling.

Hakim (1995), Handy (1994; 1995) and Hewitt (1993) claim that non-standard employment offers people the opportunity to make positive choices, but once again they ignore the power inequalities surrounding choice. Real choices can be made only where a number of real alternatives are available and when those making the choices have sufficient power to make meaningful decisions. The ability to choose is politically constrained by race, gender, disability and class. For example, middle-class women may have the opportunity to choose if they are financially secure, but only if they can avoid the social pressure to be 'Superwoman' – that is, to be carer, domestic worker and career employee. In contrast, financial necessity forces working-class women towards paid employment and many will opt (if possible) for part-time arrangements in order to avoid the stress and emotional costs associated with the double burden of domestic and paid full-time work.

Writers who are overly optimistic about non-standard employment neglect the political nature of the employment relationship. They fail to appreciate that choice in employment is not freely available to all, and that non-standard forms of employment are frequently used as a weapon against workers. Many workers have been forced to accept deterioration in their employment conditions since the use of non-standard employment releases employers from certain legal obligations and enable them to divide their workforces. For example, although Hewitt (1993) was far from happy about the situation for non-standard workers, most of the policy changes she recommended to ensure 'fair flexibility' have since been implemented. What has not changed, however, is that some employers find ways around the legislation, particularly where workers are vulnerable and have restricted options. It cannot be assumed that all workers have comparable opportunities for employment; again this is to ignore the political context within which employment occurs. Unskilled, black, disabled and immigrant workers are far more likely to be found in some of the worst forms of non-standard employment, such as homeworking (Rowbotham 1998).

Non-standard employment is not necessarily poor work and many workers do want non-standard employment. Indeed it is problematic to view the rigidity of standard work – the five days per week (or more), eight hours per day (or more) model – as an ideal to which we should all aspire. Increasingly, the pressures associated with maintaining standard work, against a backdrop of labour weakness and increased employer prerogative, have become associated with stress, ill health and personal unhappiness (Sennett 1998).

Successive governments have claimed that the UK must develop a more highly skilled workforce, and produce better-quality goods and services, in order to compete internationally. In chapter 6 we will argue that the encouragement of more flexible patterns of employment in the current political and economic context is incompatible with this aim. The current drive toward non-standard employment can be understood in many instances as an attempt on the part of employers to take advantage of vulnerable workforces, during a period of labour weakness, in order to compete with newly industrialized countries. As we saw in chapter 1, the notion of inevitable globalization is often used to legitimate these changes, without any real evidence of benefit to any of the parties concerned. We argue that the pursuit of numerical flexibility through the forced introduction of non-standard employment is incongruous with the development of a quality-based competitive economy; shrewd employers, like those in FE colleges who resisted the use of agencies to supply staff, have come to recognize this.

4

The Myth of the Female Takeover

> Socially, women's battles have been won. We have equal opportunities in the workplace and we have sexual freedom.
>
> (Edwina Currie)

> Gone are the days of women succeeding by learning to play men's games. Instead the time has come for men on the move to play women's games.
>
> (Tom Peters)

> Today's parents worry more about how their sons will make out than how their daughters will survive. . . . It is the lads, struggling with unfashionable testosterone, who find employment difficult to find and keep. It is the men who find themselves increasingly out-earned and out-ranked by women.
>
> (Fay Weldon)

Introduction

There is a poignant scene in the popular film *The Full Monty* where the group of unemployed men who are the film's heroes bewail their fate: 'We're dinosaurs, redundant,' one of them laments. 'Women don't need us any more.'

This reflects an increasingly popular view, reflected also in the quotations cited above, that men are now losing out to women in economic life. Women are entering the labour market in greater proportions with shorter breaks for childbirth and child-rearing. This 'feminization of the labour force' (Jenson et al. 1988), which is characteristic of most of the advanced capitalist societies, is linked to the growth of service-sector employment which provides increasing numbers of 'women's jobs': jobs involving caring, servicing, and performing 'emotional labour' (Hochschild 1983) for clients. Meanwhile, traditional 'male jobs' in manufacturing are disappearing, leading to declining male employment rates, increased redundancy and unemployment. In higher-level managerial and professional jobs women are now able to compete more equally with men, largely because of their increased levels of tertiary education and other credentials, enabling them to use what Crompton and Sanderson (1990) have termed the 'qualifications lever'. Considerable media attention in Britain has been devoted to the fact that girls now do better in school examinations than boys: rather than girls, it is now boys who are 'learning to lose' (Spender and Sarah 1980). This trend has also been noted in other countries, such as Denmark and Holland.

These workplace developments are matched by changes in household arrangements. In many countries dual-earner families are becoming the norm, so that men are being forced to take a more active role in parenting and housework. 'New men' who are more family-orientated are said to be emerging. At the same time the traditional role of the 'male breadwinner' is being undermined (Land 1994), especially as more women are apparently choosing to bring up children on their own. Given the rise in divorces, in single-parent families and the increasing numbers of people who live on their own, more women are accepting an independent breadwinner role and rejecting that of the traditional housewife.

Feminization, as we define it in this chapter, is manifested in varying degrees in all advanced societies, but it is in America, Britain and Australia that the trends are most advanced: for example, Britain is the only EC country where the unemployment rate for men is higher than for women. Thus it is in these countries that feminization has most clearly been mythologized as a 'female takeover', with accusations of 'men losing out' and a male 'backlash' developing against gender equality. For this reason, we use the British case to explore the 'female takeover' though research findings from other societies are discussed.

Demos, a British policy unit and 'think-tank' which has been influential in New Labour thinking, has described the changes as a 'Genderquake'. Long-standing gender roles and patterns of behaviour are in a state of upheaval. Women, inspired by popular notions of democracy which Demos endorses, along with a general spread of feminist ideas, are demanding equality with men. Men, in response, are having to adjust their own expectations, but not always willingly or without protest. Susan Faludi (1992) employed the term 'backlash' to describe the resistance of some men to equal opportunities (EO) programmes and the Genderquake. Journalistic coverage has also focused on the notion of post-feminism: that is, the idea that gender inequality is a thing of the past. Research among three generations of women carried out in Wales by Jane Pilcher (1998) found that over half of them (54 per cent) believed that equality between men and women had been achieved. More than that, it is suggested that a female takeover is occurring, with men becoming victims of a feminized work culture and 'reverse discrimination'. Wajcman (1998) speaks of the emergence of a 'discourse of male disadvantage'; Eveline reports a similar development in Australia (1999). It is men, now, who are in danger of becoming the 'Second Sex' in the face of triumphant 'girl power'.

This chapter examines these developments critically, in relation to recent research. We argue that, while the British labour force is indeed being feminized, the conditions of male and female labour remain distinct. Many of the new 'women's jobs' are part-time, and women are more likely than men to be in 'non-standard' work, as suggested in the last chapter. Established structures of gender segregation at work and in the home are remarkably resilient. Men continue to hold the majority of top jobs and to set the rules for what is normal in the workplace. Although many firms have EO policies, research findings show that women continue to report discrimination and sexual harassment in a variety of occupations.

We shall characterize women's economic position in terms of processes of *integration*, *marginalization* and *polarization*.[1] Forces of integration will first be considered, before we look at how women continue to be marginalized. Finally, it is important to stress that the fortunes of different groups of women are very different and that divisions of class, age and ethnicity may be heightened by the Genderquake.

Integration: Women Catching Up

Women are currently being integrated into the economy through processes of feminization. To explore these in a satisfactory way we need to unpick the various meanings of *feminization*, since the term is used to cover a number of developments. First, there is *feminization of the labour market*. This means that the proportion of women in employment is increasing comparatively to the proportion of men. Second, there is *feminization of occupations*, the trend for women to move into occupations which were formerly dominated by men. Finally, we distinguish *feminization of work*, whereby the very nature of jobs, tasks and skills is changed in ways said to make them more suitable for women. To see how far feminization has progressed and whether its effects are to make men and women equal, we need to consider each of these in turn.

Feminization of the labour force

There can be no doubt that the British labour force is being feminized. There has been a steady increase in women's employment rates since the Second World War; from the 1970s this has been matched by a significant fall in men's employment, especially among the older age groups. Women are now virtually half of the British labour force, 49.6 per cent in 1995. Sylvia Walby (1997) and Rosemary Crompton (1997) have offered extremely useful accounts of women's increasing participation in employment. Walby reports that women were the majority of employees in one-third of local labour markets. The activity rate for women aged sixteen to fifty-nine rose from 51 to 73 per cent between 1973 and 1993, while for men it fell from 93 to 86 per cent. Between 1981 and 1991 female employment among married and cohabiting couples rose by 16 per cent while for males it fell by 4 per cent (Harkness et al. 1996). The increase has been particularly marked among married women. More recently this has extended to mothers with young children, as the trend is for women to return to work increasingly soon after childbirth. In 1990, 41 per cent of mothers with children under five were in employment, compared to 26 per cent in 1979 (Land 1994). Susan McRae's analysis of survey data (1991) showed that, in 1988, 45 per cent of women had returned to employment within nine months of childbirth and another 20 per cent were contemplating return; this compared with 24 per cent and 14 per cent in 1979. Research among women employees in the North East of England showed that the average time spent out of the labour force for bringing up a family had fallen from ten years seven months among the oldest age group to one year among women under thirty (Bradley 1999).

As stated earlier, this increase in the proportion of jobs held by women is an international as well as a British phenomenon, typical of all the advanced capitalist economies and occurring in some developing areas such as the Far East. As Julia Brannen (1998) points out, 'growth in female employment, especially during the family formation and early childrearing phases of the lifecourse, is occurring in all European Union countries' (p. 76). Women constitute 42 per cent of the EU workforce (Drew and Emerek 1998).

The causes of feminization are complex but there is clearly a link to service-sector expansion. In most advanced countries there has been a decline in manufacturing jobs with most new jobs in services. This advantages women, since they have long been associated with service work, especially jobs involving caring and catering for the needs of clients. Women have predominated numerically in clerical work, retail, catering and the health and education professions, all of which are important providers of jobs in the modern service-based economy. Eighty per cent of employed women work in service jobs compared with 56 per cent of men (Sly 1993). The tendency for women to work part-time is another key factor, for, as Rubery et al. (1998) note, many new jobs are part-time.

The loss of jobs in manufacturing has had a disproportionate effect on men and has been associated with male redundancy, unemployment and early retirement. The oldest and youngest age groups have been especially disadvantaged. Many older men in the core manufacturing areas of Britain, such as the North East, Scotland and Wales, have found themselves 'on the scrap heap' in their fifties, unable to procure new jobs. Young men from manual backgrounds without educational qualifications face shrinking opportunities as both apprenticeships into skilled work and unskilled factory jobs diminish. In 1992, 18.9 per cent of the male potential labour force aged fifteen to twenty-four were unemployed, compared with 11.7 per cent of women in the age group (Rubery et al. 1998).

Increased male unemployment has become a major public concern, informing the discourse of male disadvantage. However, we need to consider male unemployment in relation to the position of women, as the interesting analysis by Rubery et al. shows. Britain is the only country in the EU where the unemployment rate for women is lower than that for men. In 1992, 11.5 per cent of men and 7.3 per cent of women were unemployed.[2] However, the way unemployment figures are calculated is a subject of controversy and may under-record the proportion of women who are unwillingly out of employment. Rubery et al. provide a different measure of unemployment by considering together those who are jobseekers and people who are inactive but would actually like to have a job. Here the difference between men and women diminishes, as the rates are 13.3 and 12.28 per cent respectively. Indeed, if involuntary part-time workers[3] are included as well, to produce what Rubery et al. describe as an 'under-utilization rate', then women fare slightly worse than men (14.70 as opposed to 14.41 per cent). This is not to deny the reality and misery of male unemployment; but it suggests that many of the concepts by which we categorize and study relations of production are framed in male terms and do not tally with the realities of women's lives.

None the less, the increasing proportion of women with jobs and of men without jobs is a real and important social change and significantly affects gender relations within families. There has been a decline of the 'traditional family' model based on a male breadwinner and dependent housewife. Now the most common form of partnership is a dual-earning one (Harrop and Moss 1995). Harkness et al. (1998) provide a useful account based on data from the General Household Survey (GHS). Between 1981 and 1991 the proportion of dual-earner households rose from 53 to 67 per cent, while male breadwinner families declined from 40.3 to 22.6 per cent. There was a small rise in female breadwinners from 4.5 to 6.4. Harkness et al. show that women's earnings are now a very important part of the family income; the average male share of earnings fell from 73 to 61 per cent. Among lower-income families, women's wages were vital in keeping families out of poverty. Few women now work for 'pin money,' as was revealed in the North East study (Bradley 1999). Two-thirds of the women in the study described their earnings as essential for the household and another 28 per cent stated that they were important. There are also growing numbers of women sole earners, which reflects another important social trend, the rise in single-person households: across Europe, the proportion of such households has risen from 15 per cent in 1960 to 34 per cent in 1991 (Drew 1998). Consequently, younger women recognize the need to maintain economic dependence in the face of family breakup. They anticipate having to contribute substantially to household earnings to preserve a desired lifestyle. In the words of one young North Eastern woman: 'To have a good standard of living, with your own car and holidays and that sort of thing, I think the woman has to work all her life.'

Feminization of occupations

Clearly, if women constitute a greater proportion of the workforce, we would expect there to be an accompanying change in the distribution of women and men in different occupations. The segregation of work into men's and women's jobs has been a prevailing feature in most societies, constituting a major source of male social dominance (Bradley 1989). If a female takeover were genuinely occurring, we would expect to see women moving into men's jobs.

Historically, attempts on the part of employers to feminize particular occupations have been common. For example, clerical work was feminized in the nineteenth century as new technology and bureaucratic development transformed and deskilled the tasks of clerks. Harry Braverman (1974) linked the feminization of occupations to the degradation (deskilling and de-integration) of craft work. Using such strategies, employers exploit the fact that women's work has a lower socio-economic value than male work. Employers cut labour costs by bringing in women and paying them less; women have also been characterized as less prone to collective organization and easier to control. Thus Jane Humphries, in a classic paper (1983), suggested that a tendency to feminize the proletariat might be a logical development for contemporary capitalist accumulation.

As we shall see, feminization of the labour force has not brought a major breakdown of gender segregation. However, as Walby (1997) notes, there has been some movement of women into certain areas traditionally assigned to men, notably those at the top of the occupational hierarchy. Long-standing male strongholds such as law, medicine and accountancy are currently being feminized and women have made headway in management. For example, women now comprise the majority of students in medical schools and between 1971 and 1990 they have risen from being 4 to 27 per cent of the legal profession (Crompton 1997). Between 1981 and 1991 there was a 9 per cent increase of men but a massive 61 per cent increase in women in jobs categorized as managerial in the census (Walby 1997), though women managers remain a minority. Indeed there was a slight fall in the percentage of women managers between 1993 and 1994, from 10.2 to 9.8 (Wajcman 1998).

Women make their way into these top jobs because they are increasingly well qualified and can match men in recruitment competitions. Linda McDowell (1997), in her study of women in the finance sector in the City of London, found that women under thirty had higher qualifications than their male counterparts. Walby (1997) notes the rapid increase in the proportion of women undergraduates in higher education since the 1970s, from 35 per cent in 1975 to 48 per cent in 1995. Among postgraduate students, the percentage of women has increased from 25 to 42. Crompton and Sanderson (1990) showed how women were able to use their credentials to make headway in the professions of pharmacy and accountancy. As girls are now gaining better results than boys in GCSE (General Certificate of Secondary Education) and are on the brink of surpassing them in A levels, this trend looks set to continue. But there is still a clustering of girls in the traditional female subjects (such as languages, arts and biology), while they are underrepresented in the 'hard' scientific and technical areas such as maths, engineering and computing, which might lead them into the elite jobs of the 'knowledge sector', to be discussed in chapter 7.

At the bottom of the occupational structure less has changed. Women have made little headway into traditional male jobs in manufacturing or transport which are in decline, anyway. In jobs long ascribed to women, such as clerical and retail, women have continued their advance. Rubery et al. neatly summarize the picture in the EU context: 'Women have made breakthroughs into traditional male higher level jobs at the same time expanding their share of already feminized lower skilled or lower paid occupations' (1998: 108).

Feminization of work

There is another motivation for employers to engage in feminization as well as cutting labour costs. There is a growing concern in contemporary firms with quality and customer service, which is noted elsewhere in this book. Women are seen 'innately' to possess skills considered valuable in this new service culture; 'feminine qualities' of caring, communicating and making people feel good are important employment assets. McDowell (1997) notes that the fastest-growing jobs in the 1980s in the USA included care assistants and attendants, shopwork and waitresses. Lisa Adkins (1995) demonstrates how jobs in the leisure, entertainment and catering industry make use of female employees' sexuality and bodily appearance as an inducement to customers. Women themselves may voluntarily exploit their 'feminine assets' as a way to advance: Adler et al. (1993) quote a woman as saying, 'When things get rough at conferences I just cross my legs and flash a bit of thigh' (p. 107).

This aspect of feminization is a qualitative, not just a quantitative, change. New methods of profit accumulation and new ways of organizing production call for new types of worker and different working methods. Organizations are deliberately reconstructing their work cultures and with them the requirements of working 'selves' (Casey 1995; Du Gay 1996). Male workers seeking employment in this new environment may need to develop 'feminine' aspects of themselves.

This aspect of feminization is manifested in the notion of a new 'feminine' style of management. The influential work of Rosener (1990) suggested that women operate with a more empathetic, interactive, people-orientated management style which becomes 'transformative' for the organization. This style is especially desirable in a climate of organizational change and cultural reconstruction, since women are more able to empower those in their command and encourage participation and commitment; women are ideal 'change agents'. Adler et al. (1993) list the skills which women as managers are deemed to have: they are better at listening, communicating, providing support, meticulous with detail, favour working as a team, are more concerned with justice and tackling sexism and racism. Women are said to favour participative decision-making, to be collaborative rather than confrontational and to work for consensus; while men are seen as more authoritarian, assertive, competitive, ruling by fiat rather than consultation. Male management is more likely to confirm the status quo.

However, the work of Wajcman (1998), among others, throws doubt on whether women really operate with a different style. Moreover, as Collinson and Hearn (1996) show, masculine and feminine styles are not equivalent to men and women. A woman manager may be authoritarian, trying to outperform men at their own game, while men may adopt the softer, feminine style if it is the flavour of the month. We shall discuss later in the chapter how men retain positions of domination, which will cast doubt on this aspect of the feminization thesis.

A Climate of Equality?

So far, we have linked feminization to global economic development and to the strategic objectives of management and employers. But other factors encourage feminization: notably, the role of the state in promoting equal opportunities policies and the actions and aspirations of women themselves. Taking these two factors together, we can speak of the emergence of a 'climate of equality' where it is no longer socially acceptable to discriminate against women.

EO policies are common in North America, Europe and Australasia, with the US taking the lead in progressive legislation. In Britain, since the passing of the Equal Pay Act and the Sex Discrimination Act in the 1970s, there has been a widespread adoption of EO policies. Perhaps the prime example is the Opportunity 2000 programme; this was set up by the Conservative government in 1991 to encourage organizations to improve career openings for women, by means such as setting targets or providing special training. Opportunity 2000 currently covers 25 per cent of the UK workforce (Ledwith and Colgan 1996).

Researchers have been rather sceptical about EO programmes, which are often viewed as 'window-dressing' resulting from employers' desire to appear progressive; alternatively they may be reluctantly adopted by organizations in order to avoid equality legislation prosecutions. Linda McDowell quotes one woman manager's cynical comment on her bank: 'We are an equal opportunities employer, we are an affirmative action employer, but in fact we hardly recruit any women, we fire them when they go on maternity leave, we don't like practical care arrangements' (McDowell 1997: 120). Cynthia Cockburn's research (1991) also highlights how reactionary line managers may effectively sabotage EO plans put forward by personnel staff (often women) who are genuinely committed to them.

None the less, EO programmes have brought improvements for women. For example, the Civil Service has one of the more successful EO records, having instituted special programmes for aiding women in 1984 and 1992. This has led to increased proportions of women in higher-grade posts, while career-break schemes and flexitime make it easier for women to return and continue working after motherhood; part-time staff are provided with pro rata benefits; mobility requirements which make it difficult for women to get promoted have been eased (Dickens 1994). Schemes like these have helped women to progess at work. But there is a more subtle and important effect in terms of cultural attitudes. While managers may resist and male employees resent EO policies, it is now difficult to be openly discriminatory. Gender equality has become part of the democratic agenda.

Wajcman describes this development as a 'profound cultural shift' involving 'the emergence of a new consciousness and widespread public discourse about gender equality' (1998: 1). She links it to a new spirit of independence among women which is revolutionary in its import. Women will no longer accept subordinate roles and fill secondary jobs on the grounds that men are innately superior. They are increasingly aware of sex discrimination and many are prepared to take militant action against it. This challenges the long-standing view of women as less ambitious than men, a view reflected in the work of Catherine Hakim, discussed in the last chapter. Hakim claims that only a minority of women (around 20 per cent and one-third at the highest) will adopt a lifestyle similar to that of men in which career commitment and ambition for advancement are central life interests (Hakim 1991; 1996).

Among many more recent studies which contest Hakim's arguments is Ian Procter and Muriel Padfield's research among young adult women. They conducted longitudinal research with two groups, whom they characterized as 'single employed' and 'early mothers'. Among the employed group they found evidence of strong commitment to employment. Women planned and replanned their careers, according to what opportunities were offered or withheld. Almost all rejected a traditional home-maker role; Procter and Padfield state that 'either through engaging in training, working for promotion or planning job progression, it is evident that virtually all these women were committed to developing their working lives' (1998: 135). Although the early mothers might appear similar to Hakim's 'home-orientated' women, Procter and Padfield deny this. While some had opted for motherhood because of limited labour market opportunities, most had subsequently taken either full- or part-time jobs. A majority anticipated that employment would become much more significant later in their lives. Procter and Padfield conclude that women cannot be pigeon-holed as having a single orientation: the balance between work and family priorities in their lives varies over the life-course and in response to changing circumstances. Aspirations change, expanding and contracting, as young women grapple continuously with the competing demands of work and family, and with varying 'options, possibilities and disappointments' (p. 249).

Such research suggests that the new generation of women are more strongly orientated to employment than their mothers. They anticipate earning for much of their lives and reject a future of being 'just a housewife'. This confirms Walby's suggestion of a new gender regime replacing the older one in which women were more firmly steered towards a domestic fate. It might be objected that many of the sample had unrealistic expectations, since they had not yet fully experienced the difficulties of combining motherhood and career. However, the North East research among women of all age groups confirmed Procter and Padfield's findings of strong commitment to employment and of priorities shifting over the course of their lives. The younger women appeared just as ambitious as the young men in the study, expressing desires to become managers, to 'make something of their lives', while the women in the oldest age groups were if anything keener on their jobs than their male equivalents. Such women view their jobs in contrast to the constraints of the housewife role, as these quotations from factory workers, all in their thirties and forties, show:

> I like working. I like being with people. I don't want me life revolving around me husband and kids etc. I think it gives you more of an outgoing personality when you're at work. Being stuck at home limits your interest to the family.
>
> I prefer to go to work. It gives you independence.
>
> There was no way on God's earth I would be stuck in the home. It was mind-numbingly boring being at home.

But women are still *seen* as less committed than men as this quotation from a male manager shows:

> The commitment that's being asked may be too much for a lot of ladies . . . not so bad for blokes' cos it's expected, it's a man's thing to make sacrifices. (Wajcman 1998: 103)

The persistence of such views is in part stereotyping, but also reflects the complexity of women's new life choices, as they continue to bear the major responsibility for domestic work. Bradley found that the only age group in which women were significantly less ambitious than men was thirty to thirty-nine, the age at which women's household responsibilities tend to be at their height. Similarly Perrons (1998) shows that across the EU women's activity rates are most distinct from men's in the twenty-five to thirty-four age group. But overall the evidence suggests that women's attitudes are significantly altering, with greater emphasis being placed on labour market participation.

Marginalization: Keeping Women Down

Despite these positive changes which integrate women more firmly into the labour market, gender equality has not been achieved. The feminization of the labour force does not mean an end to the distinction between 'men's work' and 'women's work'.

It is habitual to utilize Hakim's (1979) distinction between horizontal segregation (the clustering of women and men into different occupations) and vertical segregation (the concentration of women in lower tiers in each occupational hierarchy). The persistence of vertical segregation means that even if women make inroads into an organizational category they do not reach top positions within it. Women are still underrepresented in top management and the top echelons of the professions: there are only a handful of female vice-chancellors, judges and senior civil servants. In universities women lag behind men on pay scales even when they work the same number of years and are 550 per cent less likely to become professors.[4] Despite the great increase in numbers of female medical students, in 1989 only 15.5 per cent of consultants and 3 per cent of consultants in surgical posts were women: women are horizontally concentrated in the less glamorous medical specialisms, such as public health and geriatrics (Wyatt and Langridge 1996). There are many women in general practice but they are underrepresented as principals. Meanwhile in manual jobs segregation remains entrenched, with men dominating, for example, in construction, transport and metalwork while women remain clustered in female specialisms as care assistants, hairdressers and cashiers.

Since broad occupational categories obscure some of the subtleties of job and task allocation, case studies are often the best ways to explore the extent of segregation. The SCELI studies demonstrated the persistance of segregation in a variety of work settings; their survey found that 66 per cent of men and 54 per cent of women worked only or mainly with their own sex (Scott 1994). Bradley's case studies of five organizations found that only around a quarter of women and men worked equally with both sexes; vertical aspects of segregation were strong with few women managers. Traditional sex-typing of jobs, while being challenged, was hard to overcome. In a chemicals factory, for example, men worked as process operators, mixing chemicals (a job that required heavy lifting) and women worked on the automated packaging line; a few women were moving into the warehouse operating fork-lift trucks but they reported facing opposition and harrassment from male colleagues (Bradley 1999). Even in occupations which are mixed, such as banking, law or retail, women are often channelled into what Crompton and Le Feuvre (1992) describe as 'gendered niches' which carry lower status and pay: women specialize in family law, men in corporate law; women are personnel managers, men are store managers.

Robinson (1988) has suggested that gender segregation may be taking new forms with the evolution of the service-based economy: a distinction between full-time male jobs and part-time female jobs may become its most noticeable feature. This reminds us that gender difference in employment does not just involve the content of jobs, as manifested in occupational and task segregation, but the contractual basis of employment. The concentration of women in non-standard jobs is an important aspect of labour market marginalization.

As we showed in the last chapter, an increase in non-standard employment is linked to the development of flexibility. Tilly (1996) speaks of a 'part-time economy' evolving. But as Drew and Emerek (1998) point out, non-standard work is allocated differentially by gender, with men predominating in shift and nightworking, self-employment and subcontracting, while women are characteristically found in the less attractive forms of non-standard work as part-timers, home or family workers and temporary employees. In Britain in 1995, 44 per cent of the female labour force were employed part-time; and 70 per cent of part-time employees are women. Part-time employment is heavily concentrated in the service sector, especially retail, where most women are employed. A high proportion of the increase in women's employment has been in part-time work. Drew et al. (1998) also highlight the link between women's domestic responsibilities and non-standard work, reinforcing the devaluation of both. Women take non-standard jobs to juggle employment and family needs, making this choice appear a female one, which in turn deters men from taking such jobs.

There has been a small rise in part-time employment among men in Britain from 4.6 per cent of employees in 1986 to 7.7 per cent in 1995 (Delsen 1998). However, this is concentrated in the youngest (fifteen to nineteen) and oldest (over sixty-five) age groups. For men, part-time employment is, characteristically, a route into the labour market, or a way to ease oneself out of it; whereas women may undertake part-time employment at various stages during their employment history and for many reasons, but primarily in relation to child-rearing responsibilities (O' Reilly and Fagan 1998). Men resist non-standard work as incompatible with norms of masculinity, especially the breadwinner role which, as Lei Delsen states, 'retains enormous symbolic and material importance' in men's lives, even when it is actually in decline (1998: 65).

Domestic Work: the Divide Continues

Perhaps the most crucial factor contributing to women's labour market marginalization is their continued responsibility for domestic work and childcare. Studies – for example by Hochschild (1989) and Veenis (1998) have shown that while a notion of partners sharing domestic labour and childcare is increasingly becoming a social ideal, in reality women continue to perform the bulk of housework. Surveys reveal that women perform about 70–5 per cent of all domestic tasks, though the proportion decreases somewhat when they work full-time. Yet Janeen Baxter's analysis of domestic labour among dual-earning couples found that in the USA, Norway, Canada and Australia men reported themselves as doing only a quarter of total housework (Baxter 1999). Similarly Hochschild's (1989) study of Californian couples highlighted the 'triple burden' of waged work, domestic work and childcare falling more heavily on women even where egalitarian views were expressed. New men and house-husbands, though they may exist, are rare breeds.

New men supposedly want closer relationships with their children; and indeed studies show that men are spending more time in childcare. However, the gap between their involvement and that of mothers remains striking. Time-budgets collected by Jonathan Gershuny showed that in 1985 women who worked full-time spent on average 107 minutes a day looking after their young children (supermums indeed!) while full-time men spent forty-four minutes; among unemployed couples, mothers spent 137 minutes and men thirty-seven minutes (quoted in Hewitt 1993).

Veenis (1998) depicts a new family model in the Netherlands in which men are 'cuddly breadwinners'! They are increasingly concerned to build a relationship with their children and to spend time playing with them, although the bulk of routine childcare tasks, like feeding, washing clothes and changing nappies, are still done by mothers. Women, characteristically, are 'dutiful part-timers' who feel that they must work since two incomes are necessary for a decent standard of living, but continue to see household tasks as primarily their responsibility. Many families in Britain would conform to Veenis's model. While the responsibility of *individual* mothers for childcare may have weakened, the *social* responsibility for childcare remains female. Crompton (1997) provides informative data on jobs involving domestic caring. In 1991, 90 per cent of these jobs were held by women.

Discussing women's work in Denmark, Ruth Emerek (1988) suggests that women's share of the household work is characteristically 'time-dependent' such as looking after children and cooking. The traditional male household tasks, such as 'do it yourself', gardening and car maintenance are 'time-independent': they can be done at any time, typically evenings and weekends. In this way, even when men are spending considerable numbers of hours on domestic duties they are less constrained by these responsibilities than women in terms of employment options. There has not been a significant 'masculinization' of the domestic division of labour. This is one way that male labour market domination is maintained.

Men on Top: Economics, Power and Culture

Male dominance at work has been analysed by feminists in terms of patriarchy. Walby (1990) has argued that since the nineteenth century there has been a significant shift from private forms of patriarchal control, exercised by individual men in families, to public forms, embedded in the structural arrangements of paid employment and the state. A particularly influential way to explain women's inferior labour market has been dual systems theory, developed by Walby among others to show how gender disadvantage stems from the interaction of capitalism and patriarchy. We have seen how feminization is related to capitalist employers' desire for cheap labour and in this section we shall explore how men maintain positions of patriarchal authority at work. However, recent theoretical critiques have suggested that systems theory is too monolithic to capture the complexities of gendered power relations and is based on essentialist and universalist views of male and female behaviour.[5] Researchers now prefer to explore how 'the gendering of organizations' occurs through processes of everyday interaction within workplaces. This may involve study of the production and reproduction of discourses of masculinity and femininity within organizational settings; for example, ideas about the nature of management resonate with dominant views of appropriate male behaviour (Collinson and Hearn 1996). Another strategy is to conceptualize gendered power in terms of a range of resources which men and women deploy at work (Bradley 1999). Three important forms of resource which men tend to monopolize are economic, positional and symbolic.

In Britain, men still earn more than women, although the gender gap in average hourly earnings has diminished since the passing of the Equal Pay Act. Full-time women now earn 80 per cent of male wages (Walby 1997). However, since many women work part-time, men still tend to be the big earners. In 1992, 25 per cent of men earned over £420 per week, compared with only 7 per cent of women. Women are concentrated in low-paying jobs, with one-third of women and only 10 per cent of men earning less than £170 per week (Dickens 1994), despite male manual workers' recent relative decline in earnings. Analysing GHS data, Arber and Ginn (1995) found that in the majority of dual-earning households men earned more, even where women had higher occupational status. Men have greater access to overtime and other forms of bonus payments. Within organizations women move more slowly up salary scales. McDowell (1997) matched pairs of men and women working in merchant banking in terms of jobs and background and found that in most cases men earned higher salaries. Domestic responsibility is implicated in women's earnings disadvantage. Nancy Folbre (1994) calculates that a British mother will lose the equivalent of 57 per cent of her earnings because of her caring responsibilities; this involves lost periods of employment, losing out in the competition for promotion because of career breaks, and working reduced hours on initial return after maternity leave.

Ginn and Arber illustrate how women's employment patterns affect their pension rights. If women work part-time, they will have lower lifetime earnings and their chances of promotion are adversely affected. Many part-timers are excluded from occupational pension schemes. A 1988 government survey showed that 70 per cent of men and only 25 per cent of women had occupational or private pension entitlements. The median amount received by women aged sixty to sixty-nine from private pensions was £18, while men of the same age received £32 (Ginn and Arber 1998). Women in their old age face a much greater likelihood of falling into poverty. Indeed, throughout their lives women are more vulnerable to poverty than men, because of low earnings or domestic restrictions. Two-thirds of all adults in Britain reliant on income support are women (Lister 1994).

This links to vertical segregation; men hold most positional resources in organizations, occupying top posts, especially those involving decision-making and authority. Case studies of the NHS and of the teaching profession show men moving up career ladders faster than women (Healy and Kraithman 1996; Wyatt and Langridge 1996). Women still confront a 'glass ceiling' when they aspire to top jobs. Judi Marshall's research highlights difficulties faced by women managers in developing careers and fighting discrimination; some abandon the struggle for advancement and seek jobs in other more 'woman-friendly' environments (1995). The existence of 'old boys' networks' enables men to compete more successfully in the race for promotion. Men in positions of power often select and promote candidates who conform to their ideas of merit and who they think will fit into the existing team; this disadvantages both women and minority ethnic members, since white middle-class men tend to appoint in their own image.

This highlights the importance of symbolic resources in maintaining male power. Men can set the rules and norms within the workplace since they occupy top posts. They determine the criteria for acceptable workplace behaviour and the meanings of such key concepts as excellence, leadership potential, a 'good worker', commitment, even 'the working day'. Research into women managers in various industries and occupations reveals how work requirements are shaped around male norms.[6] These include the freedom to move around the country to secure promotion; the ability to work long hours, including evenings and weekends; having few restrictions on out of work time; and displaying requisite qualities of competitiveness and toughness. As Collinson and Hearn (1996) point out, the notion of 'manager' is identified with the notions of 'man', 'masculinity'; our image of the manager is male. The sober dress style of suits and tie favoured by corporate management creates problems for women, who struggle to reconcile femininity and 'businesslike' appearance (women may 'power-dress' but are discouraged from wearing trousers). Halford et al.'s (1995) case studies of banking, nursing and local government suggest that women's bodies bring into the workplace connotations of sexuality and reproduction which are deemed inappropriate in the purportedly impersonal sphere of bureaucratic organizations. The ideal form of embodiment for the workplace is male: men do not menstruate or show the bulge of pregnancy. As Young puts it: 'Women suffer workplace disadvantage because many men regard women in inappropriate sexual terms and because women's clothes, comportment, voices and so on disrupt the disembodied ideal of masculinist bureaucracy' (1990: 176).

As we saw, the notion of feminization includes the idea that women's skills are increasingly in demand because of the rise of service work. However, Judy Wajcman's book *Managing Like a Man* (1998) offers a particularly insightful picture of the way in which 'management assumptions underlying management continue to marginalize and exclude women from senior management roles' (p. 8). To succeed in this male world women have to 'act like a man', adopting male habits like working long hours and demonstrating an interest in sport. Moreover, Wajcman suggests that the whole idea of a 'worker' (especially one high in the employment hierarchy) is underpinned by the marriage contract as described by Carol Pateman (1988), in which women offer free labour to men in return for financial support. Since women cannot offer a 'corporate wife' as an asset to their employer they are at a double disadvantage: they can offer fewer hours than men and may have to expend energy on domestic tasks – as Wacjman puts it, women are seen as not bringing two people to work, but less than one! (p. 39). She found that 40 per cent of the male managers in her sample had partners who were full-time housewives and another 31 per cent had partners who worked part-time. By contrast 88 per cent of partners of female managers were employed full-time. Single or divorced women find it easier to compete in the long hours culture. But they do not have somebody waiting at home for them in the evening with a hot meal in the oven!

Other studies show how working long hours is a crucial component of an increasingly individualistic and competitive managerial culture. Catherine Casey's (1995) Hephaestus respondents emphasized the importance of their cars being seen in the car park in the evenings and on weekends. To make a mark it was considered necessary to attend 'sunrise meetings' which were held every morning at 7.20 for planning and progress review. This cult of 'presenteeism' is a key feature of contemporary organizational cultures which, far from being feminized, appear increasingly macho and family-unfriendly.

Polarization: Women Divided

The previous section focused on women in managerial positions because they are frequently the beneficiaries of current changes. However, this is the experience of a minority of women. To close the discussion we need to consider divisions among women.

The kind of changes discussed so far are likely to have the greatest effect on the new generation of women. These young women are better qualified than their mothers and can take advantage of new openings. Moreover, they are maturing under a new gender regime in which women are less pressured towards a domestic future (Walby 1997). Pilcher's (1998) interviews with three generations of women found significant differences in values between them. Older women had more traditional views on gender roles and some were suspicious of change. The middle generation had lived through the rise of the second-wave feminist movement in the 1970s; some had been strongly influenced by feminism in their views, and were very aware of gender discrimination and inequality. The youngest generation had also been exposed to feminist ideas, but were more influenced by the discourse of individualism, featuring freedom, independence and the right to make one's own choices. This kind of discourse informs the attitudes and behaviour of young women like those interviewed by Bradley or Procter and Padfield. In contrast, older women are more likely to be trapped in dead-end jobs and penalized for their absences from the labour market for child-rearing. Such women faced limited choices in their lives and look back with regret, as these quotations from a factory worker and cardiologist show:

> I wish I did something else years ago, went to college and studied and maybe got a better job.
>
> I would like to have had more education or training. In my area, the family would say what you did, you were sent to work to earn money. There wasn't a choice.

The experience of different age groups is mediated by class. Young middle-class women with higher degrees can grasp the opportunities on offer, while those without qualifications from working-class backgrounds may find themselves facing the same restricted labour market choices as their mothers, notably low-paid service work. Unsurprisingly, some of these young women opt for early childbearing and drop out of the labour market. There is an increasing polarization between the two groups in terms of employment trajectories. Harrop and Moss

(1994) showed that between 1981 and 1989 the proportions of graduate mothers in employment increased from 36 to 63 per cent compared to a modest rise from 18 to 26 per cent among mothers with no qualifications. Macran et al. (1996) found that teenage mothers were the least likely, those with degrees the most likely, to return to work.

Feminization impacts on class in different and unequal ways. The wives of wealthy upper- and middle-class men are perhaps the only group who have the luxury of 'choosing' between employment and full-time motherhood, like the wives in Rosalind Coward's (1992) study who felt overwhelmed by pressure and guilt when they tried to combine both. Most women from less affluent households feel themselves compelled to work to contribute to household maintenance. It is in the middle reaches of the class structure that the dual-earning pattern is strongest. However, manual women and wives of manual workers have most difficulty finding jobs and the jobs available to them are the worst-paid and insecure. The wives of unemployed men often find it uneconomic to work as their husbands' benefits are affected. Thus the least privileged and educated may be trapped in the home, and also have to grapple with the unemployment of their husbands and sons. This leads to polarization between 'work-rich' and 'work-poor' families which we will explore in chapter 7.

Finally, ethnic divisions are manifest among women. Historically, women from minority groups, especially recent migrants, refugees and illegal immigrants, have been trapped at the bottom of the occupational hierarchy in jobs rejected by the majority population. For example, in Britain African-Caribbean women worked in transport, low-level jobs in the Health Service and as cleaners and care assistants, while Asian women often performed low-paid textile work or homework. Disagreeable backstage work in kitchens and hotels is often performed by women from minority groups. However, the recent study of *Ethnic Minorities in Britain* (Modood et al. 1997) confirmed a picture of increasing complexity among different ethnic groups, heightened by the influence of class. African-Caribbean women are most likely to work full-time, while Pakistani and Bangladeshi women have the lowest employment rates, which reflect both cultural choices and their disadvantaged class position. In contrast, young minority women are making good use of the qualifications lever to secure professional and managerial jobs. Many young African-Caribbean women reject the options taken by their mothers, who worked as nurses and care assistants: they are also substantially outperforming their brothers, who are particularly vulnerable to unemployment.

Age, class and ethnicity combine in complex ways to influence the fortunes of different groups of women; but processes of feminization, opening opportunities for some and confirming the fate of low-paid insecure jobs for others, are intimately entwined with processes of class polarization.

Conclusion

In this chapter we have argued that, while there has been a feminization of the labour force, feminization of occupations has been limited and the culture of work has not been feminized. Gender segregation persists, men retain economic dominance and predominate in positions of power and authority, while the cultures of work organizations are deeply gendered in ways that persistently disadvantage women. Relationships in the labour market intersect with domestic relationships, in what has been termed 'the family/employment interface' (Crompton 1997). Consequently, we need to consider both productive and reproductive relations, what Glucksmann (1995) calls the 'total social organization of labour', to gain a full understanding of gendered change. Despite the rise of dual-earning partnerships, women retain the major responsibility for domestic labour, thus entering the labour market under different conditions from men; there are constraints upon their ability to sell their labour power, which continues to be less valued. Women also have to struggle to reconcile home and work demands, sometimes suffering so much psychological strain that they consider abandoning their careers (Coward 1992).

This is not to say that nothing has changed. Global economic change has opened up new opportunities for women around the world. Employment is becoming increasingly important in women's lives as they strive for independence and self-fulfilment. Equal opportunities have improved prospects for some women, though women at the top of the class structure have gained most. But the 'climate of equality' has had a broader effect upon the attitudes and aspirations of women in all classes. A new generation of well-qualified young women may be poised to take advantage of these changes, although they will have to grapple with the obstinate persistence of the domestic division of labour – and the need to change men. It is not yet true that men are 'out-ranked' or 'out-earned' by women, nor that men are being forced to play 'women's games'. Structures of male power are remarkably resilient and the feminization of the labour market does not amount to a female takeover.

5

The Myth of Technology and Science as the Solution to Workplace Problems

> Scientific rationalism – the rationalism of the mathematical models which inspire the policy of the IMF or the World Bank, that of the law firms, great juridical multinationals which impose the traditions of American law on the whole planet, that of rational-action theories, etc. – is both the expression and the justification of a Western arrogance, which leads people to act as if they had the monopoly of reason and could set themselves up as world policeman.
>
> (Bourdieu 1998: 19)

Introduction

In our discussion of globalization, lean production, non-standard work and feminization, the theme of technological change has played an important part. In this chapter we consider this in relation to a very influential meta-myth concerning the power of technology and science to transform our lives and our work.

Science and technology are not new actors in the workplace, although the post-war years have seen a rapid growth in the application of science and deployment of technology within workplaces. The scientific and technical approach to solving problems has become the 'default setting' for the implementation of change. This chapter will look at some key aspects of these interventions to challenge the ways in which science and technology are often applied in workplaces and organizations. First, we need to explore what is meant by science and technology, and to consider the nature of the myth we are examining. This is no easy task. We can think of a myriad of roles for science and technology in workplaces – for example, scientific management, new technology in production processes, high-tech surveillance – but providing neat definitions for science and technology, and neat formulations of the myth underpinning the continued application of science and technology to workplace problems, will not be easy. But we shall proceed by identifying two distinct problems surrounding the application of science and technology to workplaces, each of which is associated with a general myth of the efficacy and omnipotence of science and technology. These two distinct issues are closely related, but can be separated for analytical purposes, as will initially be done here. The first issue is an empirical one: what technological and scientific interventions can be made in workplaces, and to what extent do these solve workplace problems? We shall explore this issue by looking at a range of examples. In many ways this is actually a minor issue – we can evaluate and argue over the success of the application of technology or science to a problem from an empirical perspective. However, the second issue is much more profound: why is it that we reach for the scientific or technical solution above all other possible interventions in workplaces and organizations? Here we must examine what the role of scientific and technical rationality is with respect to contemporary capitalism: that is, we must place them in context. Why does science have, as Bourdieu puts it, 'the monopoly of reason'? Given the scope of the subject, this chapter will only scratch the surface of the topic, but we offer the reader pointers towards other writers who tackle this theoretical aspect in more depth.

Science and Technology in Contemporary Society

Science itself is a contestable concept: we can propose a range of definitions for what science is: for example, a form of knowledge, a method of inquiry, or an attitude to making sense of the world. But whichever definition we choose, we must recognize that our received version of science is often one that suggests this form of knowledge is above or beyond any social or historical context, that it is removed from social, political or cultural influence. Science is seen as disinterested, universal and transcendent. This version of science is contestable, and we shall need to grasp a social context where science is no longer seen as a neutral form of knowledge that can act as a truthful arbiter, but as a social institution that has, as many would argue, become tarnished through association with capital and with technology:

> We think that science is an institution, a set of methods, a set of people, a great body of knowledge that we call scientific, is somehow apart from the forces that rule our everyday lives and that govern the structure of society. We think science is objective. Science has brought us all kinds of good things. . . . At the same time, science, like other productive activities, like the state, the family, sport, is a social institution completely integrated and influenced by the structure of all our other social institutions. The problems that science deals with, the ideas that it uses in investigating those problems, even the so-called scientific results that come out of scientific investigation, are all deeply influenced by predispositions that derive from the society in which we live. Scientists do not begin life as scientists, after all, but as social beings immersed in a family, a state, a productive structure, and they view nature through a lens that has been molded by their social experience. (Lewontin 1993: 3)

Lewontin presents a version of science that we may call the 'new scepticism' – the view that science is not the external and immutable force that it previously appeared to be. This approach calls for the ideas and ethos of science to be located within wider social processes that have shaped them. It is also a call to see science as linked not only to technology but also to the ways in which technology is applied. From the perspective of this book, we can also read Lewontin as providing a prima facie case for the need to apply a sociology of work perspective to the productive processes of science, something that sociology of work has, largely, ignored.[1] The purpose of this chapter is to show the ways in which science is at times treated as being a neutral and external object and at other times as being a social construction or a tool of capital. Similarly, the public perception of science varies widely according to context (Fuller 1997) – a force for good that will liberate us from social and medical problems, or an evil tool, understood only by a small elite, to be used against us by big business.

Technology, too, is difficult to pin down: in a sense all tools created by people are 'technology', but this is not a commonsense definition of the term – most people apply the word 'technology' to machines that display a high degree of technical innovation: that is, machines which have been 'created' by science. Distinctions have been drawn by authors between 'technology' (machines deployed in the workplace) and 'technicality' (neutral applied science), or between 'technology' (general processes, such as microelectronics) and 'technique' (a specific technology developed for a purpose), or between 'technology' (applied science) and 'invention' (neutral idea).[2]

There is no space here for a deep analysis of what science and technology are and how they fit into contemporary workplaces, society and culture. However, we need some working parameters for the objects we are investigating. We will discuss science as the form of knowledge that is derived from the application, through rigorous investigation, of principles of rationality to the world. 'Rationality', a term central to Weber's view of social development, involves the application of the most appropriate means to gaining a given end. Systematic practices are formulated which aid rationality: such are the practices of science, laboratories, instruments, experimentation, the whole approach of 'scientific method' that is taught in schools. Science is thus a way of looking at the world where facts will be collected, organized and theories derived from these facts.

We shall also look at technology in the workplace – the machines and tools that have been derived from scientific investigation and innovation. Specifically, we focus on 'information technology' (IT), the technology generated by the invention and development of microprocessors and computers.[3] But we will encounter a third topic – 'technoscience' – which is, arguably, much more relevant than either science or technology. According to Aronowitz and DiFazio, technoscience is the state of affairs that results when science becomes inextricably linked with the technology it has created, where 'work cannot be separated from its mechanical aspects, which, in the light of the drift of the field, seem to dominate all so-called intellectual problems' (1994: 51). A different formulation is offered by Bruno Latour whose work has been central to the 'new scepticism' on science. Rather than seeing science as a remote and external object, Latour places science in a social context. The consequences of this are far reaching: where we had seen an internal logic pushing science forward, now we see external forces shaping the science that we have in a particular society:

> Scientists are the cause that carried out all the projects of science and technology, while . . . scientists are striving to position themselves inside projects carried out by many others. . . . To remind us of this important distinction, I will use the word technoscience from now on, to describe all elements tied to the scientific contexts no matter how dirty, unexpected or foreign they seem. (Latour 1987: 174)

For Latour, scientists are the 'cause' that allows projects to be carried out: we might think of the invention of the semiconductor as being the 'cause' of the microprocessor revolution. However, this does not mean that there is a direct connection between individual scientists and technology in society. Latour is saying that when we see particular pieces of technology, or particular effects of technology – say the PC sitting on your desk – we will see science as the driving force behind them, even when there is no clear link between the technology and scientific knowledge. He goes on to reflect on how this conception of technoscience could, given its broad coverage, potentially expand to include all interest groups and ideologies. But this should not be the case: for Latour, our understanding of technoscience should be based on identifying the networks of knowledges, interests and actors involved in a particular production. Thus each instance of technoscience will be judged on its own terms: Latour's technoscience is a concept to allow us to analyse the micro world surrounding a technology – how does *this* object come into being in *this* way and at *this* time? Where Aronowitz and DiFazio see technoscience as an all-pervading 'ideology' that has similar effects in different places, Latour's technoscience is subject and place specific, making it a useful tool for analysing specific technical interventions in single workplaces, but going no further. For this reason Aronowitz and DiFazio's position may be more useful in developing a broader perspective on the reasons why societies are increasingly dominated by scientific and technical rationality.

In the next sections we will concentrate on three specific topics: management science; technological interventions and applications in the workplace; and scientific rationality as an organizing principle for modern workplaces. Inevitably these topics do not neatly map on to the concepts of science, technology and technoscience outlined above. However, we will use these concepts to indicate where we think the main point of analysis should be.

Management Science to the Rescue?

It is obvious from even a cursory glance at the history of management science that science and technology are considered to be key instruments in solving workplace problems and in controlling workplaces. Taylor's scientific management was an attempt to apply 'the methods of science to the increasingly complex problems of the control of labor in rapidly growing capitalist enterprises' (Braverman 1974: 86).[4] Drucker, the management guru *par excellence* of the latter half of the twentieth century, is a strong adherent to the principles of scientific management, and an ardent promoter of management science – a discipline that will allow business and enterprise knowledge to be formalized and taught such that the right results are achieved in a 'scientific manner' (Drucker 1970). His approach rests on a conventional understanding of the methods of science and the history of technology, and his claims for the need and potential efficacy of his management science are grand: 'In fact, the future of the free enterprise system may depend on our ability to make major managerial and entrepreneurial decisions more rationally, and to make more people capable of making and understanding such decisions' (Drucker 1970: 170). Perhaps fortunately for the free enterprise system, we have seen a massive growth in management science through the 1970s and 1980s culminating in the emergence of the HRM movement in the 1990s. Total Quality Management (TQM) and Business Process Reengineering (BPR) initiatives have been particularly popular among managers and have been promoted extensively (see Hammer 1996; Wilkinson et al. 1997). While Taylorist scientific management may have its academic critics, management science is thriving. It is itself a large business, providing employment for management consultants whose sole concern is solving the workplace problems of other corporations. The management consultancy industry is worth more than $40 billion worldwide and is expanding by 16 per cent annually. In 1998, 90 per cent of the UK's 300 leading companies employed business consultants: the British Broadcasting Corporation (BBC) alone spent £22 million on them (Younge 1999).

We will look at the deployment of management science in relation to a specific case study. Royal Ordnance, Birtley, is an ammunition manufacturer that employed 1,000 people in 1990 (Stone and Peck 1992). The company is a wholly owned subsidiary of British Aerospace, a large multinational organization with interests in defence, aerospace and communications. With over 100,000 employees around the world, and major operations in the US, BAe is one of the world's largest defence equipment providers (£12bn turnover in 1999) and has extensive civil interests. RO Birtley produced the majority of its ammunition components for the UK Ministry of Defence (MoD), but exported about 40 per cent of production to foreign governments. The factory made a range of ammunition components, but not complete ordnance devices: shells and bombs on the site were not 'live' or filled with explosives. The market that the factory was involved in was one that had changed little through the latter years of the Cold War: supply to the MoD was fairly constant and foreign orders were closely regulated by the UK government.

In the early 1990s the factory faced an acute problem: sales revenue was falling, competition was rising and overheads were high. After extensive research by management scientists from BAe, the company did two things. First, it retooled parts of the factory to include new CNC (Computerized Numerical Control) machines, and it also upgraded a core element of the basic metal forming role of the factory, introducing new CNC flow-forming machinery;[5] almost the entire factory layout was reorganized. Second, it reorganized the workforce around a new 'Japanized' production system and retrained the workforce so that each machine operator would be responsible for production, quality and inventory. This lean-production process, completed by 1992, resulted in 200 redundancies as the inspector grade was abolished. The factory now boasted some of the highest-quality manufacturing in the region, based on some of the newest technology available, and a sophisticated workforce capable of running the new systems. But by 1994, over 66 per cent of the remaining 1992 workforce had been made redundant. Why had this happened? The company had apparently done everything possible to stave off further crises, had applied classic management science thinking to the situation and had tried to keep up with latest technology.

The new crisis at RO Birtley was identified clearly by the workforce in Erickson's research interviews. Although most respondents recognized that the core business of RO Birtley should continue to be weapons production, many realized that the end of the Cold War and the subsequent dramatic decline in UK government military spending meant that the company would have to develop alternative products. The armaments market had diminished so it was irrelevant whether the company was more efficient, more technically competent or even 'lean and mean': there were not enough customers for their products. It is worth pointing out that, although respondents from the workforce had the benefit of insiders' knowledge of the situation, the crisis they faced was not an isolated problem for RO Birtley: throughout the UK defence industry, companies were facing similar difficulties – years of expanding or stable markets where the customers were governments had almost vanished overnight. Between 1991 and 1993, 100,000 jobs were lost in the UK defence industry (Defence Analytical Services Agency 1993), the UK industrial sector with the highest levels of training, expertise and production technology. Faced with this haemorrhage of skilled workers, a range of national agencies – most notably trade unions and the Labour Party, but also the CBI (the Confederation of British Industry, an organization that represents the interests of large employers in the UK) – proposed conversion or diversification plans and strategies. National conferences with leading academics and politicians in attendance were held. Newspapers ran supplements on the future of the UK defence industry. Specialist publications were full of articles concerning strategies for coping with defence market contraction. Yet RO Birtley simply did not respond to this. One toolsetter summed up the new predicament: 'We'll never change. . . . There's no intention here for diversifying. And there's so many people outside that we haven't got a leg to stand on in terms of price.' Another toolmaker put it more bluntly: 'It's like banging your head against a brick wall trying to get them [management] to change.' Trade union convenors and regional officials at RO Birtley had been trying for years to get management to accept proposals for alternative production: they had produced business plans and suggested products that the factory could make – fire extinguisher bodies and industrial gas bottles. Although these approaches were considered by management to be helpful, the results of union campaigning for diversification were negative. Shop stewards interviewed described the outcome of these protracted discussions:

> [The company] doesn't respond, or if it does, it does with contempt.
>
> The bosses listened, but it went no further.
>
> We get a poor response – it's a very low priority for the company. They give a lot of excuses for not doing it, not thoughts for how to do it.

What was going wrong here? We observe a company gearing up for high technology production, applying management science to all aspects of the labour process and retraining a work-force to be individually empowered as flexible specialists. Yet at the same time, we see a factory that is collapsing, failing to attract new orders and rapidly losing current orders. Why did the high-tech initiative fail? There are two possible answers here. First, from the perspective of BAe, the parent company, this was not so much a failure as a rather large waste of money. BAe is still a major player in the global defence industry, and remains highly profitable. The company made a 'strategic decision' to focus on core business, namely weapons production, and has come to terms in a new 'lean and mean' form with the altered market circumstances. To that effect, the investment it put into RO Birtley will eventually be offset against future profits in the arms trade. However, it is indisputable that the company missed an opportunity to reapply its skills and technology to new markets, and in this respect the high-tech solution failed, not through intrinsic problems associated with technology, but through a failure to address the core problem of changing a culture. RO Birtley managers were not empowered by their parent company to carry out a radical diversification strategy. Despite having a highly flexible workforce, new technology on site and designers at the plant, BAe's decision to concentrate on core business effectively left RO Birtley having to wait for civilian companies to approach them offering subcontracts or other partnerships: an unlikely eventuality in the context of recession-hit County Durham in the early 1990s. But this lack of will to diversify was also due to intransigence on the part of managers and policy formulators in the company. When discussing general aspects of defence industry work, a frequent observation of respondents about management was the high degree of bureaucratization that accompanied many aspects of getting a job done. There are historic reasons for this: the company had been privatized fairly recently (1987) and administration was, up to that point, run on a civil service model. The heavy reliance on government contracts had induced the management to choose the path of least resistance, while hoping for a return to 'the good old days' (McIntosh 1992). No amount of new technology or scientific analysis of the workplace was going to save the workforce from redundancy: what was needed was a cultural or social solution that would tackle the problems of inertia in the company. Not only that, the new regime at the factory had resulted in an even greater level of employee dissatisfaction than existed before the restructuring.[6]

Of course, not all management science initiatives fail. Casey's study of an American high-tech company (1995), discussed in our introduction, highlights the application of management science to create new 'designer' employees who are capable of applying their skills in a competitive market, and simultaneously prepared to devote high levels of commitment to an employer. Casey presents a study of an MNC which conforms to a number of 'post-Fordist' principles. Management at Hephaestus, at least in theory, welcomed employee involvement in discussions about production or management practices, and attempts were made to integrate core employees into a new corporate culture. The company conformed to Kumar's (1995) account of typical post-Fordist management strategies: it had downsized and focused on its core, had introduced TQM and an emphasis on quality in general, and recognized the need for flexibility in the workplace; most importantly it emphasized the relations of production (in this case, methods of incorporating people into a team) rather than the forces of production (here, the nature of the technology that is present in a production process). Casey suggests that the sustaining principle of Haephaestus was 'religiosity' (Casey 1995: 191): employees believed in the corporation, while also recognizing the artifice of a corporate culture that had been created by management.

On the surface, it would appear that Hephaestus has achieved all its goals. It has created a lean and mean company, fostered employee commitment, and introduced a culture of total quality. From this perspective, Casey's conclusion that the trends seen at Hephaestus will spread throughout the world of work seems reasonable. However, a closer reading indicates a problem in creating a designer culture by means of the intervention of management scientists, namely a false display of commitment. Casey found that in significant numbers people were not conforming to the type of corporate self the company had designed. Given these findings Casey's fatalism seems inappropriate here: the case for the global victory of corporate culture and management initiatives does not seem clear-cut.

These vignettes serve the purpose of illustrating the discontinuity between technical management approaches and actual social or cultural intervention. In both cases, management approached a specific workplace and redesigned it around principles of production priorities and control of labour, utilizing wholly technical considerations. However, in neither case does the result match what the management intended. At RO Birtley, management interventions did alter the production regime but this led to an even greater dissatisfaction with the management than before. At Casey's Hephaestus corporation, the outcome of managerial intervention was to produce corporate selves who were 'defensive, colluded or capitulated' (Casey 1995: 190).[7] Many went along with the changes but without genuinely believing in them.

New Technology Improves Workplaces?

In addition to these scientific approaches to the control of labour, in recent decades there has been a rapid growth in the use of IT and the microprocessor in the workplace – as a controller and facilitator of production, or as a tool in the control of labour. The early to mid-1980s saw a rapid growth in publications concerning the implementation of IT in offices and production sites. New technology in the workplace held out a promise of a better future for all concerned:

> I argue that, as this major technological development is increasingly incorporated into yet more products and leads to the adoption of increasingly automated office and factory management and information systems, opportunities are created for the design of more interesting and fulfilling jobs and more satisfactory relationships between people at work. . . . As knowledge in this situation is power, this book

> is intended to be an aid to those who are seeking to make the new technology work, and to make it work for the common good. (Francis 1986: i)

Francis presents an academic's account of the role of new technology, based on a range of case studies carried out in 'leading edge' companies. Management consultants, too, were proclaiming the inevitable benefits of IT: 'During the next decade the challenge facing those concerned with managing offices will be how to reap the benefits of new technology whilst maintaining a highly motivated, happy and effective staff' (Birchall and Hammond 1981: vii). From this perspective, technological change is inevitable; 'as technology changes, so the co-ordination requirements change, and this is likely to lead to changes in the way work is organized' (Francis 1986: 104). Francis is prescient here: the changes wrought by the introduction of new technology have indeed been far-reaching, resulting in the emergence of new forms of labour (Aronowitz and DiFazio 1994). Later in this chapter we shall look at some technological interventions in workplaces and assess their efficacy. It will be shown that, while technology does at times provide more humanized environments, it does not necessarily improve productivity, and may even be counterproductive in terms of 'revenge effects' (Tenner 1996) and misuse of skilled labour.

There is something about new technology that makes us feel compelled to use it, impelled by its power. It is often believed that new technology is integral to economic progress, while dictating the conditions of work and production. Grint and Woolgar describe this form of technological determinism as a myth but note that it is a very persistent myth: 'Technological determinism appears to advance spontaneously and inevitably, in a manner resembling Darwinian survival, in so far as only the most "appropriate" innovations survive and only those who adapt to such innovations prosper' (1997: 11). They debunk the myth of technological determinism, largely on the grounds that it is impossible to identify any ways in which technology can have the independence ascribed to it by determinist arguments. They propose a social constructivist model as an alternative: science should be viewed as part of a network of interaction involving a number of social actors and artefacts. Thus science and technology are social products, not transcendent forces. It will be argued later that while social constructivist accounts are compelling, without a trenchant critique of the structural role of scientific and technical rationality in society we will remain unable to fully challenge this myth. First, however, we briefly review some of the promises of the myth of technological solutions, and look at some of the outcomes.

Technology Improves Productivity?

Clearly, machines can be far more efficient than human beings at producing objects or executing repetitive tasks. Yet simple forms of analysis in the mode of Adam Smith's pin factory example (the output of pins shot up when the operations of pin-making were subdivided and each worker did one task) are not sufficient to analyse fully the ways in which productivity is affected by, in this case, new computer technology. Although proponents of new technology often promise that it will liberate employees from hard work (Drucker 1970; Francis 1986), people are rarely 'working smarter, not harder', and are being 'confronted by work that is being made more intense by policies of reorganization and information technology' (Greenbaum 1998a: 167). Greenbaum notes that, far from causing work to wither away, the introduction of information technology into the workplace, the design of computer systems in particular, has been undertaken so as to ensure that work can be done anywhere and at any time: 'a redivision of labor affecting who, where, and when is done, but not necessarily resulting in less work' (p. 168). For Greenbaum there are significant changes in work resulting from these technological interventions, notably a decoupling of work from place, and a delinking of labour from labour contracts (p. 169), since employees can, for example, operate new technology from their own homes.

From employers' and owners' perspectives, surely this must be a good thing, since productivity should rise and overheads fall? However, we must be careful about making generalized statements concerning these issues: it is notoriously difficult to make an association between particular alterations in working practices and changes in productivity levels.[8] In the case of office work, the introduction of new technology has not resulted in the promised 'paperless office', but has often created a number of 'revenge effects' (Tenner 1996). Tenner provides a range of examples of new technology in the office 'biting back' against users, with effects that could not have been predicted and with negative consequences. A few examples drawn from his extensive survey of computers in the workplace will suffice to illustrate these points.

Computerization has encouraged a trend that may have unintended consequences for corporate efficiency: for example the reduction of support staff. Tenner (1996) observed that the 'American Manufacturing Association, in a much-noticed study, found that staff reductions in general did not reliably increase profits. At downsized companies, profits increased for only 43 per cent of firms and actually dropped in 24 per cent of those studied. Almost as many reported a drop in worker productivity as reported an increase' (p. 207). The diminution of support staff, facilitated by providing senior employees and managers with their own PCs, has led these latter groups to spend more time on what amounted to secretarial and clerical functions. According to Tenner, their 'jobs become more diverse in a negative way, including things like printing out letters that their secretaries once did. . . . Some social thinkers, and some people in business, believe that doing your own word processing, filing and so forth builds character. But economic theory suggests that it doesn't do much for profits' (1996: 208). He further notes that while computers create the illusion that the machine is doing all the work, a surprising amount still remains to be done by people: top executives have grasped this message and have rarely downsized their own support staff. At this point the reader may want to consider the amount of productive time that was spent in dealing with computer bugs and glitches in 1999 to forestall the 'millennium bug' – and with no guarantee of success.

In a survey of the recent history of the computer in workplaces, Greenbaum (1998a) shows that, according to most management accounts, 'the factory image of automation in the 1970s didn't result in faster document production or enhanced office productivity . . . the outcome of the 1970s was rapidly growing office employment' (p. 175). In the 1980s, she notes, there were significant disjunctions between the 'stand-alone' PC concept, and the requirements of management wedded to outmoded bureaucratic forms of organization (p. 176). The lack of productivity increases would appear to be supported by statistics: investment in advanced technology in the service sector increased by 116 per cent between 1980 and 1989, but output rose by only 0.3 per cent to 1985 and by only 2.2 per cent to 1989 (Tenner 1996). The 1990s saw a move from automated systems to distributed systems, but the increased location of skills inside computer packages has led to a shift in the work of professional staff which may generate new forms of collective action and resistance. New technology in the workplace, which can as easily now be the home as the centralized office, may be a double-edged sword, 'for just as it gives management the ability to put the pieces together, it also gives people in their roles as workers, citizens and customers the chance to communicate with each other about what they are experiencing and what they think could be done about it' (Greenbaum 1998b: 139).

New Technology is Good for You?

New technology may or may not increase productivity, but it can have significant negative consequences for those using it. Employees utilizing information technology in office environments are increasingly suffering from a range of problems. Although these may be psychosomatic (Arnetz and Wilholm 1997), Tenner (1996) has identified a range of genuine revenge effects that new technology has wrought on unsuspecting users. He argues that eyestrain, carpal tunnel syndrome, repetitive strain injury and 'mouse joint' are all common in new office environments. 'Mouse joint' was first observed in 1991 in a Californian married couple 'both of whom were using a mouse at work and at home. The male patient recovered in a month of conservative treatment with splints, rest, and ibuprofen. He apparently preferred to work in pain than to shift to other computer equipment' (Tenner 1996: 177). More complex to assess is the increase in stress brought about by the introduction of new forms of surveillance and control in computerized workplaces.

There is nothing new about technological surveillance of employees by owners and managers. Alan Warde's (1992) study of management regimes in Lancaster, UK, includes accounts of mill owners in the early 1900s using telescopes to watch workers arriving at their factories. Foucault used the image of Bentham's panopticon, a prison designed with a central watchtower from which all prisoners' activities could be observed. Foucault describes this as 'a machine' which, although at first confined to the surveillance of prisoners, rapidly expanded its 'polyvalent' applications to include the supervision of workers (Foucault 1979; 1980). However, these early attempts at surveillance were constrained by technical considerations: it was often not possible to hear all employee conversations, or to oversee all transactions between employees and customers. IT has provided a set of tools for surveillance in contemporary workplaces that, while maintaining the principles of panopticism to instil discipline in subjects, significantly increase the power of the watcher.

Students of the labour process would be unsurprised by such developments. Labour process theory has highlighted managements' persistent attempts to discipline employees and control their work output.[9] However, the rise of TQM and the increasing focus on customer service as the key source of competitive success and profitability has resulted in greater use of employee surveillance: not only to maintain discipline, but also to ensure that the company is being represented correctly. New managerial techniques – particularly those associated with the HRM movement – promote, and seek to enforce, the need for commitment, empowerment, and quality. Findlay and Newton (1998) provide an account of the ways in which performance appraisal in contemporary organizations constitutes a form of surveillance. Even more compelling are accounts drawn from parts of the burgeoning service sector: telesales, telephone advice lines and call centres in particular. Supervisors are able to exercise constant surveillance through eavesdropping on employees' phone conversations and the use of closed-circuit television (CCTV) monitors. In many offices, such surveillance is accompanied by an intensification of work. Research carried out in contemporary offices with IT-based surveillance systems in operation show a rise in reported levels of stress, although it is difficult to disentangle the effects of surveillance from the effects of work intensification. One recent American study found that, unsurprisingly, supervisors prefer electronic monitoring more than non-supervisors, and that the great majority of the latter group considered that electronic monitoring might cause heightened tension between managers and workers (Oz et al. 1999). Even in environments where work is not electronically monitored, the introduction of IT allows much closer supervision of work activities: computers networked to phone lines and databases provide stand-alone workstations where all necessary and relevant information for the work tasks can be accessed. Baldry et al. note that in one of their research sites the spatial arrangement of the office and the lack of need to leave one's desk, coupled to the very close proximity of team controllers, meant that 'surveillance and intervention form a continuous process in which supervisors and managers define the limits of acceptable non-work social interaction between team members' (Baldry et al. 1998: 175). An increase in stress and pressure was reported by 64.6 per cent of respondents with only 0.8 per cent reporting a decrease. Moreover, employers are able to access and monitor employees' use of e-mail and Internet facilities, even where they work in private offices.

Technology in the workplace provides scope for upskilling as well as deskilling, offers possibilities for improving – as well as hampering – production and gives opportunities for control in addition to resistance. However, as the examples above have shown, technology in the workplace is not a universal solution to problems, and applications of technical solutions to perceived problems can often have unintended consequences. The question that we must now address is why we feel we need to take such routes.

Why Take the Scientific and Technical Option?

Management science and technological interventions in workplaces have been used here to represent the 'empirical' aspects of the myth of science and technology. The third aspect of our inquiry is with the abstract and often hidden form of rationality that underpins the control, organization and structure of workplaces, namely scientific and technical rationality. In many ways, what we have done so far – splitting apart management science from technological innovation and deployment – is artificial. We frequently see new management techniques being deployed at the same time as new technology is introduced into a workplace. Many techniques of management science, such as closer surveillance of employees, may require specific forms of technology for their implementation. However, underlying both of these things is a form of thinking that promotes specific ways of accounting for the world around us, making sense of specific problems and structuring the way in which we will utilize knowledge and techniques. Without such techniques, there would be no possibility for the systematic discipline and education that, for example, Drucker speaks of above.

However, unlike specific, or even general, forms of technology deployed in the workplace, or management science precepts, it is difficult to identify such an orientation: simply identifying someone as being 'rational' in a work situation may not be sufficient. Yet it is vital that we place technological and scientific interventions in the wider context – political, social and cultural – if we are going to account satisfactorily for what has happened to workplaces. It is at this point that our criticisms of social constructionist approaches come to the fore. Accounts that stress actors' interpretative activities are to be applauded: they allow us to make sense of the ways in which individuals encounter, for instance, specific pieces of technology. Grint and Woolgar (1997) provide a range of examples. Yet simply leaving our analysis at this point, as the social constructionists do, is not sufficient, for such a form of analysis ignores the reasons and rationalizations that underlie such interpretative activities. Social constructionism tells us a great deal about how actors form networks with other agents or objects, and this provides insights into the enactment of work in specific settings. But it cannot explain why similar patterns of activity occur in broadly similar ways and periods. Cynthia Cockburn and Susan Ormrod (1993) provide an example of 'the woman driver' that illustrates this need for further analysis. We can identify differences between genders with respect to use of technology, and will often resort to stereotypes to explain these, for example the cliché of the 'woman driver'. But without moving beyond the specific instance of a parking mistake or a stalled car we will miss the more important point: that technologies are gendered, and arranged in a hierarchy of imperatives external to ourselves. These imperatives promote forms of evaluation that are themselves representative of imperatives that may be external to ourselves. We need to look at technology and science in specific workplaces, but must also consider what these tell us about the ways in which decisions are made in much wider contexts.

The case presented here is not so much that there is a myth of scientific and technological solutions to workplace problems: rather, that workplaces are so suffused with scientific and technical cultures that it is almost impossible to promote alternative answers to workplace problems. Indeed, not only workplaces suffer from this: late capitalist societies have assumed the pre-eminence of scientific and technical rationality above other forms of rational analysis (Habermas 1971). The issue is not just that there is a myth that science and technology can provide a solution, but that science and technology themselves have assumed mythical proportions. Marcuse describes the endpoint of such a position:

> Within the established societies, the continued application of scientific rationality would have reached a terminal point with the mechanization of all socially necessary but individually repressive labour ('socially necessary' here includes all performances which can be exercised more effectively by machines, even if these performances produce luxuries and waste rather than necessities). But this stage would also be the end and limit of the scientific rationality in its established structure and direction. Further progress would mean the break, the turn of quantity into quality. It would open the possibility of an essentially new human reality – namely, existence in free time on the basis of fulfilled vital need. Under such conditions, the scientific project would itself be free for trans-utilitarian ends, and free for the 'art of living' beyond the necessities and luxuries of domination. In other words, the completion of the technological reality would be not only the prerequisite, but also the rationale for transcending the technological reality. (Marcuse 1964: 182)

In late capitalist societies across the globe, science and technology are the source of much of our knowledge, and an influence on the status of the rest of our knowledge, but this is not always appropriate: science and technology themselves operate as myths or, as Marcuse would have it, ideologies, in contemporary industrial societies. Marcuse's comments have been seen by some commentators (such as Aronowitz and DiFazio 1994) as an idealistic prediction of a future without work, where science and technology have been expanded and applied to the workplace to the extent that there is no need for human labour power. However, we would be wrong to consider Marcuse as promoting such a view. In fact his argument is that we have become so inured to science and technology, and so seduced by their promise of rapid solutions and complex consumer products, that we can no longer see science and technology in a neutral light. We have reified science and technology, and allowed them to enter areas of modern social life in which they should play no part.

Conclusion

This state of affairs identified by Marcuse, and expanded upon by Habermas (1971), has been compounded by the rapid transformation of the workplace through introduction of new management practices and new technologies. In the last three decades workplaces have changed dramatically in terms of the levels of technology they contain, and change seems to be speeding up, with economies increasingly becoming less reliant on manufacturing and more dependent on provision of services and the expansion of IT. Technoscience – the close linkage of science and technology to work – is now prevalent in many industrial sectors. This is not due to any inherent superiority of this form of management control, nor to some innate property of the technologies themselves: it is simply that no viable alternative has emerged, or been allowed to emerge. Marcuse and Habermas both highlight the problem here: science and technology have become 'ideologies' in contemporary Western societies. Scientific rationality presents itself as the only correct form of analysis available to us, and superior to other forms of knowledge. Scientific and technological solutions emerge because those who look for solutions look only to science and technology for answers. Indeed, there is a current fashion for the techniques of scientific management, which is exemplified in the use of industrial and management experts as advisers to New Labour. Such advisers promote the application of scientific rationality to the control of people, to be further applied to the activity of government itself.

Scientific and technical rationality – the rationality of the system – is seen as the only suitable yardstick by which progress or efficiency can be measured. The consequences of this are that system imperatives are imported into situations where they may not be appropriate. Yet, according to contemporary critical theorists, this need not be the case. We can imagine a situation where decisions about workplaces and their futures are made by all people concerned. We can imagine a situation where decisions about scientific and technical research programmes are not made on the basis of increasing production of goods or military technology, but of improving the environment. We can even imagine a situation where evaluation of the efficacy of new production regimes or control processes is not made on the basis of increased profits, but on the well-being of workforces and communities. However, all these possibilities rely upon the identification and analysis of the connections between science, technology and capital in a free and unforced environment, a situation that is not so easy to imagine. Yet if we do not move towards this situation we may face the fatalistic outcomes proposed by, on the one hand, Casey, with the global victory of all-encompassing corporate cultures, or, on the other hand, the continued slide towards polarized communities of the overworked job-rich and the underworked and undervalued job-poor envisioned by Aronowitz and DiFazio.

6

The Myth of the Skills Revolution

> The key to survival in the modern world is access to knowledge and information. Without it neither individuals nor businesses nor the nation as a whole will prosper. There is a technological revolution underway.
>
> (Blair 1996: 98)

Introduction

The notion that we are entering a 'knowledge society', wherein work organizations are increasingly characterized by the utilization of better-trained, more qualified and higher-skilled employees, has lately become one of the most widely articulated propositions about employment in the advanced capitalist societies. Broad macro-level developments – occupational change, increasing innovation in new technology and communications processes and the growing turbulence associated with the emergence of a truly 'global' economy – are seen to imply a transformation in the way in which work is structured and organized. Whereas in the past, firms – and, indeed, nation-states in general – could establish and sustain competitive advantage without paying much heed to the development of their employees, increasingly it is being argued that future economic performance depends upon the employment of individuals who are capable of being adaptable, innovative and responsive to change. The prevalence of skill shortages is often seen as one of the principal causes of the relative underperformance of the advanced economies. This appears particularly important given the extent to which work is becoming characterized by the utilization of 'knowledge' and 'information' – which in turn relates to the dominance of scientific rationality, the theme of the last chapter.

Some view the development of a better-skilled workforce as an inherent feature of contemporary advanced capitalist economies. For Michael Hammer (1996), the increasing significance of 'knowledge work' is having a profound impact on employment. Organizational restructuring, allied with occupational and technological change, is liberating employees from 'drone work' (p. 40). Since the division between 'doing' and 'managing' is becoming increasingly hard to identify, people enjoy enhanced autonomy and responsibility in their jobs, giving the jobs a more discernably professional character. The former head of the CBI, John Banham, has written of the emerging 'skills revolution' (Banham 1992). However, in this chapter we question the extent to which there has been a move towards a 'high-skill' approach and show such arguments to be mythical. The persistence and significance of occupations and methods of work organization which rely upon the utilization of low levels of skill will be identified. Moreover, important constraints exist which limit the demand for skills. A case study of one recent high-profile UK policy initiative designed to help raise skill levels – the development of an improved system of vocational qualifications – highlights the way in which political and institutional factors, in particular, acted to hinder progress.

Conceptualizing 'Skill'

Before we examine the truth of the claim that there is a general shift towards a 'knowledge society', it is necessary briefly to explore the concept of 'skill', since it can be open to a number of different interpretations. Does skill, for example, refer to the formal qualifications held by an individual? Is it related to the amount of training an employee needs to do a job? Or is it bound up with the ability of individuals to perform complex jobs? As Noon and Blyton (1997) have observed, 'skill is a definitional minefield' (p. 78).

The threefold approach to defining skill elaborated by Cynthia Cockburn in her study of compositors in printing represents a useful way of unpacking the concept. She identified three perspectives on 'skill'. First, there is the skill which is located in individual workers themselves: the experience, qualifications and ability which people bring to their jobs. Second, the performance of a job also requires a certain level of ability and experience; thus there is the skill demanded by the nature of the employment situation itself. Finally, Cockburn posited a 'political definition of skill'. By this reckoning skill can be conceptualized as a social and political construct, something used as a device in the struggle for control over the labour process. The compositors, for example, had over time collectively elaborated and promoted their jobs as being highly skilled in order to restrict entry into their trade (Cockburn 1983).

Thornley (1996) has discussed three aspects of the social or political construction of skill. First of all there is a gender dimension. The prevalence of gender segregation in employment places limitations on the extent to which women's ability and experience is recognized at work. Moreover, it has been acknowledged that 'unskilled' jobs are considered and rewarded as such because they are largely performed by women. Phillips and Taylor (1986) have noted that 'skill definitions are saturated with sexual bias. The work of women is often deemed inferior because it is women who do it' (p. 55), although we saw in chapter 4 that feminization is beginning to challenge this. Second, Thornley highlights the extent to which divisions between 'skilled' and 'unskilled' jobs are established and then sustained by employers as a device for managing and subverting the collective solidarity of workers. Third, echoing Cockburn, Thornley focuses on the way in which categories of skill have been developed and sustained by workers collectively, often through trade unions, as a way of defending their sectional interests. Although Thornley highlights the distinctiveness of these three approaches to the social or political construction of skill, it is evident that in practice they are usually interrelated. In the case of the compositors, for example, during the nineteenth century male workers, through their craft union, excluded women from their trade, elaborating it as a skilled occupation with the assent of employers. Women were restricted to print-finishing work, particularly book-binding, which was then characterized as unskilled and rewarded as such (Cockburn 1985).

Our purpose in writing this chapter is not to make a further theoretical contribution to the analysis and understanding of 'skill' as a concept; rather, it is to assess critically the contention that employment in the advanced economies is typified by jobs that require ever-higher levels of skill consonant with the emergence of a 'knowledge society'. Nevertheless, in so far as it has highlighted the different ways in which 'skill' can be conceptualized, this brief discussion perhaps helps us to understand why this area has been so replete with claim and counter-claim. Most importantly, as we shall now see, whereas some writers have detected a progressive upskilling trend within the advanced capitalist societies, others have been far less sanguine.

Skill and the 'Knowledge Society'

The perception that we have either entered, or are on the brink of, a 'knowledge' or 'information' society has become increasingly commonplace within managerialist accounts of workplace change, government public policy rhetoric and some academic texts. Perhaps the most notable recent proponent of such an argument is Charles Leadbeater, an adviser to British Prime Minister Tony Blair, in *Living on Thin Air* (Leadbeater 1999). However, such pronouncements have a long pedigree. Despite the conceptual and definitional problems pertaining to the notion of 'skill', since the 1960s a range of influential studies has highlighted the existence of a general trend towards upskilling in employment and the greater importance of 'knowledge work', particularly given the more extensive utilization of new technology.

For example, Kerr et al.'s (1960) account of the 'logic of industrialism' highlighted how the development of increasingly advanced technological processes necessarily led to greater demand for more highly skilled and knowledgeable workers to operate them. Their thesis was echoed, and given further specification, in Robert Blauner's influential analysis of alienation, *Alienation and Freedom* (1964). From an examination of four American industries – printing, textile production, car manufacturing and chemical processing – Blauner concluded that although the initial impact of technology in employment had been to increase alienation, through the replacement of knowledge-based methods of craft production by machine-minding and assembly-line techniques, further automation – evident in chemical processing – then diminishes it.

Perhaps the most well-known contribution to the 'upskilling' thesis was the concept of 'post-industrial society' which was developed and articulated by the American social scientist Daniel Bell (1974). Bell argued that the increasing utilization of new technology and the growing significance of service-sector employment was having a profound effect upon the nature of work organization. Whereas 'industrial society' was typified by the presence of repetitive and unskilled manual tasks carried out to rigid specifications in a Taylorist manner, the emerging 'post-industrial society', based upon the service sector and the deployment of new technology, was characterized by the importance of knowledge work. As a result of this, Bell postulated a growth in demand for technical, professional and white-collar workers, groups for whom 'knowledge work' was central.[1]

In chapter 2 we reviewed the way in which the 1970s economic recession and the decline of profitability resulted in a crisis of

Fordism. In order to meet increasingly heterogeneous patterns of demand, firms were encouraged to be adaptable, innovative, small enough to be able to respond effectively to rapidly changing product markets and capable of utilizing new technology to its best advantage. The forging of a 'second industrial divide', characterized by the emergence of 'flexible specialization' (Piore and Sabel 1984) – the first industrial divide being the emergence of Fordist mass production – thus had important implications for employment. We have already seen that the emergence of techniques of 'lean production' was one notable response. A key claim for lean production, and indeed for post-Fordist patterns of work organization in general, is greater flexibility in production methods. To meet fragmented and rapidly shifting consumer demand requires more highly skilled and flexible employees. Wood (1989b) has focused on some of the key features of the flexible specialization thesis: the presence of high-trust employment relations within firms; the encouragement and development of responsible autonomy for employees and the imperative for multiskilling, given greater flux within product markets; and the importance attached to new technology within the workplace.

There has been long-standing interest, then, in the effects of changes in production methods – particularly the deployment of new technology – in enhancing the level of skills in the workplace. Although the terms 'knowledge work' and 'knowledge worker' have been articulated more extensively within public policy rhetoric and managerial and academic discourse in the 1990s, they are hardly new concepts. But the pressures of global economic competition have assured that they have recently received close attention.

Indeed, the further restructuring of work has been held up as a crucial generator of a more highly skilled workforce. In manufacturing, for example, the extent to which firms increasingly depend upon a smaller number of multiskilled, polyvalent and flexible employees has often been highlighted. Earlier on in this book, we subjected the concept of lean production to considerable critical scrutiny. But it is worth examining briefly the claims its proponents make in respect of upskilling. For instance, although they acknowledge that the system has its critics, Womack et al. (1990) none the less argue that lean production

> provides workers with the skills they need to control their work environment and the continuing challenge of making the work go more smoothly. While the mass production plant is often filled with mind-numbing stress, as workers struggle to assemble unmanufacturable products and have no way to improve their working environment, lean production offers a creative tension in which workers have many ways to address challenges. (pp. 101–2)

A similar message has been articulated by Peter Wickens, formerly of Nissan, who writes that, while 'not everyone has the same capabilities', beyond the need to ensure safety is maintained, 'there need be no limitations on the range of tasks employees can perform' (1987: 45). New management techniques place greater importance on giving employees responsibility for ensuring quality in the finished product. This, and the drive for flexibility, have been held up as key imperatives for the elaboration of a multiskilled workforce.

Changes in work organization, then, especially the way in which they have been driven by new techniques of production, have been presented as generating more highly skilled jobs. Changes in the occupational structure of the workforce are presented as having a similar effect. Proponents of the move towards a 'post-industrial' society, increasingly founded upon 'knowledge', base much of their analysis on the perceived growth in professional, managerial and technical occupations. In the 1980s and 1990s this trend accelerated. In the UK, for example, between 1996 and 2006, employment growth is forecast to be fastest among professional, personal and protective service, associate professional and technical and managerial occupations. Not only is employment in these expanding categories seen as inherently more highly skilled than those which are in relative decline, such as manual occupations, but it is also suggested that the greater diffusion of new technology is augmenting the already existing trend towards upskilling: 'The labour market is changing quickly and moving in directions which makes, and will make, increasing demands on the labour force. . . . Most notable is the move towards higher level jobs and rising skill requirements within jobs, including the move away from hands-on skills to monitoring, communication and understanding systems' (DfEE 1997: 1). Between 1996 and 2006 the number of employees in managerial and administrative occupations is expected to rise by 10 per cent, professional occupations by 14 per cent and associate professional and technical occupations by 17 per cent (DfEE 1997). Before he became Secretary for Labor in President Clinton's first administration, Robert Reich explored the extent and significance of such trends in the US in an influential book, *The Work of Nations*. Reich noted the increasing prominence of a cadre of 'symbolic analysts', employees whose principal activities involved the collection, processing and communication of knowledge and information (Reich 1991).[2]

Although the view that occupational and technological change are responsible for a secular trend towards upskilling in employment and the greater importance of 'knowledge work' is by no means new, in the 1990s it appears to have informed managerialist writing, public policy rhetoric and academic analyses of change in the workplace to an increasing degree. Peter Drucker, for example, has argued that 'knowledge' is becoming the principal economic resource in advanced societies, replacing capital, natural resources and labour. Whereas in the 1950s about a third of all employees were engaged in 'knowledge' or 'service'-orientated work, in the 1990s the proportion is nearer 75–80 per cent and is growing (Drucker 1993).

In the introduction to this chapter we saw that Michael Hammer has argued that increasing 'knowledge work' has a liberating effect on employees (Hammer 1996). Within Hammer's work there is an assumption that upskilling in employment coexists with a rise in high-trust employment relations. This is a theme prominent in Frenkel et al.'s (1995) analysis of change in contemporary employment. Technological development, the increasing importance of services – wherein individual employees have more scope to develop and hone their 'social skills' – and the greater prominence of Reich's 'symbolic analysts' mean that not only is there a notable trend towards knowledge-based employment, but there may also be an associated diminution in adversarial relations between managers and employees. Frenkel et al. observe that the 'trend away from routine work towards more creative, information and people-focused activity involving intellective and social skills is associated with higher levels of ambiguity and uncertainty. This in turn leads management to cede more control over the work process to employees and requires strategies to ensure reciprocated trust' (1995: 786).[3] Policy-makers are increasingly influenced by such claims (see DTI 1998c). Education and training policies, for example, need reforming to take account of the fact that 'more and more work is centred on the exploitation of knowledge, in many forms'. This might, for example, lead to the expansion of lifelong learning (Bayliss 1998: 9).

Unravelling the Myth: Skill Polarization

Although extensive attention has been directed at the apparent emergence of a 'knowledge society', it can be located as part of a long-standing body of work within the social sciences in which the notion of a secular trend towards upskilling has been articulated. However, there is an influential school of thought within industrial sociology suggesting the opposite. In his 1974 book *Labor and Monopoly Capital* the American writer Harry Bravermen argued that there was a general tendency within capitalist economies for all work to become progressively deskilled. According to Bravermen, Taylorist methods of work organization were increasingly coming to characterize all occupations in the economy, including clerical work. This involved an extension of managerial control over the workforce, principally through the separation of conception from execution in the performance of a job; the elaboration of an increasingly specialized division of labour, aided by new technology; and the transfer of knowledge about the job from employees to managers.

The publication of Braverman's book prompted a considerable amount of research into the capitalist labour process, some of which has been broadly supportive of the deskilling thesis (Armstrong 1988; Crompton and Jones 1984), and some more critical (S. Wood 1982). Among other things, Braverman's approach has been criticized for providing a romanticized view of craft work; for relying too heavily on an objective view of skill ignoring its political and social construction; for neglecting the gendered dimension of skill; and for paying too little attention to alternative managerial strategies to control employees (Grint 1998: 179–86; Noon and Blyton 1997: 108–11). Nevertheless, even if the idea of an inherent logic towards deskilling is problematic, there is plenty of evidence to suggest the existence of a generally low level of skill utilization in contemporary work situations.

For one thing, the extent to which changes in work organization have resulted in a general trend of upskilling is highly questionable. The emergence of genuine multiskilling in the UK, for example, has been somewhat rare (Bradley 1999; Cross 1988); where employers have extended the jobs of workers, it has not been from a desire to enhance their skills, but rather, to intensify their effort (Elger 1990). Although lean-production techniques have been presented as offering a more challenging environment to workers within which they can enjoy more scope to broaden their experience (Wickens 1987; Womack et al. 1990), in chapter 2 we saw that the reality is somewhat different and that Taylorist principles of job design continue to predominate. After reviewing the evidence for and against the proposition that work restructuring in the 1980s and early 1990s had led to an enhancement in skill levels, Geary (1995) concluded that:

> new forms of work organization have not led to groups of polyvalent workers charged with responsibility for managing the production process. Nor has their introduction affected employees' lives a great deal. There has been little significant upskilling and, for the main part, task specialization and gendered divisions of labour have remained as they were. (p. 391)

Earlier in this chapter we noted that the growing importance of the service sector is purportedly a key source of the trend towards upskilling, since occupations within it are increasingly believed to involve the acquisition, processing and utilization of 'knowledge'. In pointing to the diversity of employment situations which are frequently held to be filled by 'knowledge workers' – not only Reich's 'symbolic analysts', but also carers, cleaners, shop assistants, caterers, security guards and so on – Thompson and Warhurst (1998: 4) reflect on the 'sheer banality' of such a term. While it is true that the private services sector constitutes the fastest-growing area of the economy, even Drucker (1993) has conceded that many of the employees within it 'perform work that demands fairly low skills and relatively little education' (p. 76).

Two sectors where employment growth is currently strong are fast food establishments and telephone call centres, and both are characterized by regimes of work organization akin to Taylorism. The production of fast food, for example, involves simple, routine and predictable tasks which demand little skill from those who perform them (Noon and Blyton 1997). In a discussion of the increasing significance of 'McDonaldization' and 'Mcjobs', Ritzer (1998) has argued that 'the service sector, especially at its lower end, is producing an enormous number of jobs, most of them requiring little or no skill. There is no better example of this than the mountain of jobs being produced by the fast food industry'(p. 60). Case studies of the catering industry reveal that it is characterized by the presence of relatively unskilled employment (Gabriel 1988). In respect of call centres, research has shown that although workers within them find they like the 'energy' and the 'buzz', most 'emphasized they often felt frustrated by the routine aspects of their work'. One revealed that it was: 'a bit like a nineties' factory job, sometimes it's like standing on a production line'.[4]

Changes in work organization and the growth of services, then, have not necessarily contributed to upskilling in employment. Indeed, there is evidence to suggest they have had the reverse effect. Moreover, the development of a highly skilled workforce may be hindered by labour market structures (see Keep and Mayhew 1996). Three are worth identifying here. In the first place, as we saw in chapter 4, employment remains characterized by gender segregation. Given that the incidence of formal training in employment is partly related to seniority (see below), the prevalence of vertical segregation means that many women miss out on opportunities to enhance their skills. Furthermore, the persistence of horizontal segregation at work means that when women's skills are recognized, through the attainment of relevant vocational qualifications in particular, it is still only in certain areas, such as the caring professions (Felstead 1997). Second, growth in the degree of insecurity in employment may depress the level of skills. According to Richard Brown (1997b), only 'in a situation where employees have some expectation of job security is their contribution likely to include the fullest possible commitment of effort and skill, the greatest willingness to work responsibly and flexibly' (p. 83). Third, the trend towards non-standard employment which we examined in chapter 3 – part-time and temporary working in particular – has also militated against upskilling, since jobs in these areas are frequently characterized by low demand for skills (Dex and McCulloch 1997).

The advocates of increased 'knowledge work' notwithstanding, much employment remains of a depressingly low-skilled nature. The impact of work reorganization initiatives on skill has been extremely limited. According to Thompson and Warhurst (1998), 'the content of much contemporary work remains highly routinized' (p. 4); and a leading commentator on training policy has observed that 'in too many businesses, work organization and job design remain based on narrow, Taylorist thinking' (Keep 1999: 35).

Jobs in the service sector are frequently of a low-skilled character. As Philip Brown (1994) has observed: 'most damaging to the protagonists of a high skill, high wage economy, is the fact that in both Britain and the United States, the vast majority of jobs created over the last 15 years have not been high skill, high wage, but low wage part-time jobs in the service sector' (Brown 1994: 611). The operation of a 'low-skill equilibrium' (Finegold and Soskice 1988) is well illustrated by Lloyd's study of the Welsh clothing industry. She examined the way in which low pay, productivity problems and depressed working conditions were intimately linked with low levels of skill utilization. Firms in the industry were reluctant to train their employees for fear that they would be poached by other companies offering better pay; labour turnover was high anyway. There was little incentive, then, for firms to enhance the skills of their employees (Lloyd 1996).

Clearly, the elaboration of an economy characterized by 'knowledge work' is a long way off. Nevertheless, it must be acknowledged that some upskilling has occurred in employment, particularly among those managerial, professional and technical employees who are well placed to take advantage of change. Perhaps the concept of 'polarization' constitutes the best way of interpreting recent broad trends in skill levels (Ashton and Green 1996). According to the survey data used by Gallie (1994), deskilling in employment has been somewhat rare. Moreover, occupational changes have resulted in an increasing number of highly skilled jobs becoming available. Skill polarization, however, has meant that individuals who 'already had relatively high levels of skill witnessed an increase in their skill levels, while those with low levels of skill saw their skills stagnate' (p. 75). Among the groups most likely to be detrimentally affected were women workers in part-time jobs in the service sector. Other studies have revealed the extent of the polarization process. This is evident in the provision of training, for example. Both Green (1994) and Machin and Wilkinson (1995) have revealed that employees who are already skilled, particularly those who are in relatively well-paid jobs with good working conditions, are far more likely to receive job-related training than those who have fewer skills and are further down the job hierarchy.

The contention that many sectors of employment continue to be characterized by the problem of low-level skills would appear to be somewhat surprising, since in the 1980s and 1990s many governments made high-profile policy interventions which were ostensibly designed to raise skill levels. In the UK, for example, a national network of employer-led Training and Enterprise Councils (TECs) was launched; National Education and Training Targets (NETTs) were instituted as a way of measuring progress; and an Investors in People (IIP) standard was introduced for organizations judged to have been successful in integrating enhanced opportunities for employee development with business objectives. Generally, such initiatives were founded upon the assumption that the *supply* of skills to the labour market needed to be improved. Yet the paucity of *demand* for skills from employers has attracted an increasing amount of attention (Ashton and Green 1996).

Keep and Mayhew (1996) have discussed a range of factors which constrain the demand for skills: economic and employer short-termism; the low level of reward which accrues to training; the character of internal organizational structures, particularly the under-development of HR (human resources) departments; and the persistence of inequalities and segmentation in labour markets. The remainder of this chapter is devoted to an analysis of one important recent policy intervention in the UK which was ostensibly designed to enhance skill levels: the development of a coherent and improved system of vocational qualifications. In this case it will be shown that certain political and institutional factors combined to effect the implementation of policy in an adverse manner and thus restricted its capacity to contribute to improved skill levels.

The Reform of Vocational Qualifications: Reinforcing the Low-Skill Culture

In the autumn of 1986 the UK government established a new 'quango' (quasi-autonomous non-governmental organization) – the National Council for Vocational Qualifications (NCVQ) – to take the lead in the reform of the vocational qualifications system.[5] Its principal job was to develop a new framework at four levels within which existing awards could be posted and designated as 'National Vocational Qualifications' (NVQs), once they had been amended to take greater account of 'competence' in employment. Thus it was envisaged that existing vocational qualifications, offered by bodies such as City and Guilds, the Business and Technician Education Council (BTEC) and the RSA (Royal Society of Arts) Examination Board, among others, would – once they had become more competence-based – comprise the new framework.[6]

Policy-makers considered the existing pattern of vocational qualifications to be fragmented and incoherent, and that individual awards were insufficiently related to the needs of employers. By developing a new, coherent and national framework of vocational qualifications, which paid greater regard to what employers wanted, the NCVQ would play a crucial part in producing a more highly skilled workforce. According to one recent review, 'N/SVQs – work-based, competence-led awards – were to help improve on Britain's position of 13th in the world productivity table and quash concerns that the British workforce would be ill-equipped to meet the future demands for a better-skilled workforce' (Employee Development Bulletin 1999: 6).

Since it was launched in late 1986, the NVQ policy appears to have made considerable progress. In 1989 a fifth level was formally added to the framework so that many of the awards offered by professional bodies could be included. The following year, Scottish Vocational Qualifications (SVQs) were launched. NVQs and SVQs became available in areas as diverse as hairdressing, construction and business administration. In 1992–3 an amended version of the NVQ – the General National Vocational Qualification (GNVQ) – was made nationally available in five subjects in schools and colleges as an alternative, or a supplement, to A levels. By March 1998 nearly 900 individual NVQs were available and in September of that year it was reported that some 2.2 million NVQ certificates had been awarded.[7] This progress notwithstanding, by the mid-1990s it was clear that NVQ policy had failed to advance in the manner that its planners had anticipated.

In the first place, NVQs had attracted a considerable amount of criticism on account of their task-based character and the way in which theoretical and knowledge-based skills were marginalized within them (Hyland 1994; Prais 1989). Second, the rate of the take-up of NVQs by individuals developed very slowly; it took a long time for employers in particular to switch to using NVQs for their employees (Spilsbury et al. 1995). Third, although the NVQ policy was designed in part as a way of forging a more coherent framework of vocational qualifications, the provision of NVQs in fact appears to have made the system more complex and harder to understand. In constructing its new framework of vocational qualifications, the NCVQ chose to populate it with new, competence-based awards, rather than to amend the existing products of awarding bodies. Peter Robinson discovered that in 1994–5 NVQs constituted just 35 per cent of all vocational qualifications awarded. He observed that 'individuals and employers now face a wider array of qualifications than was the case before the introduction of NVQs' (Robinson 1996: 34).

From 1995 onwards, then, in order to sustain NVQs policy-makers intervened to alter the direction of the policy in a number of important ways.[8] In particular, the rather prescriptive criteria which had hitherto defined the structure of the qualifications were loosened. Related to this, greater scrutiny was given to the elaboration of a coherent framework of awards, something which had hitherto received scant attention. Thus ways in which non-NVQs could be incorporated within the system were explored, and renewed attempts were made to develop greater co-operation and consistency in the approaches taken by the large number of bodies responsible for awarding the qualifications. From October 1997 onwards this work was supervised by the newly established Qualifications and Curriculum Authority (QCA) which replaced the NCVQ.[9]

Although the NVQ policy was one of the UK government's flagship policies, designed to contribute to the desired 'skills revolution' by helping to forge a more highly qualified workforce, in the first ten years of its existence it none the less faced profound difficulties – so much so that since 1995 policy-makers have had to make considerable changes in an attempt to sustain it. In the remainder of this chapter we will focus on the key political and institutional factors which combined to undermine the effectiveness of the NVQ policy from the outset. This will provide a useful example of how policies which are ostensibly designed to help raise skill levels in the UK economy can in fact have adverse effects.

In the first place, the progress of NVQ policy was undermined by the generally weak level of political commitment accorded to enhancing vocational education and training. Although it was devised and launched largely under the auspices of the Manpower Services Commission (MSC),[10] where the importance of improving skill levels in employment was given a high priority, after the MSC was wound up in 1988 NVQ policy slipped down the political agenda. Officials in the Department of Employment (DE) continued to offer support, but successive Conservative government ministers were less enthusiastic. Generally, they were committed to a model of education in which traditional academic standards and values were seen as defining 'excellence'. Vocational education and training was seen as something inferior. According to one senior NCVQ official, 'I think there was always . . . a certain ambiguity. They (the Conservatives) didn't want it to fail because it was their initiative; but they didn't want it to succeed either because it was actually contrary to their deepest instincts' (quoted in Raggatt and Williams 1999: 167).

For the most part, the NVQ initiative, indeed vocational education and training policy in general, was furthered by Conservative governments only in so far as it constituted a way of coping with high levels of youth unemployment. While there was much rhetoric in the 1980s about how a reformed system of vocational qualifications could act as a catalyst for improving skill levels in the UK, and this was certainly something that MSC and DE officials believed, politicians were largely only interested in ways of managing unemployment. Thus a key rationale for the launch of NVQ policy was the urgent need for qualifications in the new Youth Training Scheme (YTS), since existing arrangements – principally the YTS leaving certificate – were deemed woefully inadequate and policy-makers were coming under increasing pressure to improve quality (Ainley and Corney 1990; Finn 1987). Since the vast majority of YTS programmes were typified by a low-skill ethos (Lee 1989), this was inevitably reflected in the structure and content of the early NVQs, most of which were based on the YTS experience.

The NVQ policy also suffered from the renewed ethos of voluntarism which increasingly characterized UK labour market policy from the mid-1980s onwards. There were four aspects of this. First, the abolition of the MSC in 1988, and the devolution of many of its functions to a new, ostensibly employer-led network of local Training and Enterprise Councils (TECs), meant that crucial strategic support for the NVQ policy was diminished. Second, we have already noted that NVQs were designed to be based on 'competence' in employment, consistent with the overall aim of increasing employer ownership of and commitment to vocational education and training. Policy-makers had envisaged that a small number of sectoral 'lead bodies', such as the Construction Industry Training Board, would be responsible not only for drawing up the new standards of competence, but also for making sure that they were of a broadly based character and not just a reflection of narrow, task-based functions. However, by 1993, 162 of these 'lead bodies' were eventually established. Given the ethos of voluntarism and the imperative that the NVQ system be employer-led, policy-makers found it difficult to reject proposals for lead bodies. Thus, the standards of competence they drew up were frequently narrow and sector-specific, reflecting the content of low-skilled existing jobs rather than promoting upskilling.

Third, although the CBI supported the principle of NVQ policy and criticized the narrowness of the early awards (CBI 1989), it was too weak to co-ordinate the efforts of employers in a voluntary system. Fourth, we have seen that the design of the NVQs was adversely affected by the importance attached to voluntary arrangements. Their delivery suffered likewise. The original idea had been that existing vocational qualifications would be made more competence-based and – once they had been hallmarked as 'NVQs' by the NCVQ – inserted in the national framework. However, awarding bodies were under no compulsion to submit their awards to the NCVQ for accreditation. Many continued to offer their existing, traditionally assessed qualifications, for which there was often considerable demand, alongside the new competence-based NVQs. By 1996, eight years after the first NVQs had become nationally available, they still constituted a minority of vocational qualifications awarded (DfEE 1998). Thus the establishment of a coherent, national framework of vocational qualifications was as far away as ever.

Nevertheless, we should recognize that the failure to develop such a framework cannot be ascribed only to the government's preference for voluntary arrangements and the operation of market forces in vocational education and training, but also to the actions of the NCVQ, the new body given responsibility for building the new system. Although an original aim of policy-makers had been the establishment of a framework of vocational qualifications, within which existing awards could be posted once they had been amended to become more competence-based, in 1987 – the first full year of its existence – officials in the NCVQ chose to encourage more profound reform. They specified that awards would not be accredited as NVQs, and placed in the nascent framework, unless they were based on a particular competence-based approach. Initially, this was the 'task analysis' method which had been developed for application in YTS programmes. This policy generated considerable discontent outside of the NCVQ, since such an approach was perceived to result in narrow and task-specific NVQs, as even one of the NCVQ's own officials later acknowledged (Jessup 1991).

The MSC, and subsequently the DE, therefore developed the concept of 'functional analysis' as a way of defining competence in employment, and by 1991 lead bodies were mandated to use such an approach for occupations in their particular sectors.[11] However, although functional analysis was designed to produce broad-based standards of competence, upon which high-quality NVQs could be founded, lead bodies rarely utilized it properly, largely because it was a highly technical approach and they had difficulty understanding it, and so interpreted it in a very narrow manner. Intervention by the DE notwithstanding, lead bodies generally continued to produce narrow, task-based standards of competence to underpin NVQs. Furthermore, the perceived complexities of functional analysis discouraged employers' commitment and participation and helped to ensure that other vocational qualifications continued to attract a healthy, and in many cases growing, demand.

Consequently, the DE and the NCVQ came under increasing pressure, both internally from government ministers and externally from critical media reports (Smithers 1993), to reform NVQs; from 1995 onwards review mechanisms and programmes of improvement were initiated by the DE (Beaumont 1996). Thus NVQ policy was adversely affected by the vicissitudes and tensions generated by the process of 'government by quango'. In the first few years of the organization's existence, NCVQ officials appear to have enjoyed considerable latitude to implement NVQ policy as they saw fit, even though this did not accord with the remit they had been given. From 1991 onwards, however, there was a significant shift the other way as the NCVQ fell under the increasing control of the DE and became, in effect, 'a general factotum for the Department' (DfEE 1996: 4). Significantly, throughout the lifetime of the quango the NCVQ's council – which consisted of lay representatives from industry, educational bodies and trade unions, for example – appears to have had little influence in establishing, monitoring and evaluating policy objectives.

Finally, the progress of NVQ policy was impeded by further intra-government tensions, this time on a departmental basis. There were three dimensions to this. In the first place, during the late 1980s the NCVQ faced stiff opposition in Scotland when it proposed to extend the NVQ system there; it also received scant support from the Scottish Office. Following inter-departmental discussions SVQs were launched in 1990 as a compromise. Although the structure of these new awards meant that they were consonant with the NVQ framework, they were none the less distinctive qualifications in their own right and were not accredited by the NCVQ, but by the Scottish Vocational Education Council (SCOTVEC).

Second, in England and Wales the Department of Education and Science (DES) was rather cool about the whole affair.[12] Although it had been jointly responsible, with the MSC, for the original 1985–6 Review of Vocational Qualifications in England and Wales, and it formally co-sponsored the NCVQ, the DES was largely uninterested in progressing vocational qualifications policy. According to a former MSC official, the DES

> had their own agenda . . . [it] was very much that of attempting to maintain the pristine quality of A levels and GCSEs and so on, and to keep totally clear of the vocational education system. No, that's not true – to keep their presence in the vocational education system, but not to allow any sullying of the pure waters of particular school qualifications. (quoted in Raggatt and Williams 1999: 183)

The launch of GNVQs in 1992–3 increased the involvement of the Department for Education in vocational qualifications policy, but its interest was still predicated largely on maintaining the perceived sanctity of the 'Gold Standard' academic A levels. It is interesting that after the 1995 amalgamation of the Employment and Education departments, supporters of NVQ policy observed a decline in its importance in the newly established DfEE, since the ethos of the old education department appeared to hold more sway.

Third, NVQ policy was adversely affected by the reluctance of the Treasury to support it with adequate funds. The Treasury believed that employers should bear most of the costs. Between 1986 and 1995 financial support for the NCVQ was conditional on its working towards becoming self-funding through the levy it charged on accredited NVQs. The slow pace of progress meant that the NCVQ never even came close to achieving this, and on at least two occasions in the 1990s its work was jeopardized by insufficient resources. The parsimony of the Treasury was detrimental to NVQ policy in one other important respect. From 1990 onwards it specified that an increasing proportion of the money used to support government-funded training programmes should be released only when certain tangible outcomes had been achieved, including the attainment of a recognized vocational qualification by an individual. A number of studies have shown the adverse effect of this 'output-related funding' (ORF) policy, a form of payment by results, had on NVQs, given their competence-based assessment regime. Training providers came under pressure to certify trainees as 'competent' even if they did not meet the required standard (Steedman and Hawkins 1994). Furthermore, not only were training providers encouraged to offer programmes which guaranteed quick and cheap outcomes in order to release the ORF element, typically in service-sector occupations, but the scope for fraud was also increased (Felstead 1994; House of Commons Employment Committee 1996; M. Jones 1999).

In summary, then, this case study of an important policy intervention, the production of an improved system of vocational qualifications ostensibly designed to raise skill levels in the UK, has shown that significant political and institutional factors hampered its progress. The introduction of NVQs may initially have made matters worse. The quality of the new qualifications was detrimentally affected by the connection with managing youth unemployment, the employer-led basis of the system, and restrictive funding arrangements. Furthermore, the ethos of voluntarism precluded the development of a coherent framework of NVQs, particularly since the NCVQ took the opportunity to forge more fundamental reform than the government had originally anticipated. Related to this, the effectiveness of NVQ policy was further undermined by the paucity of broad, governmental support both on a political and – outside the DE – departmental level. Since 1995, policy-makers have taken major steps to rectify some of the perceived faults of the NVQ system, and there is some evidence to suggest that NVQs have gained popularity as a result (Employee Development Bulletin 1999). Nevertheless, the difficulties which affected their implementation were considerable and have had a lasting, adverse effect not only on the structure and content of the qualifications, but also on the wider perception of them.

Conclusion

Early on in this chapter we examined the view that occupational and technological change were the driving forces behind a secular trend towards upskilling in contemporary societies. Such has been the degree of change that some commentators have written of an emerging 'knowledge society' wherein employment is increasingly characterized by the utilization and deployment of information. Clearly there have been, and continue to be, major changes in the ways in which economies and societies are organized that appear to support such a proposition: the progressive displacement of manufacturing industry by services; the more extensive use of new information technology; and the growing speed of communications. In assessing the significance of such developments, Manuel Castells in particular has acknowledged the emergence of an 'information age' (Castells 1996). But he has further argued that while some groups are benefiting from the changes wrought by economic and technological advances, many others are becoming increasingly excluded from the advantages accruing to the privileged.

With this in mind, it is important to recognize that while some groups of employees, principally those working in managerial, professional and technical occupations, are witnessing an increase in their skills, many others are not. Jobs commonly retain a low-skill character, especially in the fastest-growing sectors. Attempts to improve skill levels have often floundered because of the general low level of demand for skills, something which is reinforced by structural characteristics of the economy, such as the persistence of segmented labour markets, for example. The case study provided of UK vocational qualifications policy revealed the way in which political and institutional factors also impeded the progess of an initiative ostensibly designed to raise skill levels. Altogether, then, the 'skills revolution' is as yet little more than a myth.

7

The Myth of the Death of Class

> In virtually every manufacturing activity, human labor is steadily being replaced by machines. . . . By the mid-decades of the coming century, the blue-collar worker will have passed from history, a casualty of the Third Industrial Revolution and the relentless march onwards ever greater technological efficiency.
>
> (Rifkin 1995: 140)

> Make no mistake about it, I'm proud of being working class, I'm not changing my attitude or culturing my voice or even getting my grammar correct.
>
> (John Prescott, Deputy Prime Minister)

Introduction

This chapter explores a third key meta-myth, that of the death of class, which has been particularly influential in framing broad accounts of the future of work relationships. Jeremy Rifkin is one of many writers who have proclaimed the imminent disappearance of the working class in the face of contemporary changes. American writers like Rifkin have been riveted by the power of new forms of technology characteristic of the 'Information Age' and the phenomenon of 'jobless growth' – that is, the ability of corporations to increase productivity and efficiency with a diminishing number of workers. While Rifkin's book (1996) focuses especially on the loss of jobs in agriculture and manufacturing, he is sceptical about the often vaunted ability of the service sector to provide jobs to replace them. He looks forward prophetically to the day of 'the last service worker'.

Similarly, another influential American commentator, Peter Drucker, speaks of 'the disappearance of labour as a key factor of production' (1993: 61). Drucker rehearses the idea formerly elaborated by Daniel Bell (1974), that knowledge has replaced both labour and capital as the key resource in society, becoming the driving force behind social dynamics, the 'axial principle'. The implications of such change are weighty for sociological theorizing, given the central place accorded to labour and production in the classic theories of Marx, Durkheim and Weber. In particular, Marx's vision of societies powered by the dynamic between labour and capital would be made obsolete if Drucker's vision of 'post-capitalist society' was realized.

European theorists have been more circumspect in their visions of the future, but broadly similar ideas about the decline of the working class have made regular appearances. An early discussion of 'post-capitalism' by Ralf Dahrendorf (1959) announced an end to class conflict, since the working class had been successfully incorporated into the system through various mechanisms of industrial and political citizenship. In the 1980s Andre Gorz (1982) provided an account of the 'death of the working class' very similar to that of Rifkin and Drucker. His 'farewell' to the proletariat was based on the notion that computerized technologies had the power to produce all the goods and services necessary for society while utilizing the labour of only a small core of full-time employees. The rest of the working class would become virtually redundant, transformed into a 'neo-proletariat' who would suffer long-term unemployment or be engaged in insecure and casualized work. As a result, claimed Gorz, work would no longer hold the central place in people's lives.

These arguments connect to more general debates around the key sociological concept of class. Politicians are fond of heralding the imminent arrival of a meritocratic and 'classless' society (an idea particularly tenacious among Americans, who like to see their 'new world' as a meritocracy free from the invidious legacy of the feudal and hierarchical European past). Among sociologists, the utility of the concept of class has also been contested. Many see it as an obsolete notion grounded in the analysis of modernity and industrialism and no longer applicable in a new postmodern, post-industrial world. While class was once possibly *the* central sociological concept, it has been displaced by other concerns, 'either decentred by race and gender or subordinate to political ideological relations' (Aronowitz and DiFazio 1994: 279). For example, a recent book by postmodern sociologists Jan Pakulski and Malcolm Waters was entitled *The Death of Class* (1996). They argue that the concept of class should be abandoned as untenable, discredited and outdated; class societies produced by the industrial revolution have now have been replaced by what they call 'status-conventional' societies: these are characterized by multiple status cleavages and differentiated lifestyle groups, so that aspects of social difference such as gender, ethnicity, age, religion and especially consumption activities replace class in people's lives.

Pakulski and Waters produce an extreme version of the case against class, but weaker versions of the same arguments appear in the work of other authors. In *Risk Society* (1992) Ulrich Beck argues that old collectivities such as class are weakening, eventually to disappear with the rise of individualistic values and cultures. Alternatively, class relations in the advanced economies are seen as drastically altered and fragmented by the processes of post-industrial change so that old theorizations are no longer relevant. As in Gorz's account, this is often linked to a notion of 'a decentring of work' in people's lives: work relations cease to be an important influence either on individual identities or on collective forms of action. Attention shifts from the analysis of production relations as a source of collective interests, consciousness and action towards the study of cultural consumption as a source of meaning in individuals' lives, lifestyle choices and identities. This is linked to political change: the old redistributive politics of class, exemplified by the trade union movement, is replaced by the politics of identity and difference, embodied in the new social movements (such as feminism, green activism, the gay and lesbian liberation movement).

This chapter surveys these various tenets of the 'end of class' meta-myth and challenges them. We focus especially on those aspects of the myth which deal with changes at work, although some attention will be given to the persistence of class inequalities more generally in society. In Britain and other advanced industrial economies the gap between rich and poor has been steadily increasing and people in working-class communities continue to be disproportionately subject to insecurity, unemployment, illness and poverty. As opposed to the decentring of work, we shall argue that production relations remain highly significant as a source of identity. Relations at work are still characterized by alienation and exploitation rather than harmony; as indicated in chapter 2, they remain potentially conflictual, even if class conflict and industrial action have been muted by the political climate of the New Right era and the tactics of lean production. Workers continue to hold collective and solidaristic values as well as individualistic and instrumental ones. The chapter concludes that while class relations are changing they continue to have crucial effects on our lives.

The Decline of Labour and the Death of Class

As we have suggested, ideas about the end of class are not new. However, they have gained in urgency towards the end of the twentieth century in relation to significant changes at work which we have discussed in this book. We will start our discussion by looking at two influential contributions to the debate, those of Zygmunt Bauman and Catherine Casey.

Bauman is a leading exponent of the idea that consumption relations have replaced production relations as a driving force in our society. He has developed these ideas in a number of publications and provided a concise summarization of them in *Work, Consumerism and the New Poor* (1998). The core of his argument is that, with the onset of a postmodern society, capitalism has moved into a new phase. The proletariat are no longer needed as producers: capital mainly relates to them in their other social function as consumers. He speaks of a 'gradual yet relentless passage . . . from a "society of producers" to a "society of consumers" and accordingly from a society guided by the work ethic to one ruled by the aesthetic of consumption' (p. 2). People's sense of themselves and their personal identity has consequently altered. In the past 'work was the main orientation point, in reference to which all the other pursuits could be planned and ordered' (p. 17). It acted as the compass by which people located themselves in the social whole; it informed standards of living, lifestyle and leisure pursuits; it was the main mechanism of social integration, binding people into society; and it 'stood at the centre of the lifelong construction and defence of a man's identity'. In short 'the type of work coloured the totality of life' (p. 17).

By contrast, Bauman believes that 'in its present late-modern, second-modern or post-modern stage, society engages its members – again primarily – in their capacity as consumers' (p. 24). The desire to consume becomes the primary force in shaping selfhood. Bauman asserts that this shift makes 'an enormous difference to virtually every aspect of society, culture and individual life' (p. 24) although his discussion does not clarify exactly what this entails. He does claim that, since a stable job is now an impossibility for most people, they must construct their personal identities around other aspects of life. Consumer choices become the main way in which people can assert themselves as persons. Like other contemporary theorists of the self, such as Kenneth Gergen (1991), Bauman suggests that identities are changeable, volatile and disposable; we make for ourselves temporary 'aggregate identities' constructed from what is 'currently available in the shops' (p. 29). Bauman concedes that for some people work remains the central life focus, but this applies only to a small minority of elite workers, a point we shall contest later in the chapter.

A slightly different though related account is provided by Casey (1995), who links the end of class to the decline of occupational identities. She describes how at Hephaestus somebody joining the company as a research chemist or engineer might end up working as a manager or marketing expert. Loyalty and sense of identity were attached to the company, conceived of as a 'team' or a 'family', not to occupational groupings. Thus the distinct class cultures developed by occupational groupings, especially through the medium of trade unions, are fading, as union attachment disappears from all but a core of blue-collar workers. In this way, Casey claims, 'Hephaestus makes over old class selves and reconstitutes them in its own image' (p. 136).

Casey is more equivocal than Bauman about the role of work in people's lives, claiming that it remains 'a dominant activity' (p. 21), while posing a question as to whether work and production will 'endure as central organizing elements at this post-industrial juncture and beyond' (p. 2). But she shares with Bauman the conviction that we have entered a new phase in society, with radical effects on processes of self formation and identity. In the old industrial phase, she argues, 'social class . . . provided a primary sense of identification and solidarity' (p. 132). However, in a post-industrial phase, 'a polarized corporate workplace without the intricate divisions of labor of industrial society and with a requirement for flexible technologies and workers . . . hastens the erosion of traditional class and occupational identities' (p. 134).

There is some difference in orientation in these two influential accounts. Bauman is not so much talking of an end of class relations *per se*, but rather, of a radical change in their nature, involving an end to oppositional class identity as envisaged by Marxists. Casey is less certain about the decentring of work, but asserts more strongly that class consciousness and action are on the wane. The implication of both, however, is that work is no longer a site of solidaristic class meanings and identities: social divisions no longer rest upon production relations. How true is such a claim? The rest of this chapter presents evidence to question it.

The Decentring of Work?

Let us start by considering Bauman's claim about the decreasing centrality of work. This sits uneasily with his own acknowledgement that, for the professional and managerial elite, work is taking over an increasing proportion of time. As we saw in chapter 4, numerous studies have highlighted a 'long hours' culture', or what Simpson (1998) has described as 'presenteeism', resulting from restructuring and competitive managerial cultures.[1] People work twelve-hour days and over weekends, attending optional meetings, courses and training sessions outside working hours; the fax, modem, laptop computer and, above all, the mobile phone allow the activities of the office to spill over into the train, the pub, the restaurant and the living-room – even the beach! Bauman ascribes this behaviour to an elite group of 'workaholics . . . with no fixed hours of work, preoccupied with the challenges of their job twenty-four hours a day and seven days a week' (p. 34).

But evidence from studies suggests that this 'cult of work' is expanding, not declining. Aronowitz and DiFazio point out that in America long hours of work are not confined to the professional and managerial groups, although they may be at the sharp end of what the authors consider a 'social pathology of overwork' (1994: 315), rather than a personal pathology of workaholism. Millions of ordinary working people need two or more jobs in order to earn what a single good manufacturing job would have brought them in previous decades.[2] Thus 'an alarming number of workers, both intellectual and manual, surrender nearly all their waking and even dreaming time to labor' (p. 350).

This contention is supported by Arlie Hochschild in *The Time Bind* (1997). Observing employees in a typical American small town, Hochschild noted that both sexes used work as a means to escape from home, inverting the old relationship where home acted as a refuge from work. Hochschild suggests that women experienced a sense of value and respect at work which was lacking in the drudgery of housework – and even childcare. Although the major employer in the town offered family-friendly options, such as job share or parental leave, Hochschild noted that few employees took them up; working less than full-time was interpreted as lack of commitment and ambition which might affect career advancement.

Wajcman (1998) and McDowell (1997) observed the same phenomenon among British managers and finance workers. British studies show that men in particular are unwilling to sacrifice earnings in order to work shorter hours (Hewitt 1993). This casts doubt on the findings of Ray Pahl (1995) who studied successful men and women, highlighting their expressed desire to achieve a better balance between working and home lives. Pahl suggested that the materialist and individualist culture of the 1980s might be changing, with people putting more value on family life and leisure activities. But Wajcman's research suggests that expressions of this kind do not tally with people's actual behaviour and choices. Men may profess a desire to 'spend more time with the children' but continue to work all the overtime they can get.

Research studies also show that not only high-flying professionals and ambitious managers place value on their work. Interviews with employees in the middle ranks of the employment hierarchy carried out by Bradley (1999) revealed that work was an important source of interest and self-respect to many, as the following quotations from North East workers show:

> It's changed my life going out to work. I couldn't bear to stay in the house and not to work . . . I used to be very quiet. Coming out to work has changed me. (female factory worker)

> You get satisfaction from it, feeling you're doing something . . . I enjoy using my mind. (female laboratory worker)

> After a couple of weeks on the sick, you want to go back to work. You get bored, you get lazy. . . . You need something to get up for in the morning. (female factory worker)

> It's brilliant . . . job satisfaction, to see people get better. The team work between all the staff, there's never a dull moment on the ward. I look forward to every shift. (male nurse)

Academic commentators often undervalue less glamorous types of job, unable to believe that people can get satisfaction from work which is routinized and less intrinsically varied and interesting. But such jobs still offer a range of 'valuables' (Jahoda et al. 1972): companionship, escape from domesticity, structured time, self-respect, as well as financial rewards. Women especially are emphasizing the need to 'make something of their lives' by developing careers, as we saw in chapter 4. Of course, there are many people who are bored with their jobs, especially where they have been stuck in them for some time. But unemployment, given its low status and lack of money, is not an enticing option for most. Recent research by Trickey et al. (1998) confirmed the finding of earlier studies, that most of the unemployed display considerable work attachment and devote energy to jobseeking.

To be sure, studies cannot tell us whether people's attachment to work and career is a matter of individual inclination and choice or the result of internalizing broader social values. Certainly our culture continues to place high value on labour market participation. The espousal of a 'workfare' approach to welfare provision by both British and American governments reinforces the view that responsible citizens are those who support themselves by wage-earning rather than dependency on the state. Schools labour to promote the work ethic in children. Ruth Levitas's analysis of New Labour social policy (1998) suggests that the notion of being 'included' in society is conceived of in terms of employment, while other contributions like unpaid or voluntary work are ignored and devalued. But whatever the reasons, there is little sign as yet of any real decentring of work in the lives of most people in Britain, America or Europe.

The Persistence of Social Inequalities

Having established the continuing importance of jobs in people's lives, we need to explore the link between work and class more explicitly. We start by considering the issue of inequality. In a classless society one might suppose that inequalities would diminish; such differentials as existed would be based on merit, but nobody would be excluded from a share of society's wealth and compelled to live in poverty. But in reality poverty and inequality are currently increasing both nationally and internationally. In Britain in particular the gap between rich and poor has been steadily increasing since the coming to power of the 'New Right' government in 1979; and in America, too, the espousal of liberal free market policies after the ending of the postwar Keynesian epoch has increased economic polarization. In the words of one American economist, Scott Burns, 'the 80s will be known as the decade of the fat cats, a time when entrepreneurial pieties were used to beat the average worker into cowed submission while America's corporate elite moved yet higher on the hog' (quoted in Rifkin 1995: 169).

In Britain, some levelling of income differentials occurred between 1959 and 1979, but since then the gap between high and low earners has been steadily widening, as research carried out for the Rowntree Foundation revealed: between 1979 and 1992, the real incomes of some of the poorest tenth fell by 17 per cent (Hills 1996). At the same time, there was increasing polarization between 'work-rich' and 'work-poor' households (Gregg and Wadsworth 1996). In 1993, 14 per cent of the British population lived in households with no work. Levels of unemployment doubled in the OECD countries between 1972 and 1992, and between 1990 and 1995 male unemployment increased in all EU countries (Lawless et al. 1998). The spread of mass unemployment and low wages has brought increased poverty, concentrated in the 'work-poor' households. It is estimated that 40 per cent of children live in poverty in contemporary Britain, compared with one tenth in 1979, most of them in homes without workers.[3] According to United Nations' measures, only Ireland and America among the developed nations have higher levels of poverty than Britain.[4] Research also indicates that people's economic position, especially poverty, is passed down from parents and even grandparents, a clear sign of the reproduction of class disadvantage (Elliott 1999).

Globally, the gap between rich and poor nations continues to increase. It is estimated that 25 to 30 per cent of the 3 billion people who make up the world's labour force are underemployed (the more common situation in developing countries without fully developed state welfare systems), while 140 million workers are unemployed, with 60 million young adults aged between fifteen and twenty-four unable to find jobs (ILO 1998). In Zimbabwe and Indonesia, 41 per cent of the population earn less than one US dollar a day and in South East Asia and Africa some 30 per cent of children under five suffer from malnutrition.[5]

Wealth also became more concentrated during the same period. Banks et al. (1996) analysed Inland Revenue returns and found that the richest 4 per cent of the British population own 43 per cent of the wealth. The spread of home ownership and holding of pension funds is often cited by proponents of 'classlessness' as a sign of meritocracy. However, Banks et al. show that the ownership of financial forms of wealth (shares and other assets like savings accounts) is highly concentrated among top earners.

These growing inequalities are clearly related to changes in employment relations. The work of entrepreneurs, managers and a top elite of professionals and technical experts has been considered increasingly worthy of high economic rewards, while rank and file workers have been subjected to pay restraints and wage cuts. Gosling et al. (1996) report on the widening gap between skilled and unskilled workers, along with increasing disparities within skill categories. Generally the picture is one of polarization between the well qualified and unqualified; between 1979 and 1993, the median wages of those with higher education rose by one third, while for those who left school by sixteen the figure was 10 per cent.

Throughout the 1980s and 1990s, chief executives and directors received massive pay rises, along with huge bonuses and stakes of shareholdings in their companies; for example, in 1998 Sir Richard Sykes of Glaxo Wellcome had a 53 per cent increase to bring his salary to £1.7 million, Sir Geoff Mulcahy of Woolworths and B&Q a rise of 39 per cent to reach £1.5 million.[6] In America Rifkin (1995) reports that the 4 per cent of what he terms the 'knowledge elite' earn as much as the bottom 51 per cent of wage-earners: their gains were made at the expense of the mass of employees, who faced lower pay levels, loss of jobs and declining state benefits: 'While millions of urban and rural poor languish in poverty, and an increasing number of suburban middle-income wage-earners feel the bite of re-engineering... a small elite of American knowledge workers, entrepreneurs and corporate managers reap the benefits of the new high-tech global economy' (p. 180). The prosperity of the super-rich is shown in the fact reported by Kirby (1999a) that the ten richest men in the world earn more than the total wealth of the forty-eight poorest countries in the world, whose populations total some 560 million people. The UN estimates that $40 billion would be needed to achieve basic education and health care for everybody in the world, along with adequate food, water supplies and sanitation: $40 billion is less than 4 per cent of the combined wealth of the world's 225 richest people.[7]

Class and Difference at Work

The link between these increasing inequalities and work arrangements is evident. Differences in income and wealth spring from the way people are differently located in the labour market and from the different roles they fill in the system of production. Those who are excluded altogether from participation in production fare worst and are most vulnerable to poverty. In recent years, an increasingly competitive and globalized capitalism has heightened differentials of power and rewards within companies and organizations. In the developed societies global competition has brought increased unemployment and legitimated the use of tactics to increase flexibility, as discussed in previous chapters. Consequent increases in non-standard work bring lower earnings to many households. In the developing societies, MNCs are able to exploit the desperation of people to find jobs by utilizing them as cheap labour, especially women. Nation-states may offset some of these effects by employing devices for redistribution of earnings and wealth (such as progressive taxation policies), by provision of public-sector employment and by welfare and social security policies. However, the trend since the 1980s has been for the removal of market impediments, in line with currently orthodox free market economics, for privatization of the public sector, and the slimming down of welfare states. Thus, with a few exceptions, nation-states have actively promoted economic polarization.

It is precisely these processes of economic differentiation which sociologists refer to by the shorthand of 'class'. At a very abstract level these result from processes of global capital accumulation. But although sociologists share this basic conception of class, there has long been disagreement about how exactly these processes inform concrete social relations and how to define distinct classes.[8]

Classic Marxism works with a model of class that focuses on the dichotomizing relationship between capital and labour, bourgeoisie and proletariat, or refines that model in terms of contradictory locations between the polar positions, such as the various class maps provided by Erik Olin Wright (1976; 1985). But currently orthodox in British sociology has been the neo-Weberian approach, developed by John Goldthorpe and Gordon Marshall among others (Goldthorpe 1982; Goldthorpe et al. 1980; Marshall 1997). This arranges clusters of occupations together as social classes on the basis of common employment features and lifestyle chances, and has without doubt been the most influential model because of its utility in empirical investigation. Goldthorpe specifies three major class groupings, the service class (sometimes known as the salariat) of high-level service workers, professionals and managers; the working classes; and an intermediary class of low-paid service workers. A similar occupational approach has informed the development of social-economic categories (SECs) used by the government statistical services, including the new schema devised by David Rose and Karen O' Reilly, who draw on Goldthorpe's work. Their seven-class category system distinguishes different labour market clusters on the basis of various aspects of employment relations, especially the distinction between a service relationship, typical of white-collar employees, and a labour contract typical of manual work (O'Reilly and Rose 1998).[9]

But this occupational model of class has provoked considerable criticism. One major problem is that it does not cover the situation of people who are not in employment (such as the unemployed, the retired, full-time 'housewives' or students). Yet these various groups of people are subject to class processes. Rose and O' Reilly have tried to address this by including an eighth group in their new class schema composed of people who have never worked; yet this is not entirely satisfactory, as it assumes all non-workers are in the same class position, which is unlikely to be true (for example, there are rich men's wives, long-term invalids, middle-class dropouts and 'New Agers' as well as young unemployed men on 'sink' estates).

This points to a more fundamental problem with the occupational approach: class must be conceived of as a set of relationships in which individuals are located, rather than as a property of an individual. In fact all class theorists have acknowledged that families, communities and workplaces are important transmitters of class. We suggest that class should be seen as a complicated set of economic, political and cultural relationships arising from the way societies organize the production of goods and services. These include market and labour process relationships, but also those of distribution and consumption

(Bradley 1996). Aronowitz and DiFazio (1994) call for a multidimensional account of class which will deal with the complexity of class situations, situations which are continuously changing. Aptly, they describe class as 'a project in the making' (p. 292).

However, whatever definition of class is used, work arrangements have a key role in the formation of class divisions. As well as the overarching division distinguished by Marx between the owners of the means of production (along with their agents) and the non-owning wage-labourers, contemporary capitalist employment generates lesser divisions among the wage-earners, on bases of skill, qualifications, nature of the job (manual or mental labour) which have constituted the base of neo-Weberian accounts. There is also a fundamental cleavage between those who are employed within the production process, deriving their wealth or income from it, and those excluded from production who must be supported by others (families, husbands, charity, the state) or starve. All these divisions are still being reproduced by contemporary employment relations, though we should emphasize again that this is only part of the complex nexus of class relations. Nevertheless, work remains a site of class reproduction, in opposition to the 'death of class' thesis.

In fact, critics of class such as Pakulski and Waters concede the existence of economic inequalities and divisions at work although they may reconceptualize them as forms of status distinction. Their claims about the death of class rest more on the issue of declining class identity and action, which we will discuss shortly. But a persistent strand of thinking *has* suggested a decline in work-related divisions. For example, Peter Saunders (1990) and Peter Drucker (1993) have both suggested that the development of pension funds has blurred the fundamental capital/labour distinction: we are all petty capitalists now. This line of thinking informs managerial views of organizations as 'unitary' institutions in which all employees from top managers to cleaning staff have common interests and stakes in the company, sometimes in the form of share options.

Moreover, during the 1980s, linked to the trend towards Japanization in British companies, there was considerable talk of 'harmonization' between the layers of the hierarchy, especially the merging of blue- and white-collar work conditions in what was referred to as 'single status'. Flexibility was said to be breaking down the traditional distinction between manual and mental labour and overriding longstanding occupational distinctions, in the way described by Casey (1995). Organizational restructuring in the 1980s often involved 'delayering' of some tiers and grades and the 'flattening' of employment hierarchies. This implied an upgrading of the conditions of lower-level workers, as suggested by Bell in his original account of post-industrialism. There is however, a counter-view, the Marxian notion of proletarianization, which suggests that higher-level workers are having their conditions degraded to those of manual workers.

We will revisit the notion of proletarianization, but deal first with the issue of upgrading. All the evidence from statistical sources and research studies suggest that traditional divisions are still strong. We have noted the increasing division between the highly rewarded elite of directors and top managers and the mass of employees. We have also noted the increasing polarization between work-poor and work-rich households. Research studies also confirm that internal differentiation among tiers of wage-earners hold strong. For example, Price and Price (1994) found that the status divide between manual and non-manual workers continued to be a 'pervasive feature of the workplace for many British employees' (p. 558). The pay differential remained: while the average weekly earnings of non-manual men had increased by 37 per cent between 1979 and 1990, the increase for manual men was only 11 per cent. Similarly O'Reilly and Rose (1998) reported that the distinction between the 'service relationship' and the 'labour contract' was confirmed by a number of indicators in their survey of employment conditions: for example, higher occupational groups had more autonomy, control over their tasks and working day, better promotion prospects and different types of pay arrangements (monthly salaries as opposed to weekly wages). Bradley (1999) found in her case studies that even where management had tried to flatten hierarchies and erode job distinctions to promote functional flexibility, employees had a very firm sense of their own job designation and were attached to their occupational identities.

There is little evidence of an end to divisions among wage-earners or to occupational identification. However, the persistence of inequalities and distinctions does not in itself mean that employees have a strong awareness of these issues. This brings us to the heart of the 'death of class' thesis: the contention that worker collectivism and individual class identification are both on the decline.

Class, Collectivism and Conflict

'The management and factory are separate: they are the bosses and we are the factory. It's like that with men and women' (Jenkins 1999: 193). This classic statement of a 'them and us' imagery comes from a woman factory worker interviewed in the North East of England by Sarah Jenkins. Her research indicated that collective attitudes are still to be found among both manual and lower-level service workers. Bradley's study (1999) uncovered a similar sense of worker solidarity and opposition to employers and managers among many employees:

> I think the union are on our side and I think the management are against us.
>
> You're talking about two classes. All those who have to work. Britain's run by the class who do the employing. They're the people who have the power.

Many manual workers resented the way they were viewed by managers;

> They assume you're stupid because you're a production worker. There's no prospects.
>
> Sometimes you feel you're at infant school. They treat you like you're a bairn.

Both Jenkins's and Bradley's respondents showed attachment and loyalty to trade unions even when workers were disillusioned with their own unions and saw them as powerless. Unions were considered necessary to protect individual workers from victimization, to represent them when they had a grievance, and also to act for the workers as a collective body to negotiate for pay and conditions:

> Without the unions there's nothing to look after the interests of the ordinary person. We'd just be walked over.

Collective and individualistic motives mingled in the accounts offered by these employees of the need for unions and their reasons for membership (Bradley 1994). But what emerged strongly was a sense that, in a period when managerial power had been strengthened and the threat of redundancy was widespread, unions were more than ever necessary to protect employees. In the next chapter we explore in more detail the debates about the decline of trade union membership and counter-arguments about union revival.

It could be objected that the North East workers were untypical, coming as they did from a region with the highest level of union membership in Britain and strongly established working-class communities. But similar findings emerge from studies in other regions. Andy Danford (1996) found a strong sense of opposition to management in a study of South Wales factory workers. Gail Hebson observed considerable levels of class awareness among women unionists in Bristol.[10] At the other end of the class spectrum, McDowell (1997) found a strong sense of class in the financial organizations she studied in the City of London. Class background was a crucial factor in recruitment. Most of the employees had attended elite universities, such as Bristol, Durham and Exeter, if not Oxford and Cambridge. People spoke of the necessity to have 'the right kind of background' (p. 126) and reported how their co-workers grilled them about their family origins. This indicates how we like to pigeonhole the people we encounter in a class bracket.

Evidence from national surveys also confirms that class awareness is not dead and indeed might be on the rise. Kirby (1999b) reports a Gallup poll of 1996 in which 76 per cent of respondents believed a class struggle existed in Britain, as compared to 48 per cent in 1964. Similarly, a national poll in 1998 found that 68 per cent of interviewees believed that Britain was 'class-ridden'.

Why, then, do writers such as Pakulski and Waters claim that class collectivism and identities are vanishing? Two objections, which must be taken seriously, can be raised to our arguments so far. First, a sense of class might be confined to the more traditional class groupings: the working class who still inhabit older communities and housing estates, and the upper and entrepreneurial classes who maintain dominant social hegemony. Perhaps the growing mass of middle-class people lack class awareness? The same is true of younger people who are no longer subjected to traditional patterns of class socialization in families, through apprenticeship and through union membership. Paul Willis and colleagues (1990) argue that young people are much more likely to find their identification through involvement in music-based subcultures and other consumption activities: style wars replace class wars. Second, even if residual class identities and collective impulses linger on, they no longer find expression in class-based protest or organizations, such as the unions, the old Labour Party or the parties of the far left. Political action, especially among the young, is more likely to surround the 'new social movements' (NSMs), such as the fight for animal rights, against genetically modified food or to save the countryside from roads.

There is some truth in these contentions. Goldthorpe et al. (1980) described the middle classes as being of 'low classness' in comparison to the 'mature' working class; they have a less coherent social and political identity. Many middle-class people have traditionally identified with the ruling elite and voted for their political parties, while others, especially those working in the public sector, have sympathies with the working class and support parties of the left. Middle-class people may therefore demonstrate lower levels of specific class identification and collectivism.

On the other hand, some middle-class groups have seen their positions eroded in the past decades. The Americans talk of the 'squeezed middle'. The threat of redundancy and unemployment has reached many formerly protected groups, including public-sector employees and middle managers. Aronowitz and DiFazio (1994) suggest that this amounts to a distinct proletarianization of the middle classes, which is likely to be sustained as the power of the state and corporations over professionals tightens. There has been some support for such a view in Britain, too, although it is rejected by others (for example, Devine 1997; O'Reilly and Rose 1998); Devine claims that even low-level service workers are likely to identify as middle class. However, some groups of middle-class employees have seen their autonomy and job security eroded, especially those in the lower professions and the public sector. Control over such groups has become much tighter, often at government instigation. For example, university lecturers now have both their research output and their teaching quality monitored and evaluated at regular intervals, with individuals who do not come up to scratch targeted for early retirement or redundancy. Such changes can be seen as limited proletarianization, although many distinctions remain between manual and white-collar work. As a result there has been an upsurge of unionism among some middle-class groupings and signs of industrial militancy among occupations, such as nurses, teachers and airline pilots, who were wary of industrial action in the past.

But class identification is not a simple process. We emphasize that class is not an individual attribute or identificatory label. Rather, class is a set of relationships in which people are located, which inform their life chances, choices and behaviours. People may respond to their class situation in different ways, sometimes by positively embracing a class identity ('working class and proud of it', as John Prescott states in the quotation at the head of the chapter), sometimes by rejecting it. The work of Skeggs (1997), for example, emphasizes the importance of 'disidentification' in certain cases. She studied a group of young women training for care work and found that they developed a strong cult of respectability to distinguish themselves from 'the poor' or 'lower class'. For some, belonging to the working classes can be seen as a stigma (Mahony and Zmroczek 1997), a reason for being 'looked down on'.

Moreover, in the course of their lives people's position in the class nexus often changes (as they become upwardly or downwardly mobile, marry into other classes, gain higher education, or move into a different residential area, for example). The changing nature of the service-based economy increases the difficulty of locating particular occupations in class terms. There has been considerable disagreement among sociologists, for example, about the class situation of retail and clerical workers. This mixed experience, which may be referred to as 'class hybridity', leads to further confusion about identity and belonging. It is not surprising that many people express what Marxists have described as 'contradictory' class responses.

Such changes contribute to the declining role of traditional class-based movements. Class is now more ambiguously implicated as the basis of political party membership. In part, this reflects the growing prominence of political mobilization round other sources of social difference, such as gender, ethnicity or disablement. These movements compete with the older political bodies for people's affiliation, calling on other aspects of their social identification. Note how the quotation from the factory worker which headed this section drew attention to polarities of both class *and* gender.

However, class meanings and interests may still be at play in the new political alignments, even though relatively submerged. Indeed, Klaus Eder sees the NSMs as being the class movements of the middle class (1993), and, one might add, of the disenfranchized young. Many of these political campaigns, although they do not centre on the workplace, are profoundly anti-capitalist and opposed to big business. Many of them specifically target the actions of multinational corporations. The libel case brought by McDonalds over charges made by Helen Steel and Dave Morris about the farming practices that lie behind their hamburgers is one famous example of a moral challenge to the power of a transnational giant; the campaign against Monsanto over genetic modification of crops is another. NSMs can be interpreted as part of a long tradition of opposition and resistance to the economic interests and ideologies of the dominant classes, even if they take novel and diverse forms. In this respect, it is interesting that young people are so often involved in them. This suggests that young people are not merely addicted to individual consumption and will take up causes based on collective interests. Indeed there is no real evidence that young people's class behaviour is significantly different from their parents. Although they are less likely to be union members, this is partly because they are typically employed in less unionized sectors or in temporary jobs: there is limited evidence that they have any strong ideological resistance to unions, though their lack of a long work history may make them apathetic (Cregan 1999).

Class and Change

In this context, we should reaffirm that class relations are by nature dynamic and fluid. We should not expect classes to be produced and reproduced as they were in the earlier stages of the industrial epoch. Behind some of the accounts of the decline of class, such as those of Casey or Pakulski and Waters, there lurks a false conception of some Golden Age of class consciousness, when people were clear about their class location, collective impulses were strong and class was the basis of politics. But were things ever like that? Rather, as Marshall et al. (1988) have argued, collectivist and individualist motives and actions have always coexisted. Unions have always struggled to gain and retain membership, though their fortunes have ebbed and flowed over time. Processes of class identification have often been contested and ambiguous, although, as Devine (1997) points out, in many ways class has been remarkably resilient over the course of the twentieth century.

Changes in the economy inevitably bring reconfiguration of the class nexus: we suggest that this process is particularly intense at the moment. Service-based or 'post-industrial' capitalist economies have characteristically evolved new class formations: a small, highly concentrated and more internationalized capitalist elite; a large service class, typically divided in separate groupings with distinct interests and assets (Butler and Savage 1996; Savage et al. 1992); a growing group of intermediate workers who may be termed a 'service proletariat' (Esping-Andersen 1993); a shrinking manual working class; and a solidifying excluded or labour surplus class. Study of such new class formations has focused recently on the excluded group, often labelled by the rather derogatory term 'underclass', or on the expanding middle classes. New insights about class and identity may emerge from this ongoing work.[11]

The American writers cited in this chapter tend to a rather apocalyptic view of class developments. Their accounts feature the notion of a 'knowledge sector' or 'technical elite' of highly skilled workers, with all other groups becoming of increasingly marginal importance in production. They suggest that mass unemployment will increase exponentially unless dramatic steps are taken to halt it, such as the drastic reduction of the working week coupled with some form of job sharing or rationing.

This scenario is underpinned, however, by a blinkered vision of *what work is*, derived from the industrial past. The 'worker' who is vanishing is the male factory worker. If we operate with a broader vision of work we can envisage a different future. In Europe there has been a focus on the emergence of new forms of service work, many of which are associated with women. The ageing of the population, a demographic phenomenon found in all advanced economies, necessitates new arrangements and institutions for the care of elderly people, inside or outside their own homes. Gregson and Lowe (1994) document how the increase in women's employment has led to the rapid expansion of demand for domestic workers (they studied two distinct groups, cleaners and nannies). Sex work and work in the tourist and leisure sectors are increasing around the world. High levels of crime, mental illness and other social problems mean there is still plenty of work that needs to be done, if societies are willing and able to pay for it: we need more researchers, medical workers, teachers, social workers, childminders. The reparation and reclamation of destroyed and damaged environments is another social task which could absorb armies of the unemployed.

Whichever scenario is correct, the further shrinking of employment, or the expansion of service and community work, the changes will have profound effects on class relations and meanings. But in this chapter we have argued that this does not mean an end to class, merely its constant refiguration in new and unpredicted forms. However, to grasp the nature of these changes we must abandon some of the old orthodoxies about class in favour of a more flexible, multidimensional form of analysis which is sensitive to the interaction of class with other dynamics of social differentiation, such as gender and ethnicity.

Conclusion

This chapter has criticized many aspects of the 'death of class' myth. We have seen that work is still central in many people's lives. Work arrangements continue to generate class differences and inequalities that persist over generations and are currently increasing. Indeed, rather than the disappearance of class, we highlight increasing class polarization. Those in the labour surplus class and the manual working class are disproportionately likely to experience low educational attainment, unemployment, insecurity, poverty, illness and early mortality.

Class, however, must be viewed as a complex nexus of relations which constantly change. For this reason, processes of class identification (or disidentification) are equally complex and uncertain. The growth of the middle classes, now numerically dominant, has disrupted traditional class loyalties and affiliations, bringing new patterns of political allegiance. Opposition to the dominant capitalist orthodoxy may take new forms and promote new alliances between different disadvantaged groups. Despite this it is wrong to say that class is dying and that the working class is disappearing; class relations are reconfiguring and the working class is taking new forms.

8

The Myth of the End of Trade Unionism

> It is the job of the company to create an environment in which a trade union becomes irrelevant . . . the very nature of the unions, sitting in there in a divisive capacity, stops the employees and managers of an organization getting together as one team.
>
> (Chief Executive, Zurich Insurance)

Introduction

One of the most notable recent developments in work and employment has been the deterioration in the social, economic and political influence of the trade unions in many parts of the world. Three factors have been highlighted as particularly important causes of this trend. First, in academic circles there has been a growing interest in how trade union decline may be the expression of a weakening of work-based collectivism, an interest linked to the issue of the death of class, discussed in the previous chapter. Second, the changing structure of employment – the shift of jobs from the highly unionized primary and manufacturing sectors to relatively non-unionized private services – appears to have undermined union power. According to Moody (1997), 'millions of industrial jobs, many of them higher-paid union jobs, evaporated as industries like steel, shipbuilding, machinery and automobiles closed facilities and reduced production capacity across the West' (p. 182). Third, many employers have become increasingly concerned to exclude unions from their workplaces. The elaboration of techniques associated with the unitarist philosophy of HRM – in which it is assumed that employees and managers share common goals, principally organizational success, and that relations between them are harmonious – are perceived to further a less conflictual climate of industrial relations.

Although the power and influence of the trade unions have diminished in many countries, the trend has been particularly acute in the UK. Between 1979 and 1997 successive Conservative administrations passed legislation which restricted the powers of trade unions in the labour market. Equally importantly, their broader social and macroeconomic policies further weakened the position of the unions, undermined their legitimacy and reinforced the prerogative of employers. Although the Labour government which was elected in 1997 has partially reversed the trend of hostile legislation, it none the less espouses quasi-unitarist rhetoric about the importance of 'partnership' in the workplace and the need to replace conflict at work with common aims and values. Given the intensity of the anti-union climate, an assessment of how the unions have fared, and of their future prospects, in the UK is particularly instructive. Evidence is reviewed to show that, first, adversarial and low-trust relationships continue to be an important feature of the industrial relations scene; and second, that this gives the unions an opportunity to expand their role and influence on a collective basis.

The Political and Legislative Assault on the Unions

In recent years there has been a marked political and legislative assault on trade union power in the UK. In the 1960s and 1970s the trade unions, largely through the auspices of their confederation – the TUC (Trades Union Congress) – played an increasingly important part in the formulation of public policy, especially in economic-related matters, on important bodies like the National Economic Development Council (NEDC) and the MSC. The role of the trade union movement in contributing to policy formulation was such that commentators were able to refer to it as an 'estate of the realm' (Taylor 1993) or a 'governing institution' (Middlemas 1979). Although both Hyman (1989) and Waddington and Whitston (1995) have cautioned against overstating the influence of trade unions in governmental decision-making, union participation was accepted as legitimate even by Conservative administrations of the time. Yet perhaps the high point of the unions' influence occurred when the Labour Party was in office between 1974 and 1979. In exchange for a commitment to wage restraint, which in reality could not be delivered by union leaderships, the then Labour government under James Callaghan offered a 'Social Contract', which included supportive measures for trade union organization in the workplace. Between 1979 and 1997, however, the scale and scope of union influence was reduced by successive Conservative administrations. As we saw in chapter 6, the MSC was wound up in 1988 and its functions were largely dispersed to a network of TECs. Three years later the Conservatives abolished the NEDC. According to Davies and Freedland (1993: 427), the 'distancing of unions from the corridors of power' was a distinctive feature of politics in the 1980s and early 1990s; in particular, the TUC was excluded from participating in the formulation of public policy (Heery 1998b).[1]

Not only did the Conservative governments of 1979–97 weaken the legitimacy of the trade unions by excluding them from the political arena, but they also enacted a legislative programme designed to constrain their operations. Unlike many other countries, until the 1980s most of the activity of unions in the twentieth century went ungoverned by statute (Kahn-Freund 1964). They benefited from immunities granted by various acts of parliament so that they could organize collectively or take strike action, for example, without being challenged in the courts by employers. Between 1980 and 1993 the Conservatives progressively reduced the scope of these 'immunities' in a series of laws. The Trade Union Act of 1984, for example, made it unlawful for a union to engage in industrial action without having conducted a secret ballot beforehand, and the 1993 Trade Union Reform and Employment Rights Act required unions to give employers a minimum of seven days' notice of any industrial action.

Both Davies and Freedland (1993) and Dickens and Hall (1995) have provided a detailed examination of the Conservative's legislative agenda. For the purposes of this chapter it is simply necessary to indicate that the programme of reform, while it was initially incremental in nature, and not the expression of a grand design, was guided by two imperatives. In the first place there was an obvious concern with reducing trade union power in the labour market. Second, the legislation appears to have been designed to undermine collectivism and to promote individualism as a way of further diminishing the legitimacy of the unions (Martin et al. 1995; Smith and Morton 1993). Nevertheless, the efficacy of the legislative programme has been questioned. Dunn and Metcalf (1996) prefer to ascribe the reduced power of trade unions to changes in the economy and the composition of the workforce. However, in a case study of shop-floor industrial relations in an auto components factory Andy Danford has demonstrated the extent to which changes in the law have weakened the power of the unions. Most notably, they have induced perceptions of 'impotence' and 'defeatism' among workers who feel that they have reduced scope to challenge the actions of management (Danford 1997: 117).

During part of the 1980s, at least up to the 1987 General Election, union leaders looked forward to the return of a Labour government which they hoped would revoke the Conservative's trade union legislation. When the Labour Party did eventually return to office in 1997, such hopes had long been dashed. Historically, there have been extremely close links between the unions and the Labour Party; indeed, the unions were largely responsible for establishing it as a political institution in 1900. This connection notwithstanding, the relationship between the Labour Party and the unions has often been fractious (Minkin 1991). Following the disastrous electoral performances of the 1980s under the leadership of Neil Kinnock the Labour Party tentatively began to distance itself from the unions (McIlroy 1995). After the fourth successive election defeat in 1992 this process accelerated. Within the Labour leadership there was a perception that the link with the unions gave the electorate the impression that the party was beholden to a special interest group, one that was associated, particularly by the media, with damaging and unnecessary industrial conflict and disruption in the 1970s (McIlroy 1998). The Labour Party had already conceded that, when in office, it would not seek to abolish most of the Conservative's industrial relations legislation. Between 1992 and 1994, under the leadership of John Smith, the link between Labour and the unions was weakened; for example, the scale of the union 'block vote' in leadership elections was at first reduced and then replaced by a system of 'one member – one vote'.

Following Smith's death in 1994, and the election of Tony Blair as his replacement as Labour Party leader, the distancing of Labour from the unions speeded up. According to David Farnham, Blair's aim was to 'reduce union power within the Party' (Farnham 1996: 587). At the Labour Party Conference of October 1996 one leading shadow minister, Stephen Byers, reportedly advocated ending the trade union links with the party entirely.[2] In respect of its policy aims, between 1994 and 1997 the Labour leadership placed an increasing amount of emphasis on wooing business support. Labour strongly stressed its support for competitive markets and for creating the conditions in which industry could thrive. Within this broad approach to economic policy, industrial relations was conceived of in unitarist terms (McIlroy 1998). Unions were seen to be a legitimate part of the institutional infrastructure of the UK, but their major role was to engage in 'partnerships' with employers in order that the economy could be 'modernized' (a favourite 'New' Labour word) and improved.

The Policies of Employers

In the postwar period strong workplace trade unionism developed, particularly in the engineering and manufacturing sectors. This was often based on sophisticated shop stewards' organization and strongly asserted the primacy of collective bargaining as a way of regulating the employment relationship (Terry 1983). In the 1960s and particularly the 1970s equally vigorous union growth occurred in many parts of the public sector (Terry 1982). From the beginning of the 1980s, however, it appears that union organization in the workplace has been weakened in a number of important respects. For one thing, the trend towards smaller workplaces has been identified as inimical to trade unionism (Hyman 1991).

Furthermore, many employers took increasing advantage of the changed economic environment, particularly high unemployment, and a more sympathetic political climate, to reassert managerial prerogative – the 'right to manage'. During the early to mid-1980s there was a growth of interest in 'new industrial relations', comprising single rather than multi-union bargaining arrangements, work flexibility, single status for employees and 'no-strike deals'. In a spirit of 'new realism' some unions, notably the EETPU (Electrical Electronic Telecommunication and Plumbing Union), reacted favourably to such developments (Bassett 1986). But as Kelly (1996) has noted, often the motives of employers stem not from a desire to advance genuine social partnership in the workplace, but from a keenness to weaken unionism.

The decline of trade union organization can be examined with reference to three related developments. First, there has been a significant increase in the proportion of employers who do not recognize unions for collective bargaining. Millward et al. (1992) showed that between 1980 and 1990 the proportion of establishments recognizing trade unions declined from 64 to 53 per cent, with the fall being even more marked in private manufacturing. Yet outright de-recognition of unions by employers appears to have been rare, and particular to certain sectors such as newspaper publishing and shipping (Claydon 1996; Kelly 1990). The fall in the incidence of recognition reflects the reluctance of employers setting up new plants on 'greenfield' sites to deal with the unions (Blyton and Turnbull 1998).[3] In the 1990s, however, the trend towards de-recognition appears to have accelerated (Gall and McKay 1994), with one observer noting that 'a cumulative trend towards de-recognition might be emerging' (Claydon 1996: 163). Data extracted from the Labour Force Survey (LFS) show that between 1993 and 1997 there was a decline of 4.6 per cent in the proportion of employees working in establishments where unions were recognized (Cully and Woodland 1998).[4] According to Storey and Sisson (1993), 'trade unions are concerned with representing the collective interests of employees, whereas management may want to place more importance on the individual' (p. 202).

Second, collective bargaining arrangements themselves have been the subject of considerable reform. During the 1980s there was a trend away from national bargaining towards a system of company- or plant-specific negotiations (Blyton and Turnbull 1998). More significantly there is evidence that the incidence of collective bargaining has diminished (Millward et al. 1992). One commentator has observed that 'in the course of the 1980s . . . the scope of collective bargaining has narrowed . . . the depth of union involvement has diminished and that organizational security offered to unions by employers has deteriorated' (W. Brown 1993: 197).

Third, many employers also appear to have given greater consideration to techniques of HRM. In the United States, Kochan et al. (1986) found that HRM was increasingly coming to replace collective bargaining as the predominant way in which relations between workers and their employers were regulated. It is notoriously difficult to define HRM, not least because it has often been used by employers and by some academics as a conceptual peg on which to hang a wide range of otherwise unconnected managerial innovations.[5] Nevertheless, perhaps the most distinctive aspect of the adoption of employment practices associated with HRM is the way in which they are deployed to undermine trade unionism (Sisson 1993). As Guest (1989) has noted, HRM is predominantly 'unitarist and individualistic in contrast to the more pluralistic and collective values of traditional industrial relations'. The 'values underpinning HRM leave little scope for collective arrangements and leave little scope for collective bargaining. HRM therefore poses a considerable challenge to traditional industrial relations and more particularly to trade unions' (p. 43). Thus the trend towards HRM is largely indistinguishable from the general attempts by employers to exclude trade unions from their workplaces. There is an assumption – and this now appears to be held by the UK Labour Party as well – that in modern, well-run companies where there is an increasing emphasis on the contribution made by individuals to corporate success, there is little need for the collective and oppositional influence of workers organized in unions.

Social Change and the Challenge for the Unions

In reviewing the experience of trade unionism in the 1980s, a number of writers have suggested that it weathered the hostile political, economic and industrial climate relatively well. Kelly (1990), for example, pointed to the general resilience of workplace organization, and, on the basis of substantial empirical research in six diverse geographical areas, Gallie et al. (1996) observed that there was no 'evidence of a general tendency for union power to be undermined' (p. 14). The presence of robust trade unionism in some areas notwithstanding, the considerable decline in union membership in the 1990s is perhaps a reflection of more profound difficulties for the unions. Until 1989 official data pertaining to aggregate trade union membership was drawn from the returns made by the unions to the Certification Officer. They reveal that between 1979 and 1989 the number of union members in Britain fell from 13,289,000 to 10,158,000, a decline of some 24 per cent. Between 1989 and 1996 union membership contracted by a further 22 per cent to 7,900,000 (Cully and Woodland 1998). Since 1989, data on trade union membership have also been collected by the annual LFS. They show that from 1989 to 1997 aggregate union membership fell by about 21 per cent to just over seven million (Cully and Woodland 1998).[6]

The extent of the decline in membership raises the question of how far the weakening of trade unionism is an expression of broad social change, especially the shift away from class-based collectivism towards greater societal individualism. According to a prominent historian of the American labour movement, trade unionism is 'by definition, the collective effort by workers to advance their job interests' (Brody 1993: 43). Not only might continuing falls in aggregate membership reflect the diminution of this work-based collectivism, but the decline in the incidence of overt industrial action can also be cited as a further example of an increasingly individualistic climate. In 1997, for example, only 235,000 working days were lost through strike activity, the lowest figure ever recorded (*Labour Market Trends*, June 1998), and a stark contrast with the 1970s when, on average, strikes accounted each year for over 12,000,000 working days.

We have already examined the ways in which former Conservative governments and employers sought to undermine collectively based trade unionism in Britain. But as we saw in the last chapter, it has been increasingly commonplace for sociologists to argue that there has been general trend away from work-based collectivism, particularly in so far as it is associated with class identity (Bauman 1998; Casey 1995). As early as the mid-1980s it was being acknowledged that broad social and economic changes were adversely affecting labour movements. In their analysis of the shift from 'organized' to 'disorganized' capitalism, for example, Lash and Urry (1987) acknowledged a 'decline in the collective identity of each national working class' (p. 234). They attributed this development to the widening fissure between private and public sector workers, the growing internationalization of the economy, the challenge to the largely male labour movement posed by the increasing number of female employees, and the declining significance of the manufacturing sector. In a pessimistic vein Touraine (1986) asserted that 'class conscious union movements have not been able to maintain themselves anywhere. . . . There has been a general decline in Europe of collective efforts aimed at transforming industrial society in the interest of the working class' (pp. 161, 165).

The challenge to the trade unions posed by the diminution of class as a source of social identity appears to be twofold. On the one hand, a greater degree of societal individualism has been identified. The diminution of the salience of class- and work-based collectivism and the rise of more fragmented, fluid and individualized identities is a prominent feature of postmodern accounts of social change. On the other hand, some writers have noted the emergence of new, more contingent and non-class-based forms of collective organization and action – those based on the politics of the environment, for example (see Crook et al. 1992). Given the decline in the significance of working-class identity and consciousness, the importance of trade unions, in so far as they are class-based institutions, is bound to diminish (Phelps Brown 1990).

Unions, then, have been encouraged to adapt to the apparently more individualistic climate of recent years. Bacon and Storey (1996), for example, have argued that the 'fracturing of collectivism' means that unions should focus more on responding to the individual needs of their members. Such an approach has also been recommended by both the CBI and the left-leaning think-tank, the Fabian Society (House of Commons Employment Committee 1994; Fabian Society 1996). Perhaps the most notable expression of this view, however, came in a booklet written for the Fabian Society by Bassett and Cave (1993). They argued that unions should concentrate on representing and servicing members more explicitly as individuals; in fact they should treat them as 'customers' in order to 'perform better in the changed, more individualistic, markets for trade unions' (p. 16).

There is some evidence that unions have begun to adopt policies that reflect such an analysis of their plight. The notion of 'managerial unionism', in contrast to the 'professional unionism' and 'participative unionism' of previous eras, has been developed to conceptualize changes in trade unions in the 1990s (Heery and Kelly 1994). It includes, among other things, an increased emphasis on managerial effectiveness, the greater centralization of decision-making and organizational matters, and a new concern with identifying the needs of members as individuals rather than as part of a collective group. Heery (1996) has cogently summarized the essential characteristics of the new, managerial unionism of which he states that the GMB general union is the most notable exponent:

> At its heart is a managerial servicing relationship, in which unions seek to research members' needs and design and promote attractive servicing packages in response. This relationship rests on the assumption that members are largely instrumental in their orientation to unions and behave as reactive consumers who can be attracted or alienated from unions by the quality of the service which is provided. (p. 187)

Thus far in this chapter we have examined how the collective, social and industrial power of the trade unions was weakened in the 1980s and 1990s. As the quotation which opened this chapter indicates, there is a widely held perception that in a modern economy the workplace should increasingly be characterized by partnership between individuals and their employers, rather than workers' collective organization and adversarial relations. That a textbook on 'employee relations' (Hollinshead et al. 1999) can now be published which includes no analysis of the pattern and causes of strike activity, or even of industrial conflict in a broader context, may be considered a noteworthy development in this respect. The ongoing fall in aggregate trade union membership in many Western economies not only appears to bear out the view that adversarial industrial relations are relatively insignificant now, but it also indicates that the decline of trade unionism might well be the expression of long-term social change, and thus difficult to halt, let alone reverse.

The Resilience of Collective Action and Organization: Three Exemplars

Notwithstanding the very negative picture for the unions that has so far been presented, the remainder of this chapter is devoted to an examination of the continuing resilience and significance of collectively based trade unionism. The provision of some exemplars of union activity is an instructive way of highlighting some relevant issues.

First, during the 1980s and early 1990s the vehicle manufacturers Vauxhall claimed to have taken substantial steps towards improving employee relations, involvement and participation at its Ellesmere Port and Luton plants.[7] However, the adoption of 'lean-production' techniques (see chapter 2) generated a considerable amount of discontent among Vauxhall workers, which found expression in a dispute lasting from September 1995 to February 1996 and involved an overtime ban and unofficial strike activity on the part of workers represented by the TGWU and the AEEU. Formally, the disruption centred on demands for improvements in pay and conditions of service, but the intensity of the struggle was a reflection of the workers' dissatisfaction with new working practices. Eventually the dispute was settled after six months of workplace conflict, and, although the demands of the unions were not entirely achieved, the negotiated settlement represented a considerable victory for collective action. Despite the elaboration of sophisticated and innovative employment practices at Vauxhall, Stewart concludes, perhaps a little too strongly, that 'the unions, by virtue of their ideological hegemony continue to outpace management . . . when it comes to delivering on promises to their members' (Stewart 1997: 6).

Second, in 1998 the industrial action that affected the construction of the extension to London Underground's Jubilee Line represented another example of how collective action by workers organized in unions can result in important advances.[8] The rapid completion of the Jubilee Line extension was important politically because it was designed to serve the government's flagship Millennium Dome in Greenwich and had to be finished before the beginning of 2000. By the autumn of 1998 the project was eighteen months behind schedule and was in danger of not being completed on time. The US-owned firm Bechtel – renowned in its home country and elsewhere for being belligerently anti-union – had already been brought in by the government to oversee the work and make sure that it was finished as quickly as possible. During 1998 the climate of industrial relations on the site deteriorated markedly and workers mounted an unofficial overtime ban. In November 1998 workers installing electrical systems underground raised worries that the speed of the work was endangering health and safety. The immediate cause of the dispute was the main electrical contractor's decision to order the transfer of twelve union activists to a different site after they had complained about faulty fire alarms in the tunnels. About 500 workers, mainly members of the AEEU, then walked out and a strike began which lasted nearly two weeks. Under the law, because it was an unofficial dispute, AEEU officials were obliged to renounce the action and encourage the strikers to return to work. Furthermore, managers had the option of hiring a replacement workforce. It was recognized, however, that not only would new workers be difficult to procure at short notice, given the shortage of adequately skilled individuals, but that this would also exacerbate and perhaps extend the dispute. After less than a fortnight the union and management negotiated a settlement whereby the twelve transferred workers were reinstated and an agreement on matters including mobility, productivity and health and safety was arrived at. According to Seumas Milne, management 'effectively backed down'.

It might be argued that these exemplars are unrepresentative of UK employment relations in the 1990s. Vehicle manufacturing, for example, has traditionally been characterized by strong workplace trade unionism in the UK,[9] and the dispute on the Jubilee Line extension attracted attention as an expression of discontent by a small group of relatively privileged employees who benefited from skill shortages in an acutely sensitive political environment. Yet there are also sectors, particularly in the public services, where increasingly robust collective organization is being forged, even in areas where it has hitherto not been strong. One of these constitutes our third exemplar. During the early and mid-1990s the National Health Service was subjected to considerable processes of restructuring by the UK government. Hospitals and other major health care providers were reorganized as quasi-autonomous 'trusts' and, in the interests of efficiency and cost-effectiveness, the development of a market-based culture between these providers and their 'customers' (principally local health authorities and general practicioners) was encouraged to develop. In the North East of England hospital mergers and closures were among the main results of this policy. Interviews carried out by one of the authors in 1994 and 1995 with representatives of the Manufacturing, Science and Finance (MSF) union, covering hospital technical staff, speech therapists, clinical psychologists and radiographers, highlighted the level of insecurity permeating employment in what had hitherto been a stable environment. Although employees saw union membership largely as an 'insurance policy', MSF representatives reported that there was a heightened level of interest in the collective protection that the union could offer. A number are quoted below:

> Recently we've had a few new members because of the political situation. They're so scared they join out of self-preservation.
>
> In the last few months or so we must have recruited about twenty new members. Which is a knock-on effect of the merger problem. People are looking to the union for protection.

> They're going to get representation; there's always somebody in the union that's going to know more about procedures and terms and conditions.

> The problems they have here will make them think they need someone to speak for them.

The Resilience of Adversarialism and Collectivism at Work

The brief exemplar of MSF organization points to both the changing character of trade unionism and the continuing significance of adversarial industrial relations. Until about the 1970s trade unionism was identified largely with full-time male employees working in primary, extractive and manufacturing industries; as we saw in chapter 3 employment in manufacturing has contracted considerably, and the proportion of employees working in the service sector has increased.[10] Although the unions have experienced difficulties in expanding their organizational base in private services (Macaulay and Wood 1992), in public services (including those which have recently been privatized) they still retain a considerable presence and influence. Notwithstanding the adverse pressures described earlier in this chapter, Bailey (1996) has shown that in many public services union organization continues to be robust. Furthermore, although trade unions in the public sector have traditionally had strong, central and overly hierarchical characteristics restructuring processes have thrown up opportunities for the development of more participative and 'bottom-up' forms of organization.

Fairbrother (1994) has explored such processes of 'union renewal'. He shows that while employment in the public services has been affected by the elaboration of decentralized managerial structures, the furtherance of market principles, including privatization, and greater intensification of work, paradoxically such developments provide an environment within which collective, democratic and participative workplace trade unionism can increasingly flourish, since there is a greater need to challenge managerial prerogative. Nevertheless, as the example of union organization in local government shows, in some cases public-sector restructuring can strengthen the authority of more bureaucratic and centralized forms of unionism (Fairbrother 1996).

An instructive case study of workplace union renewal in Girobank has been provided by Dundon (1998). Established in 1968 as a part of the Post Office, Girobank was in 1990 sold to the Alliance and

Leicester Building Society, a firm which did not recognize unions elsewhere in its operations. The privatization of Girobank 'intensified the pace of restructuring, managerial devolution and decentralized business units' which had already been set in train under the ownership of the Post Office (p. 131). However, largely on account of the increasing authority and independence of local shop stewards, the accommodation of immediate managers and the collective identity generated by a local dispute, workplace trade unionism in the privatized Girobank strengthened in the 1990s. In conclusion Dundon considers that although it 'would be wrong to infer that the "balance" of power has shifted to labour', none the less 'the ability for local unionism to question and challenge the managerial prerogative appears to be both renewed and above all legitimized' (p. 133).

In general the presence of robust trade unions in traditional private services has been less evident. Yet in the banking and finance sector – an increasingly important part of the economy in the last two decades, with notable employment growth – trade unionism appears to have increased in significance. For example, the membership of BIFU (Banking, Insurance and Finance Union), the major union in the sector and now known as UNiFI, rose from just under 60,000 in 1965 to peak at over 170,000 in 1990, before settling back to just under 135,000 in 1995. Between 1989 and 1993 the proportion of employees in banking and finance who were union members – the union density – rose from 49 to 52 per cent (Gall 1997). Furthermore, contrary to the view of Price (1983) that the union membership of white-collar workers is largely predicated on instrumental and economic factors, and is not the expression of a 'strong general commitment to trade unions' (p. 175), there is evidence that the growth and consolidation of trade unionism in the banking and finance sector has been an expression of greater support for its functions and purposes.

During the 1980s the previously rigid, bureaucratic and paternalistic employment practices and career structures that had typified the major banks in particular (Crompton 1989) were disrupted by economic restructuring and the elaboration of new technology. The financial services sector especially has become dominated by retail operations at the expense of the traditional emphasis on accounting practices and procedures, and this has been accompanied by an increase in job insecurity and deskilling. Gall (1997) suggests these developments have accelerated the 'unionateness' of employees in financial services. There has been an increase in the proportion of employees who are union members, a growth in the incidence of industrial action, and even the quiescent institutional staff associations – which traditionally competed with BIFU for the allegiance of bank workers – have become more akin to proper unions. The staff association in Barclays Bank, for example, renamed itself UNiFI in 1994 and subsequently joined the TUC before merging with the BIFU in 1999. Case study evidence supports the contention that the increased 'unionateness' of workers was an important facet of the finance sector in the 1990s. In a comparison of the French bank Crédit Lyonnais and the British Co-op Bank, Thornley et al. (1997) discovered that, despite attempts by the employers to individualize the employment relationship, there was a strong degree of adversarial industrial relations in evidence: union members were not only attracted to trade unionism for instrumental reasons, but also because of the need to provide collective restraints on managerial action.

The ongoing significance of adversarial industrial relations in the 1990s – something that does not bear out the politically and employer-inspired rhetoric of partnership in the workplace – has been identified elsewhere. In a study of three food-processing plants, for example, Scott (1994) found that in two of them, where unions were present, although managers had tried to reform industrial relations so as to induce a more co-operative climate at work, the traditional pattern of adversarialism could not be overcome; moreover, unions remained influential in production matters. He states that while 'many commentators have argued that trades unions have become universally weak or irrelevant in recent years . . . managers ought not to take such a state of affairs for granted' (p. 153). Where unions retain a presence in the economy, low-trust relations between managers and workers are sufficiently significant to ensure that they continue to play an important part in articulating the collective discontent of their members. But what of the increasing numbers of areas within the economy where employers have sought to exclude trade unions? Here the prospects for a revival of trade unionism appear to be somewhat healthy.

The 'Representation Gap'

One general conclusion drawn from the research into the deployment of HRM practices – which supposedly constitute a new model for regulating the employment relationship, as a successor to collective bargaining – is that their incidence is associated with workplaces where trade unions are recognized (Millward 1994; Storey 1992). As Kelly (1998) has argued these findings should cause no surprise. Given that

HRM practices are introduced to marginalize unions and collective bargaining, they would hardly be needed in workplaces where unions were weak or non-existent. Nevertheless, a further implication is that, given the decline in collective bargaining and union recognition outlined above, there are an increasing number of workplaces where few mechanisms for mediating the relationship between workers and employers exist. Guest (1995) has referred to the growing number of workplaces where neither unions nor the practices associated with HRM or the 'new industrial relations' are present as a 'black hole' for employee representation.

Thus there has been a growing amount of attention directed at the size and nature of the 'representation gap' in many parts of the UK and elsewhere (Towers 1997). Two points can be made regarding this 'gap'. First, contrary to the views of many employers, it is not an expression of workers' contentment with the way in which their workplaces are governed. Indeed there is evidence that points to the opposite being the case. For example, John Kelly uses data obtained from Citizens' Advice Bureaux to show the high degree of discontent about workplace governance which exists among employees. In 1983 the Bureaux received 469,000 work-related complaints. Ten years later the number had nearly doubled to 882,557 and in 1997 there were 610,000 complaints (Kelly 1998: 45). Moreover, the British Social Attitudes survey has traced 'a significant underlying deterioration over time in employees' perception of workplace relations' (Bryson and McKay 1997: 29). The survey found, for instance, that the proportion of respondents who reported that relations with management in their respective workplaces were 'not very' or 'not at all' good was 15 per cent in 1983, but had risen to 24 per cent in 1995 and 20 per cent in 1996. (Bryson and McKay 1997: 28).

From this and other data the authors conclude that, in

> the eyes of employees, the working environment has clearly deteriorated since the early 1980s. Nowadays employees are far more likely to feel that the gap between the high and low paid at their workplace is too high, that management and employee relations are poor, that their jobs are insecure, that their workplaces are not being managed as well as they could be, and that they do not have much say over how their work is organized. (Bryson and McKay 1997: 38)

Second, the disclosure that many workers are treated akin to 'factors of production' (Millward 1994) gives unions an opportunity to expand their constituencies and organize among otherwise unrepresented workers in the UK and elsewhere. According to Richard Hyman, the 'space for independent forms of employee representation is considerable' (Hyman 1997: 320); and Brian Towers has noted that in the UK there is 'an untapped demand for the collective defence provided by unions against arbitrary management decisions' (1997: 237).

What have the unions been doing to meet the 'untapped demand' for employee representation, which has increasingly been highlighted? As we briefly noted above, during the late 1980s and early 1990s a common approach among union leaderships was to assume that collectivism was in decline and that workers were becoming more individualistic in their attitudes and values. Indeed, some commentators argued that unions should adapt their policies accordingly (Bassett and Cave 1993). However, there are two major problems with such an analysis. First, given the resilience of adversarial industrial relations and the evidence of a 'representation gap', it is apparent that the constraints on authoritarian managerialism that unions can provide – particularly in so far as they are collectively generated in the workplace – might represent the most effective way for unions to reassert their role in society.

Second, the view that the decline of trade unionism has been an expression of increased individualism, at the expense of collectivism, is misplaced in two respects. For one thing, Kelly and Waddington (1995) have argued that a cultural shift, such as that towards a supposed greater individualism, is an inherently long-term process and cannot explain the rapid diminution of trade union membership during the 1980s in particular. Unionism, they stressed, has not been weakened by the growth of more individualistic values among the populace; rather, it has increasingly been excluded from the workplace by hostile employers. Moreover, the 'individualistic' explanation for trade union decline misrepresents the complex relationship between collectivism and individualism within trade unions and greatly overstates the extent to which there was ever 'a golden age when workers were spontaneously collectivist, and labour organizations joined ranks behind a unifying class project' (Hyman 1992: 159).

The point of these arguments is to establish that trade unionism is not the victim of secular decline, given adverse social trends. Not only have trade unions long accommodated their members' individual goals and aspirations, but there is also significant latent demand among unrepresented workers for the collective social and economic power that unions can provide in the contemporary workplace, especially where the actions of authoritarian employers would otherwise go unconstrained. Indeed, there are indications that there has been a revival of collective activity, based on participative local trade unionism, at a global level (Moody 1997). In respect of the UK, from a large-scale survey of union members Waddington and Whitston (1997) discovered that collective reasons, such as 'if I had a problem at work', for 'improved pay and conditions' and 'because I believe in trade unions', largely underpinned people's decision to join unions. They rule out an increase in individualism as an explanation for the decline of trade unionism and surmise that it is more likely to be an expression of employers' preferences for, and their capacity to establish, non-union arrangements. Waddington and Whitston (1997) recommend, therefore, that to improve their prospects unions should look to expand their organizational bases and, in particular, consider the appointment of dedicated, full-time recruitment officials who could 'recruit at unorganized workplaces and among workers at organized sites which existing local representatives are unable to contact' (p. 539).

This is a conclusion union leaderships appear to have accepted. In sharp contrast to the earlier recommendations of its Special Review Body in the 1980s, which, among other things, proposed that unions should expand their individual services to members, from the mid-1990s onwards the TUC has increasingly fostered the elaboration of novel organizing strategies. In June 1996, the TUC launched a 'New Unionism' strategy, the principal aim of which was to encourage 'unions to shift resources from servicing existing members to recruiting and organizing new ones' (IRS 1997: 4). In particular, heavy emphasis was to be placed on instituting recruiment drives aimed at women workers, young workers and service-sector workers (Heery 1998b). The new emphasis on organizing stemmed in part from the TUC's analysis of developments in the United States trade union movement as well as those in Australia and the Netherlands. Moreover, during the 1990s the AFL-CIO (American Federation of Labour/Congress of Industrial Organization), the US trade union confederation, has devoted an increasing amount of its budget – as much as 30 per cent – to organizing campaigns, including the establishment of an 'Organizing Institute', and in 1996 it reported the first rise in its membership for thirty years (Heery 1998b; IRS 1997). The combative recruitment campaigns that the US Service Employees' International Union has mounted among health care, nursing home and cleaning workers, among others, constituted important (albeit isolated) examples of how a greater emphasis on organizing can boost union membership and activity (Towers 1997).

As part of its 'New Unionism' campaign in 1996, the TUC established a task group to examine how a greater organizing culture could be elaborated within the British trade union movement. The task group recommended that an 'organizing academy' should be set up to train and develop union recruiters. In January 1998 the academy came into existence with thirty-six trainee organizers in its ranks, sponsored by seventeen TUC-affiliated unions (Labour Research 1998). The TUC claimed that this initiative resulted in a number of successes, including a recognition agreement at the FCI Scotland computer assembly plant. In February 1999 it launched the second year of the programme with the recruitment of a further tranche of trainee organizers (TUC 1999).

As a way of reviving trade unionism, it is perhaps too soon to assess the impact of the TUC's increased emphasis on organizing workers. Nevertheless, it represents a recognition among union leaderships that trade unionism in the UK and elsewhere has been weakened not by the reduced interest of employees, but by the increased antipathy of employers – buttressed by supportive political and economic contexts – and the inaccessability of unions for many employees, particularly in the private service sector. An increased emphasis on recruitment, then, might release the 'untapped demand' (Towers 1997) for the collectively secured representation that unions can offer individuals at work. However, not only does the commitment to the organizing initiative exhibited by some of the TUC's affiliates appear to be somewhat brittle (Heery 1998b), but there is also a broader obstacle to be overcome, since there is a potential contradiction inherent in a centrally originated and directed policy designed to boost greater workplace organization and participation from the bottom up.

Nevertheless, in the UK at least the effort of the unions to expand their coverage may be made easier by an easing of the political climate. Despite the distancing of New Labour from the unions described above, in its 1997 manifesto the Labour Party made a commitment to introduce legislation which would compel employers to recognize trade unions where a majority of the relevant workforce was in favour. During the preparation of a consultative document in 1997–8 there was considerable concern in union circles that the government, following representations by the CBI in particular, was conceding too much ground to employers. However, in the resulting White Paper – Fairness at Work (DTI 1998a) – it was suggested that employers must recognize the union where a ballot shows that a majority of those voting, and at least 40 per cent of those eligible to vote, are in favour of recognition. Furthermore, if more than half of a workforce are union members, the White Paper recognizes that there is a *de facto* desire for union recognition and that this should then be facilitated without a ballot.[11] The 1999 Employment Relations Act incorporated the Fairness at Work proposals and even before the legislation took effect there was already evidence that union efforts to secure recognition from employers were bearing fruit (see Labour Research, November 1998: 6). While it is important to acknowledge the timidity of the Labour government's legislation, a result of its eagerness to keep business leaders sweet, it none the less mean that the unions face a less hostile climate than they have been accustomed to (Heery 1998b).

Conclusion

In this chapter we have reviewed the recent experience of trade unionism, focusing in particular on the decline in its power and influence in the UK. Although the weakened state of the unions appears largely to have been the result of increased employer antipathy and a more hostile political climate, there is a widely held assumption that their decline is secular in nature and the expression of long-term, adverse social trends. Some academic sociologists locate the diminution of the unions within the broader context of the dissolution of (working-) class-based identities and politics, and argued that the fracturing of work-based collectivism implies that unions, as organizations based around the politics of the workplace, are condemned to decline. Among employers there has been a perception that changes in the workplace make the role of the unions irrelevant in the modern economy, as the comments made by the Chief Executive of Zurich Insurance indicated. The paradigm of industrial relations is held to be represented by the 'high-commitment' organization wherein managers and employees work together, as partners, to ensure competitive success. The old 'them and us' attitudes of the past had, it would seem, become anachronistic. Since employees now shared the same goals and objectives there was no need for the conflictual presence of unions.

There is an increasing amount of evidence showing this picture of harmonious industrial relations to be a myth. As the evidence reviewed in this chapter and elsewhere in the book shows, workplaces continue to be characterized by adversarial relations, a fact ensuring that there is an ongoing need for a trade union presence. Moreover, the exemplars discussed above provide a useful response to those who argue that industrial conflict has vanished (McKinstry 1996). Indeed, as the global examples cited by Moody (1997) indicate, the prospects for a revival of trade unionism world-wide are encouraging. Placing developments within a framework in which the ongoing importance of class is attested, he writes that the 'pressures of globalization and lean production, the transforming powers of renewed struggle, and the fresh forces that have come to the working class in recent decades are all pushing the working class and its organizations in a more aggressive and confrontational direction' (p. 289). Given this state of affairs, an easing of the hostile political climate and the efforts they themselves are making to expand their organizational capabilities, it seems clear that the trade unions will continue to maintain a presence in the future and may well even expand their influence.

9

The Myth of the 'Economic Worker'

In *The Jobless Future* Stanley Aronowitz and William DiFazio address the question of 'is work a need?' by prefacing their discussion with a quotation from David Lodge's novel *Nice Work*. Lodge presents a conversation between Vic Wilcox, the managing director of a light industrial factory, and Robyn Penrose, an English lecturer at the University of Rummidge (i.e. Birmingham, UK), that, for Aronowitz and DiFazio, sums up the fact that 'the "self" is constituted, at least for most of us, by membership in the labour force, as a member of either the job elite – the 'professions' – or the working class' (1994: 329).

> 'Men like to work. It's a funny thing, but they do. They may moan about it every Monday morning and they may agitate for shorter hours and longer holidays, but they need to work for their self-respect.' [Wilcox]
>
> 'That's just conditioning. People can get used to a life without work.' [Penrose]
>
> 'Could you? I thought you enjoyed your work?'
>
> 'That's different.'
>
> 'Why?'
>
> 'Well, it's nice work. It's meaningful. It's rewarding. I don't mean in money terms. It would be worth doing even if one wasn't paid anything at all. And the conditions are decent – not like this.' (Lodge 1989: 126–7)

Aronowitz and DiFazio raise an important point here, and one that we will return to, namely that work is central to the construction of identity. But a point they ignore is as significant: despite over a century of sociological analysis of work, workers and workplaces, academics still tend to impute motives to others that they do not hold themselves. Quite simply, Penrose had never thought that other people in jobs that she herself would not choose to do – indeed, is glad not to do – could have similar motivations to herself with respect to work. We should bear this in mind in considering what we call the 'myth of the economic worker'; academic and managerial accounts of people's motivations for working frequently employ an explanatory framework that proposes a simple formula: people work primarily for money, therefore our explanations of work and workplace behaviour should adopt this as the primary point of explanation. What is striking is that few managers and academics would consider that their own primary motivations for working are purely financial, yet they still uphold the myth and apply it in managing and in formulating academic analyses of work. The question of how and why this myth has arisen, whether it has a basis in fact and what correctives we can offer against it, are the main themes of this chapter.

Like all good myths, there is a core of truth at the heart of the myth of the economic worker. It is true that when asked, many people in employment will reply that they are working to provide a living for themselves and their families. However, such statements are only the tip of an iceberg of motivations with respect to work, as the following examples from Swan Hunter Shipyard workers show:

> I do it to make money to live. No one goes to work in a shipyard for pleasure. (shipwright/foreman)

> Why do I work? For a purpose in life. I've been on the dole at times and you are not contributing to society. I want to work and it isn't just for the money. You get more respect from people if you are in work – more than if you are on the dole – and I know that's wrong, but that's the way of it. (wood machinist)

Two workers, both men, similar in age, experience, qualifications and social class position, offer two very different accounts. Neither respondent is 'right' or 'wrong' here, but what would certainly be wrong is the elimination of a whole raft of rationalizations and motivations concerning work to produce a sociological account that will conform to a theoretical perspective. Yet were we to apply some standard sociological paradigms to this study of a shipyard, that is almost certainly what we would be doing: reducing a range of human motivations to a simple formula equating work with employment and, thus, with subsistence and remuneration.

It may seem that this critique of sociological theory is too extreme or is insensitive toward the complex and nuanced workplace accounts that many writers have produced. One need only to look at Huw Beynon's *Working for Ford* (1984), for example, or Paul du Gay's *Consumption and Identity at Work* (1996) for accounts of work that do not reduce workers to characters playing out the role of *homo economicus*. However, these examples are exceptions, produced against the grain of overarching theories that prioritize and privilege the economic as a mode of explanation. It is not our intention here to eradicate such lines of analysis entirely: we recognize that financial rewards, and differentials within them, are highly significant to people involved in formal employment. But we also stress that explanations pitched purely at the level of the rational pursuit of economic goals are insufficient to explain the range of workplace attitudes and behaviour. Such an approach may contribute to the misrepresentation of the role of work both as an aspect of personal identity and as a crucial factor in structuring broader social relations such as class, issues which have been discussed in previous chapters.

Indeed the myth of the economic worker has complex links to the myth of the death of class. While Marxists have often been accused of economic determinism in their accounts of social relationships, economistic arguments have also frequently been used by opponents of Marxism and by conservative politicians, who argue that human beings are both 'naturally' lazy and 'naturally' greedy and competitive: economic incentives at an appropriate level must be offered to induce them to work. These ideas were central to the work of the early political economists such as Adam Smith and J.S. Mill, who incorporated them into their accounts of the operation of the free market and their suggestions for social policy. But the prime exponent of this idea, that rank-and-file workers are natural 'shirkers' and can be made to co-operate with employers only by a mix of tight control and economic inducement, was surely the key management thinker, Frederick Taylor, whose techniques of scientific management enshrined them. As discussed in chapter 3, Taylor's work was hugely influential throughout the twentieth century and across the globe, and elements of Taylorism have survived a putative switch from Fordism to post-Fordism. This includes the premisses that workers will act rationally to serve their best economic interests and avoid negative consequences and, specifically, that their attitudes to work will be rationally orientated to maximize monetary income (Braverman 1974).

Our aim here is to offer an alternative account of workplace motivations that will allow us to place work, in its wide variety of forms, in social, structural and personal context. A further aim is to analyse why the economic mode of explanation has retained its primacy and prevalence in formal analyses of work: have we not yet been able to shake off Adam Smith's doctrine of capital accumulation being an expression of the human subject? For Smith, man had a 'natural' propensity to barter and exchange and this gave rise to a 'natural' economic form: this idea became the basis of Smith's main argument in *The Wealth of Nations*, that an economy would develop and should be left to its own, natural devices, free from 'unnatural' interventions, such as state-imposed restrictions (Kumar 1986: 17). As with the rest of the present book, a fundamental goal is to produce accounts and theories that reflect what workers have actually said about their work, their identities and the realities of work. In the case of this chapter, the examples will be drawn from a recent investigation examining the attitudes towards work held by defence industry workers. This chapter will also examine the possibilities of applying contemporary critical theory to develop a more complete account of the nature of work.

Sociological Approaches to Work

Any good introductory sociology textbook will tell you that a central tenet of sociological argument is the construction and application of concepts. How can we make sense of social stratification without the construction and delineation of the concept of social class? Equally, how can we make sense of the role of work for individuals without an analysis of what work actually is? But this is what the sociology of work has traditionally done. It failed to produce a fundamental analysis of *what work is*, preferring instead to equate work (the concept) with employment (the economic category). Only recently, with the critique offered by feminist social scientists, has the notion of work been extended to cover less formal types of 'purposeful activity' such as caring, domestic work and 'emotional labour', what Glucksmann (1995) has termed the 'total social organization of labour', in order to cover reproductive as well as productive activities. Ruth Schwartz Cohen's (1985) analysis of the role of technology in American households concludes: 'The productive work which is still being done in American homes is difficult to "see" because the reigning theory of family history tells us that it should not be there, and the reigning methodology of social sciences cannot be applied to it' (Cohen 1985: 120).

The tradition of thought that extends backwards from contemporary critical theory also provides us with some fundamental analyses.

An examination of this work is revealing not only of the nature of work itself, but also of the ways in which such analyses have been obscured by contemporary sociological accounts of work, accounts that have taken economic motivation as the primary orientation towards work. Contemporary critical theory draws on a wide range of sources of inspiration. Notwithstanding this, it is possible to identify some core commonalities concerning the nature of work in the background of contemporary critical theory, specifically the analyses offered by Marx, Weber and Arendt of the nature of work. As with Aronowitz and DiFazio, writing in the 1990s, the concern of these social theorists is with the question 'is work a need?'.

Both Marx and Weber, the two main sources of inspiration for sociological studies of work, offer an understanding of work based on the concept of employment or occupation, although they do so for wholly different reasons. It is in Marx's early works that he offers his deepest examination of the nature of work; here he does not make a straight connection between work and employment. In *The Economic and Philosophical Writings of 1844* (Marx 1975) he clearly identifies the 'emancipatory' power of labour, of transforming nature and satisfying individuals' inner needs:

> It is therefore in his fashioning of the objective that man really proves himself to be a *species-being*. Such production is his active species-life. Through it, nature appears as *his* work and his reality . . . man reproduces himself not only intellectually, in his consciousness, but actively and actually, and he can therefore contemplate himself in a world he himself has created. (Marx 1975: 329)

Marx distinguishes this form of labour (creative and transformative) from the forced labour that is imposed by capitalism. It is, of course, the latter form of work – forced labour – that becomes the subject for all of Marx's later writings, the core of his critique of capitalism and the basis of his key notion of alienation. Marx shows the ways in which employment – either being an employer or being employed – is the key determining feature in social stratification along class lines, and that the capitalist organization of employment for the extraction of surplus value is a fundamental tool for the analysis of capitalism itself. Without the extraction of surplus value – the generation of profit from capitalists' paying workers less than their labour power (transformed into commodities) is valued in the market place – capitalism cannot function. Weber, conversely, uses employment as a category to highlight commonalities between different social groups. Both being employed and being an employer are merely different expressions of rational economic activity; there is fundamentally little difference between the meanings and motivations attached to 'work' by different social groups. Such differences as we do perceive are caused by factors external to the employment situation – traditional attitudes, religious beliefs, obligation to kin or family group:

> All economic activity in a market economy is undertaken and carried through by individuals acting to provide for their own ideal or material interests. This is naturally just as true when economic activity is oriented to the patterns of order of organizations, whether they themselves are partly engaged in economic activity, are primarily economic in character, or merely regulate economic activity. (Weber 1978: 202)

Inside work situations, Weber notes that the degree of monotony or repetitiveness of tasks may affect the ways in which workers will seek reward, but does not take the point further, preferring to stress the ways in which productivity or performance can be enhanced by financial incentives: 'in the capitalistic system, the most immediate bases for willingness to work are opportunities for high piece-rate earnings and the danger of dismissal' (Weber 1978: 151).

Some might be critical of the analysis just offered and claim that Weber also provided an insight into motivations to work through his description of a 'calling': for Weber, modern lives are defined, to a large extent, by having a duty to follow a vocation. Weber uses the accepted metaphor of a calling – namely, that of being 'called' to a religious vocation – but he applies this to everybody, not just the religiously inclined. However, a closer examination of Weber's analysis and use of this concept reveals a strong economistic flavour. Weber's concept of a calling is central to his thesis of *The Protestant Ethic and the Spirit of Capitalism*, which describes the emergence of capitalist societies in Western Europe. He identifies an elective affinity between the religious calling to an ascetic monasticism of the early Protestant reformers, and the 'spirit of capitalism' which suffuses the now secular lives of people living in modernity. The spirit of capitalism promotes the earning of money, but also the rational pursuit of profits and the avoidance of 'spontaneous enjoyment of life' (Weber 1938: 53). Weber continues:

> The earning of money within the modern economic order is, so long as it is done legally, the result and expression of virtue and proficiency in a calling. . . . It is an obligation which the individual is supposed to feel and does feel towards the content of his professional activity, no matter in what it consists, in particular no matter whether it appears on the surface as a utilization of his personal powers, or only of his material possessions (as capital). (pp. 53–4)

Weber echoes Adam Smith in his attribution of a 'natural' orientation towards economic values, beyond the meeting of mere subsistence needs: 'Man is dominated by the making of money, by acquisition as the ultimate purpose of his life. Economic acquisition is no longer subordinated to man as the means for the satisfaction of his material needs' (p. 53). Despite Weber's deriving his concept of a calling from the Puritan ethos of choosing to leave behind earthly matters, in capitalist societies a calling is not purely a matter of individual choice. On the contrary, Weber notes that 'The puritan wanted to work in a calling; we are forced to do so' (pp. 180–1). For Weber, the calling – that is, the rational pursuit of money and being impelled to carry this out – is what is most characteristic of 'the social ethic of capitalistic culture, and is in a sense the fundamental basis of it' (p. 54). Ultimately, Weber describes our motivations in work as being fundamentally economic.

Both theorists present an understanding of 'work' that is formal and structural: by using concepts based on employment and occupation they choose to ignore aspects of work that can be seen as essential to the construction of meaning associated with productive activity. While both Marxist and Weberian perspectives provide useful insights into aspects of employment, there are omissions which must be rectified to provide an adequate sociology of work, sufficient to explain the ways in which workers make sense of their work and their lives at work. To offer a corrective we must turn to an analysis of what 'work' actually is.

The substitution of 'employment' for 'work' in much sociology of work would be unimportant were it not for the fact that many people's understanding and experience of practical activity extends much further than the boundaries imposed by the category of employment. Employment is a formal relationship: it describes a contractual position arrived at by an employer and an employee. While it would be foolish to deny the relevance of this relationship as being the basis of many people's experience of work, we have to note two things about this reduction. The first is obvious: employment simply does not include many forms of practical activity that the participants would describe as being work. Housework, caring for children or relatives and voluntary work are three obvious cases in point. The second point may not be quite so obvious, but it is perhaps more significant: that people in employment will frequently use their work as a resource for the construction of their identity, but will rarely do this in a way that actually reflects the formalities of the employment contract.

Marx's work and Marxist approaches to wage labour give us insights into the ways in which production and the labour process will be organized and controlled to maximize profits for owners. To this end, we find that Marxist studies of work focus on formal mechanisms for control, formal and informal resistance to such control, and the effects that the labour process has on the lives of those involved in production. Weber, taking capitalism and the market economy as a given, focuses our attention on the ways in which individuals involved in employment will motivate themselves to achieve self-interested goals, and will make sense of occupation by reference to external value systems. Weberian approaches to sociology of work tend to look at the ways in which status and hierarchy are constructed in the workplace, and the ways in which occupational groups will coalesce as communities. Interpretative accounts of work, informed by the Weberian framework, focus on aspects of interaction and social action at work and highlight the necessity for reference to the individual frame of meaning. However, such approaches rest on a formal understanding of production as employment, rather than seeing work as a complex form of social action that, while it may retain features of rational economic action, can also be a central resource for the construction of identity.

The work of Hannah Arendt provides a useful staging post between the foundational and reductive analyses of work produced by the later Marx and Weber, and the contemporary critical theory of Habermas and Aronowitz. In particular, her deconstruction of productive activity into two distinguishable components – 'work' and 'labour' – can be used to aid the reconstruction of a sociology of work that takes into account the social conditions within which work is carried out, and the personal processes by which work becomes a resource through which individuals make sense of their world. Arendt's opposition of 'work' and 'labour' is fundamental to her understanding of the human condition: 'The work of our hands, as distinguished from the labour of our bodies . . . fabricates the sheer unending variety of things whose sum total constitutes the human artifice' (Arendt 1959: 119).

Interestingly, neither the early Karl Marx nor Adam Smith would argue with this formulation – although later commentators (Grint 1998) dismiss this point as being irrelevant, since few of us in contemporary society are involved in producing artefacts. Such a critique misses the point of Arendt's thesis: her aim is to draw together the connections between the material world we are involved in making and the interpersonal world of social communication that we are also involved in making. Arendt is presenting us with the opportunity for making sense of all, and not just the economic, aspects of the labour process under capitalism, albeit in a somewhat abstract form.

Arendt describes the ideal form of life as resting on three fundamental human activities: labour, work and action. Labour is activity orientated towards subsistence needs, work is creative production, and action is the human condition of plurality – social action, interaction and communication. For Arendt, we are in a situation where we need to achieve all three of these components to maintain the active life which will fulfil our needs as humans. We need to labour to meet our subsistence needs; we need to work to meet our creative needs; we need to interact and be heard to meet our communicative needs.

Arendt does not concern herself with applying this framework to actual studies of workplaces or attitudes of workers, and this is a drawback in applying her thesis. However, it is possible to reconstruct and apply her conceptual scheme to the world of work by using the ideas of some more practically orientated critical theorists – notably Jürgen Habermas and Stanley Aronowitz, two contemporary writers who have used the debate about the nature of work to analyse the contemporary condition of work. Habermas agrees with Marx that the fundamental distinguishing characteristic of human beings is work, viewing it as transformative action that makes us confront, interpret and change nature. However, Habermas makes a move similar to Arendt in adding a further fundamental characteristic: that human beings distinguish themselves by interacting through language. We both work *and* interact, and do these things socially. For Habermas, we understand and apprehend the internal and external world through work, and it is thus deficient to consider work to be the purely economic category that Weber and the later Marx both identify. Habermas's resonances with Arendt are emphasized in his description of the split between work and interaction, but he modifies this further, identifying a split in the category of work itself, to see work as both practical activity and a series of choices: 'by "work" or purposive-rational action I understand either instrumental action or rational choice or their conjunction' (Habermas 1971: 91).

For Habermas, while work may be governed by purposive rationality, and structured by rational choices, it is also informing us about the world and our part within it. It thus becomes a key resource for making sense of our personal and public lives. It should be noted that Habermas's definitions of work do not restrict themselves to the world of formal employment: this definition would include all forms of purposeful human activity that lead to particular goals being achieved. Subsistence, of course, may be one such goal, but need not be the only one.

Habermas does not offer us a specific sociology of work. However, his critical theory provides a basis for more recent investigations into the nature of work, notably that of Aronowitz and DiFazio. Their wide-ranging project explores recent trends in the rapidly changing Western industrial landscape, focusing on the imposition of scientific and technical rationality and the creation of a new work culture based on this that they refer to as 'sci-tech' work (Aronowitz and DiFazio 1994). They combine, through a critical analysis, elements of the work of Marx, Weber, Arendt and Habermas to analyse how work and employment will change as we enter the twenty-first century. They are critical of Arendt's abstract thesis, suggesting that while it has core components of value it is ultimately a 'privileging of politics over labor' (p. 334) in that it sees genuine human interaction only occuring inside the sphere of politics. Similarly, they are also critical of Habermas's later turn towards the linguistic sphere as being the denial of the importance of the world of production and materiality: 'According to this school of thought, work, however necessary, is ultimately no measure of man. The repository of truly human action is language' (1994: 334).

This is, we would suggest, an overly critical line to take of Habermas, who strives to retain work at the core of his social theory. Regardless of this, Aronowitz and DiFazio take the most useful parts of these theories and combine them with Marx's analysis of capitalism and Weber's conception of a 'work ethic' to identify ways in which we are surrounded by a 'dogma' of work that continues to impel us into forms of employment counterproductive for genuine human needs.

Aronowitz and DiFazio's thesis ultimately rests on their desire to change a system of employment which denies human value and puts profit first. Work should not be like this, but is forced to be by the inappropriate imposition of the imperatives of the system. The 'dogma of work' keeps us in this system, ensuring that profits are made and the system reproduced. But ideally we should be in a situation whereby human beings can achieve their creative potential, can satisfy subsistence needs, and can have their voices heard without being submerged under the weight of system imperatives. Their final plea is for a transformation of the nature of capitalist production such that ecological needs and freedom will be achieved.

By deconstructing work into its socially constructed components of 'work' and 'labour', by incorporating Habermas's theories of the human need for interaction, communication and the recognition of mutual human interests, by considering the ways in which we are surrounded by a 'dogma' or 'ethic' of work and by maintaining the perspective on the exploitative and divisive nature of capitalism, we can begin to move towards a sociology of work that, while considering the structural implications of formal employment under capitalism, will also acknowledge that work, as an activity and a set of social relationships, may provide meaning and identity for the individual. By removing the reliance on the formal employment bond as a foundation for analysis, this approach allows us to investigate the ways in which identity construction is not solely attached to the labour process. Rather, it allows us to see how individuals relate their work to their social situations, to the values they perceive society to hold of their endeavours, and to wider perspectives on the nature of the social world. This is a particularly fruitful approach to take when considering workers who are involved in forms of work that do not conform to the stereotype of 'normal capitalist production'. In a recent study of defence industry work this framework was applied to make sense of why defence industry workers saw themselves as being different from other workers and how they constructed their identity in a workplace that was often surrounded by a sense of moral disquiet. The myth of the economic worker was not a useful frame of reference for explaining defence industry work in the round.

Making Sense of Defence Industry Work

The research material presented in this paper is taken from a study of attitudes towards work in the defence industry in the North East of England. Two research sites were investigated: namely, Royal Ordnance, Birtley, and Swan Hunter Shipbuilders, Wallsend. As we saw in chapter 5, RO Birtley was privatized in 1987. Swan Hunter, too, was recently privatized; in this case as a result of a management buyout in 1986.

At the time of commencing the research (October 1992) these two companies employed 4,500 people between them (Swan Hunter 3,700 and RO 800). When the interviews were conducted in 1994, this number had declined to 1,300 (Swan Hunter 1,000 and RO Birtley 300). Thus, both companies had suffered job losses in excess of 66 per cent in the space of eighteen months, and Swan Hunter was at the time in receivership. Swan Hunter Shipbuilders closed in November 1994, although the receiver maintained a skeleton staff in the shipyard in an attempt to keep open the possibility of selling the yard as a going concern. The shipyard was finally bought in June 1995, eight days before the assets of the yard were to be sold at a public auction, by the Dutch-owned THC Group, who intended to refit oil supply vessels and offshore platforms. In May 1996 the first workers were hired by the company to work on the conversion of the bulk carrier *Solitaire* into a pipe-laying vessel.

The research attempted to cover as wide a range as possible of defence industry workers. The methodology was therefore designed to include defence industry personnel of all grades, and involved in all aspects of the operation of the companies under study – from production to administration, security and ancillary staff.

Why did defence industry workers see themselves as being different from other workers? Some, admittedly, did not, preferring to identify themselves with other people who did similar tasks in similar (civilian) workplaces. But many did. When asked to explain their perception of difference, some were incredulous, since for them the reason was obvious: the products they made at work made them different. They were involved in a form of morally contestable work: 'I make products that kill people' (machine tool setter).

'Traditional' sociology of work approaches have great difficulty in 'seeing' the product of work. For Marx, and subsequent Marxist analysis, what was made at work was of no specific interest to the sociologist: it was the conditions under which production took place that were important. Similarly, for Weberian approaches, it is not the product *per se*, but the social organization of the workplace, or the status ascribed to the job type, or the position in a hierarchy or labour market that is significant to the sociologist. While in no way wishing to deny the importance of these points, for defence industry workers the product, and particularly its end use, was of great importance.

Similarly, when we consider motivations to work, many defence industry workers identify needs beyond the purely pecuniary suggested by the myth of the economic worker. It is significant here that many of those interviewed identified a 'need' that was, to a certain extent, satisfied by working. Here are some responses from Swan Hunter workers to the question 'Why do you work?':

> I want to provide for my family, but I enjoy the trade union side of my work. I like going to meetings, negotiating and helping people. (design engineer)

> To keep my family. But I think it's important to do something you enjoy. (draughtsman)

> The pay packet. But work is a necessary ethic when you work all your life – it governs your existence. (welder)

> For self-respect – I don't want to become a social parasite. And I don't want to be bored. It's good for meeting people and I get a lot of job satisfaction, and for the money too. (sheet-metal worker)

> Making a living and getting the self-respect of doing something productive. It gives me peace of mind. (driller)
>
> To exist. I like the job. I come to work to use my skill and to make enough money to have a decent way of life. (plater/foreman)
>
> It's all I know. (caulker/burner)

Out of twenty-one Swan Hunter workers interviewed, eleven offered similarly qualified responses as to why they were working, while one said that the money was not important at all. This figure of 50 per cent of interviewees identifying something in addition to money as their motivation to work is significant in itself. We must, however, be wary of overgeneralizing from this data: Swan Hunter workers were part of a particularly tight-knit occupational community, and a threatened one at that. These are factors that could overemphasize the non-pecuniary aspects of work to individuals. Nevertheless, in chapters 4 and 7 we saw examples of other groups of employees who similarly regarded their work as a source of social, not merely economic, valuables: self-respect, interest, companionship, pride in accomplishment and skill. For many Swan Hunter workers, their work provided them with much more than just subsistence: it was an outlet for their skills, a source of social interaction and a foundation upon which they constructed their identities. This served as a basis for resistance to the closure of their shipyard and a way of distinguishing themselves as a distinct community.

To put this in more formal terms, we are suggesting that people's reasons for working are much more complex than would be suggested by the myth of the economic worker. In terms of Arendt's conception of human practical and social activity, the above responses provide a clear example of people recognizing labour, work and action as components of their employment. The workers interviewed all identified a 'labour' component in that they described their work as providing for their subsistence needs. They also indicated – although not in so many cases – that their work provided them with a form of satisfaction that was related to production. This is a complex issue concerning the nature of skills being deployed, the nature of products being made and the use to which the products were being put. Finally, from Arendt's perspective, there are important action components inherent in their working situation: interpersonal interaction, political action and general socialization. The defence workers showed that their work combined these factors, and at various times in the accounts they provided to outsiders they might accord greater significance to one of these elements over the others.

This was particularly clear in the identity constructions that they offered. Occupation and work are a resource for identity construction for two prime reasons. Firstly, work as goal-orientated practical activity is the most 'valued' form of social activity in our society. It contains purpose and order, and provides satisfaction to many workers. Aronowitz and DiFazio (1994) rightly urge caution when considering the nature of this satisfaction. It may derive from our need to create, deploy our skills or 'be useful', but equally it may be constructed by individuals as a response to the social nature of work (as we pointed out in chapter 7). This point illustrates the second reason that work becomes a resource for identity: it is the site of the majority of social interactions for many people, and is the place where people enter into communication and discussion with others, making and forming relationships that are meaningful and long-lasting. Many people marry workmates. This is not to suggest that interactions outside work are unimportant. On the contrary, many defence workers spoke of their families as their primary reasons for working, and many identified significant relationships and identity-forming activities outside the workplace. However, clear occupational identities were forged around the tasks performed at work, the products made, the institutional location of their industry and the deployment of skill in the labour process.

Finally, having considered motivations, identity formation and the nature of work, we will briefly look at the points raised by Aronowitz and DiFazio concerning the nature of work in contemporary capitalism. Defence industry workers believed that their voices were excluded from any consideration of the future of their jobs. At both research sites workers had presented proposals to the management outlining strategies to allow their companies to move towards civilian production. Their motivation for such proposals was twofold. First, many workers were opposed to the production of military goods. Second, they identified the crises that the international defence industry faced with respect to the end of the Cold War and the subsequent decline in military spending. Despite such plans receiving trade union sponsorship, backed by extensive research, management at both sites rejected these out of hand.[1] Similarly, many workers identified continuing worries that they might be forced to participate in the production of nuclear, chemical and bacteriological weapons and would be denied any choice in this matter, in the face of downsizing and restructuring of their workplaces. Clearly, the situation described by defence industry workers illustrates the exclusion of the voices of workers from genuine discussion in workplaces and exemplifies the orientation of management and employers, but not necessarily workers, towards economic goals.

UK Government Policy and the Myth of the Economic Worker

Why is the myth of the economic worker so prevalent? While traditional sociological theorizing has contributed to this, as we have shown, it is within the world of work itself and also the realm of politics and policy formation that the myth is most strongly promoted. This is well evidenced by the introduction and imposition of performance-related pay (PRP), a particular favourite of the Blair government. Faced with allegedly poor performance in public services, the UK New Labour government has initiated and imposed a range of performance-related pay schemes to improve 'productivity' and 'standards'. This is a basic premiss of the reductive financial analysis of work: if people are paid more they will produce more (of course, the corollary never seems to concern those in power).[2]

How can the government improve the performance of teachers? There are significant pressures facing the UK education system: pressures from prospective employers for well-trained and skilled school-leavers, pressures from the media to ensure that basic skills and discipline are imposed in schools, pressure from parents to ensure that their children are given a good education. The government response has been to institute a new package of financial incentives for teachers, to promote good practice and punish poor teaching. The PRP package offered to teachers in 1999[3] will assess teachers' performance on the basis of classroom tests and examination results obtained by pupils, effectively a return to the discredited 'payment by results' strategy utilized in the nineteenth century.[4] Those teachers achieving the appropriate grade will be rewarded financially through a new promotion scheme. These proposals have met with stiff opposition from teachers and unions: 'I already work 60 hours a week. Very often I am at school by 7 or 7.30 a.m., working to get ready for the day. How can I work any harder?' (Sarah Fryer, Association of Teachers and Lecturers conference delegate).[5]

Teachers and their unions point to the chronic underfunding of their profession, the ideological assaults made on teachers through the 1980s and 1990s by education ministers and the continuing erosion of status and value attached to teaching. Teachers see themselves as being overworked, underpaid, but most significantly as undervalued. In an industrial sector notorious for its trade union fragmentation it is noteworthy that the issue of PRP has united the teaching profession and unions as no other issue in recent times has done. The government's proposals for PRP for teachers constituted an attempt to redress the chronic slump in demand for undergraduate teacher training but there is evidence that graduates' disinclination for entering the teaching profession is set to continue.[6]

PRP will not be confined to primary and secondary education. The recent *Independent Review of Higher Education Pay and Conditions*, chaired by Sir Michael Bett (Bett 1999), proposes similar strategies for the remuneration of university staff. Bett's recommendations for the introduction of more performance-related increments in staff progression through salary scales, although vague, relied heavily on 'evidence' from outside the HE sector (paras 114; 130). Again, such proposals have met with stiff opposition from HE sector trade unions.

The UK government has not confined itself to the public sector in promoting the benefits of PRP. Recent controversy concerning large boardroom pay rises, and concerns about the practice of providing senior executives with 'golden parachutes', has led to the government's attempting to use PRP as a cure for public dissatisfaction with high levels of pay in the private sector. A recent survey has shown that the highest-paid directors in the UK received pay rises of 26 per cent,[7] roughly three times higher than the rate at which profits have grown, while most employees were receiving pay rises of between 4 and 5 per cent, with public-sector employees being awarded an average of 3.5 per cent in the 1999 round of pay settlements. This has faced the government with a dilemma: it is unwilling to restrict top levels of pay, for fear of being seen as the party opposed to the free market and the 'incentives' approach, while at the same time it wishes to rein in top salaries to show commitment to the principle of classless meritocracy. The UK Trade and Industry Secretary, Stephen Byers, in responding to the debate about boardroom pay levels, offered a new formula based on the principles of PRP. He announced that the government fully supported 'world-class pay for world-class performance' at the same time as introducing proposals for shareholders to veto top executives' pay awards at annual general meetings. Byers's claim that, with the new measures for shareholders' review of boardroom pay, 'if salaries are high it's because directors are doing a good job',[8] rings somewhat hollow in the light of the overall performance of UK industry. The slogan certainly fits the image that the government wants to project of the UK as a leading global economic and military force. However, as commentators have pointed out, very few of the UK companies providing top pay for executives could actually be considered world-class.[9]

The government is committed to applying the PRP formula in both the public and private sector, against fierce opposition from trade unions, the traditional constituency of the Labour Party. Despite research to the contrary, in political debates about the future of work, the nature of work in contemporary society and the role that work plays in the construction of identity, it would appear that the cash nexus is the 'bottom line' – and now the only line that the government can see. This line has been wielded against public-sector workers, accused by Prime Minister Tony Blair of being adverse to change and opposed to entrepreneurialism.[10] We are now in a situation where poorly paid public-sector workers are being told by their employers that they do not even deserve their low (and government imposed) wages, an assault leading to an even further erosion of recognition and status for groups of workers who traditionally have worked not just for economic rewards but out of a desire to provide a good service for clients, to serve the community and to contribute to building a better society for all.[11]

Conclusion

So why does the myth of the economic worker still abound? Again, it is contemporary critical theory that provides us with the most helpful insights here. In sociology, as we have seen, work – and aspects of work – have often been reduced to 'employment', meaning that analysis is conducted at the level of formal or contractual relationships rather than at the level of subjective meanings that participants in work attach to actions or situations.

As noted above, this can be a useful device. Such forms of analysis allow us to see clearly the relationship between the operation of capital and the position of the individual. But they serve to obscure other important points. In this way, such sociological analyses actually reflect the ways in which system rationality and system imperatives predominate in the articulation of formal knowledge. It is not that such approaches are invalid. Rather, they serve to conceal and devalue the commonsense understandings of society that people hold, and render invisible those aspects of working, such as caring, household or voluntary work, which do not conform to the contractual norm. We need hardly point out how frequently such forms of work are undervalued, ignored and not seen as 'real work'.

A critical perspective, drawing on the work of Habermas (1984; 1987), illuminates the ways in which system rationality – the rationality that describes the imperatives of the economy and the state – permeates academic discourse at the expense of communicative rationality, the rationality of our everyday lives. However, it also illustrates a core problem in the political discourse of Western industrial societies; namely, that our public arena for discussion has been colonized with the imperatives and rationality of the capitalist system. It is as if the 'default state' for discussion of the future of work, the nature of work and the economic structure of society can only be a form of discourse that always prioritizes the needs of capital over the needs of individuals and communities. As Aronowitz and DiFazio point out, we need to put labour and work back into perspective so that we can achieve self-managed time and move away from the 'endless work' situation and cult of presenteeism (see chapter 4) that now afflicts us. We should recognize the political and thus transformable nature of the labour process. Such recognition can only be achieved through a genuine reconstruction of civil society and political institutions:

> We envision a civil society as the privileged site for the development of individuals who are really free to participate in a public sphere of their own making. In such a civil society, politics consists not so much in the ritual act of selection, through voting, of one elite over another, but in popular assemblies that could, given sufficient space and time, be both legislative and administrative organs. The scope of popular governance would extend from the workplace to the neighbourhood. (Aronowitz and DiFazio 1994: 358)

This is no mean task, and analysis of the steps required to achieve such a transformation are beyond the scope of this book. We can, however, point to the ways in which the myths surrounding the world of work indicate the need for a different approach to work itself. Without placing work in its wider social, cultural and political context, we will continue to focus only on employment aspects and ignore the ways in which work provides people with resources other than the purely financial. But such analyses require that we investigate work closely and from the perspective of those most closely involved in it. Such studies will require a wider brief than a focus on the nature of the labour process if we are to understand work in wider contexts, most crucial of which, we have argued here, is the political context. We need to recognize the commonalities between the 'myths' that abound in workplaces and public discussions of work. These are not mere coincidences but indicators of the degradation of public debate about the role of work and employment, and the distribution of employment chances in society. Finally we must recognize the need for innovative, but grounded, theoretical approaches to making sense of work. These concerns will be dealt with in our final chapter.

Conclusion: Beyond the Myths?

> The class war is over. (Tony Blair, British Prime Minister)

> We are talking about investing in human capital in the age of knowledge. To compete in the global economy, to live in a civilizing society . . . we will have to unlock the potential of every young person.
>
> (David Blunkett, British Minister for Education)

In this book we have explored a series of interconnected myths about how the world of work is changing and the effects of these changes for all of us. The myths we have identified are not exhaustive: we could have discussed, for example, the myth of the work-shy 'dole scrounger'; or we could have looked in more detail at some of the subsidiary myths we have touched on along the way: for example the myths that women lack ambition, that they do not make good managers, that women workers are 'bitchy' about their fellows; or the view that Japanese industrial relations are superior and more harmonious and should be copied by all other nations. However, the set of myths that we have selected are, we believe, currently the most influential. Together they constitute a prevailing view of work which is uncritically espoused by most employers and by government and other policy-makers.

This view links irresistible forces of globalization to the 'knowledge society' and the 'skills revolution': flexibility in the labour market is seen as absolutely necessary for countries to compete in this economic environment. The centrality and power of these meta-myths have also been identified by Pierre Bourdieu (1998) as crucial to the maintenance of capitalist hegemony. Like Bourdieu, we see these myths as serving to legitimate practices that bring a deterioration of conditions for many working people and subject them to a regime of threatened insecurity, as highlighted in Richard Sennett's account (1998) of the effects of 'flexible capitalism' in America. While purporting to empower, all too often they disempower.

While accepting that important changes are under way and that the myths have some bearing on them, in this book we have consistently criticized the universalistic and monolithic account of change offered by the myths' proponents. This concluding chapter pulls together our critique and offers some pointers to alternative ways of understanding workplace change. The main points of critique which are developed here can be summarized as follows:

1 The accounts offered are determinist and inevitabilist, suggesting that there are no alternatives to the identified trends.
2 Discussion of the changes tends to gloss over variations and therefore present a one-sided and universalistic view of changes which in fact are very complex and often display contradictory tendencies.
3 Often commentators make claims that are not backed with convincing empirical evidence.
4 Continuities with the past and the effects of past events and traditions are often ignored.
5 The changes need to be placed in political context in order to reveal the possibility of other political options.

Previous chapters have emphasized the variability of change in different contexts and countries, the importance of continuities from the past in shaping events and the existence of a range of possible political options that societies could adopt in response to global challenges. Above all, we have tried to expose the determinism of these myths and their tendency to endorse the view that there is only 'one best way' to run a modern economy and society. To Mrs Thatcher's 'There is no alternative,' we would respond: 'It doesn't have to be this way!'

In defence of this stance, we have highlighted alternatives and demonstrated how working people in their daily lives are resisting and questioning those aspects of change that have led to deterioration in their working lives: the long hours' culture, the flexibility of non-standard employment, PRP and performance appraisal. We have also explored the changing social relationships to which globalization and the knowledge society are linked; we have rejected the idea that gender and class inequality are things of the past and that social harmony has been achieved and we show how the fight against class and gender injustice remains an important motivating factor in many people's lives. Thus the workplace is not simply the site of irresistible economic forces but remains, in Richard Edwards's classic phrase (1979), 'a contested terrain', where a variety of interest groups struggle for recognition and fairer distribution of resources.

Myths about work are nothing new, and, as another counter to fatalism and determinism, it is worth mentioning some earlier myths that were equally influential in their time. The nineteenth century threw up a long-lasting one, the notion that married women's employment was undermining family life and that they should be persuaded to give up jobs and stay at home. The 1960s was the time of the 'leisure society' scenario. Technology and automation would free societies from the necessity for long hours of work and consequently people, especially youngsters, would need to be 'educated for leisure', taught to spend the extra free time creatively, rather than hanging about in the streets and indulging in antisocial behaviour. Then in the late 1980s we heard repeatedly of the 'demographic time-bomb'. Owing to falling birth rates there would soon be insufficient numbers of young people to satisfy employers' needs, so they would have to turn to alternative sources of labour, such as married women and older people. These discredited examples show the folly of attempts to read the future in an inevitabilist way: married women's work has become socially acceptable, the leisure society never came into being, rising unemployment offset the declining numbers of young people and defused the demographic time-bomb.

Substantiating Myths: the Dangers of a 'Top-Down' Approach

This points to another key weakness of many versions of the myths examined in this book: that there is little, if any, empirical evidence offered to support them. In some cases this happens because, although the myth is unfounded, it supports a particular ideological or political position. Such is the case of the myth of the end of secure employment, which Pollert (1988a) claims was promoted by 'New Right' governments as part of a 're-education' of working people to induce acceptance of tougher conditions in their jobs. In a similar vein, the myth of the end of trade union power has been used as part of a process of undermining workers' confidence that they can still effect change within their workplaces.

A second reason for the unsubstantiated nature of these myths is that in some cases researchers have tended to ignore workers' opinions and activities in order to concentrate on the views of managers and what they perceive (or hope) is happening. The response of workers is either unexplored or even assumed. This is a failing displayed by the authors of some influential sociological macro-accounts of social change, such as Giddens (1998) or Bauman (1999). It is also characteristic of many management writers, who, driven by a belief in the superiority of the managers' vision of the workplace and accepting a necessary logic of capitalist enterprise, pursue a 'top-down' approach that skews research findings in a number of ways. The 'disappearance' of the worker predictably brings about the apparent disappearance of workplace resistance. However, as Thompson and Ackroyd (1995) assert, 'it [resistance] is there if workplace researchers have the time and inclination to look' (p. 629). For example, as discussed in chapter 2, detailed exploration into the experiences and views of lean-production workers reveals that, despite the outward success of the strategy, lean production presents managers with many problems, some of which stem from workers' resistance. Managers themselves would sometimes prefer to deny this, as exemplified by a personnel officer in an organization studied by one of the authors who simply refused to accept the existence of a massively hostile response to current changes, which the researcher uncovered by talking to employees.

The 'top-down' approach also means that the subtleties of the cultures of work can elude researchers. The dangers of this are well illustrated with reference to the perceived 'female takeover' of the workplace. From the outside (or the top-down), women appear to be succeeding in unprecedented ways. However, a detailed examination of the views and activities of those affected by this apparent change reveals that patterns of gendered behaviour at home and at work still reflect cultural views about domesticity and stereotypes about masculinity and femininity which ensure male advantage.

By contrast, *Myths at Work* has drawn on detailed case study evidence that places workers at the centre of research, establishing what is really going on in the workplace. In the current climate it can be difficult to gain access to workplaces for lengthy periods of time, so that long-term ethnographic study of labour processes is hard to accomplish. Nevertheless some researchers have achieved this, while others have sought detailed insights into changing workplaces through a range of other research methodologies, including focus groups and qualitative interviewing. By placing workers at the centre, while investigating the impact of the cultural, ideological and material constraints brought to bear on their lives, it is possible to correct past errors and put labour back into the sociology of work. It is also likely that overzealous emphasis on change will be corrected since workers' accounts are often cynical about rhetoric and surface gloss surrounding developments such as team-working or empowerment. Rather, their accounts point to continuities in industrial relations.

Continuities and Change

In recent years texts offering critical assessment of trends in work and employment in the UK have appeared almost duty-bound to consider the relative effects of change and continuity. This is perhaps inevitable, given the strong claims for change that have been made by politicians and managers. More considered analyses of developments are therefore helpful. In the field of industrial relations, P. Edwards (1995) has stressed the importance of positing a 'balance sheet of change and continuity . . . to indicate how the regulation of employment is developing' (p. 599). He suggests that in considering the 're-regulation' of labour that occurred during the 1980s and early 1990s, including the reassertion of managerial authority, its cyclical nature must be acknowledged. Blyton and Turnbull (1998) also argue against seeing developments in employment relations solely in linear terms, as is common in managerial accounts, since this results in an overemphasis on change and novelty. However, they also caution against relying on cycles as a device for conceptualizing the relationship between change and continuity, since in these interpretations too much stress may be placed on continuity and stability. Rather, they introduce the concept of 'spiral time', a metaphor they suggest is more adequate to capture simultaneous aspects of 'change and continuity, progression and reversal' (p. 12). More prosaically, Noon and Blyton (1997) identify important aspects of recent change in work and employment – the rise of the service sector, increased managerial authority and the growth of job insecurity, for example – as well as the resilience of more long-standing trends, such as the gendered division of labour and Taylorist patterns of work organization.

In our critical evaluation of myths at work we, too, need to consider the relative impact of change and continuity in relation to the predominant managerialist and political representations. We are frequently assured that new social and material technologies of production are helping to create more flexible and highly skilled employees, committed as 'partners' to organizational objectives, unsullied by attachment to trade unionism and imbued with individual self-belief that if they work hard the meritocratic character of contemporary capitalism will ensure that they are appropriately rewarded. Change is not only presented as characteristic of contemporary work arrangements but as an emphatically positive feature. Indeed, those who express reservations may find themselves denounced as part of the 'forces of conservatism' that stand in the way of progress!

Yet the discourse of change, and its positive ethos, has not become so well established just from the efforts of politicians and business. Its deep-rootedness is also an expression of the instrumentalist concerns of many writers and researchers. Academic and managerialist writers have introduced and debated such concepts as 'post-Fordism', 'flexible specialization', the 'knowledge economy', the 'third way' and 'lean production', among others. The novelty of such concepts and trends is frequently asserted, and the significance of continuity downplayed, simply because it helps to sell books, establish careers and sustain reputations. We must recognize that there are important vested interests present in maintaining that work and employment are constantly characterized by change.

By challenging the myths and highlighting the realities of work and employment, we have perhaps exposed ourselves to the criticism that we have erected a 'straw person'; placing too heavy an emphasis on setting out the myths, and thus making them easy to knock down. But we believe that our analyses have drawn out the complexities and nuances of each topic area. In our discussion of British trade unions, for example, we have not contested that they were severely weakened during the 1980s and 1990s; however, we stress that the UK continues to be typified by adversarial industrial relations, something that gives the unions scope to recover from their recent difficulties. Nor have we argued that non-standard work has not increased in significance. Rather, we have challenged the assumption that it is becoming ubiquitous and is universally beneficial. Finally, in our discussion of skills we accepted the existence of some upskilling, but indicated that it was not commonplace and has been frustrated by institutional factors. Thus we have not simply highlighted the various myths and then criticized them. We have also offered distinctive, up-to-date and critically informed discussions of key topics relating to the world of work and employment, discussions that have been informed by the voices of employees to whom we have listened.

The Political Context of Myth-making

Listening to alternative voices is one way to guard against the inevitabilism discussed above. We must also grasp that myths about work are products of specific political contexts. Here we discuss primarily the British political context, as this was the frame for our own research, but similar accounts could be offered for other societies.

The 'globalization' and 'knowledge society' myths proliferated during the rise of 'New Right' governments in the 1980s and 1990s, the era of 'Reaganomics' and 'Thatcherism'. This period witnessed attacks on the collectivist and redistributive social policies that were developed in the postwar period. It was marked by the reintroduction of 'incentives' and consequent widening of earnings and incomes disparities (see chapter 7), along with the dismantling of parts of the welfare state and the privatizing of public services. Unemployment was allowed to reach high levels, while trade unions, having been denounced as 'the enemy within' by Margaret Thatcher, were deprived of some of their powers and their hard-won involvement in political decision-making. To legitimate the sufferings and setbacks imposed on many ordinary working people as a result of such developments, 'New Right' governments sought to promote a culture of individual responsibility and entrepreneurial initiative: 'stand on your own two feet', 'get on your bike' and cut the 'apron-strings' of the 'nanny state'.

In the 1990s some 'New Right' governments have been replaced by left-centre parties, espousing some version of a 'third way' as exemplified by Tony Blair, Bill Clinton and Lionel Jospin. Currently these parties retain an attachment to neo-liberal 'free market' economic policies, while promoting progressive and democratic social policies (positive action for women and ethnic minorities, employment rights for gays and lesbians, opening access for disabled people and so forth). In Britain this has opened up the way, at the very least, for some renegotiation about social change in the workplace, as trade unions and other representative bodies are allowed back into the policy-making arena. Despite this, the voices of employers' groups, such as the CBI, are still the most powerful influences on governments in deciding what 'can' and 'can't' be done. Thus the myths that developed in the 1980s still retain their power.

For example, British Prime Minister Tony Blair is known to be influenced by the work of Anthony Giddens (1994; 1998), whose account of the 'third way' strongly promotes a view of triumphant globalization and new technology transforming our lives. In *Beyond Left and Right*, Giddens suggests that the Japanese pattern of industrial relations should be the model for the future. He sees class as being of diminishing importance in politics as 'the traditional working class has largely disappeared' (1998: 104) and presents an image of society marked by increasing individualism, 'self-reflexive' management of identities and careers, with lifestyle choices increasingly salient as sources of identification: in sum, Giddens presents a rather benign, optimistic version of the bleak visions of Bauman, discussed in chapter 7. Such ideas have clear resonance with Blair's conception of a democratic, pluralist society and his declaration to the TUC Congress on 14 September 1999 that class antagonism in the workplace was a thing of the past, to be replaced by constructive 'partnership': 'Business and employees, your members, aren't two nations divided. That's old style thinking. That's the thinking of the past'.

Another influence on Blair's thinking has been Charlie Leadbeater of the Demos think-tank, whose book *Living on Thin Air* (1999) endorses a very strong version of the 'meta-myths' of globalization and the scientific and technological revolution. Leadbeater explicitly describes himself as one of Handy's 'portfolio workers' and Drucker's knowledge workers 'armed with a laptop, a modem and some contacts' (p. 1). Globalization is depicted as irreversible and irresistible, 'the swirling forces which are shaping our economic lives' (p. 3) and, while acknowledging the disruptions it has brought to people's lives and established working practices, he is adamant that 'globalization is good' (p. ix) and must be embraced: 'Nor will we get very far by reining in the dynamic and creative forces which are driving the global economy, in particular the creation and spread of new ideas and technologies which are the well-springs of higher productivity and improved well-being' (p. 4). To compete and survive in the global economy, countries must undergo processes of modernization, embracing innovation and flexibility; here the public sector comes in for special criticism: 'The public sector needs more innovation, creativity and entrepreneurship . . . Government will only become more effective and adaptive in an era of rapid social and economic change if public employees at all levels become engaged in a continuous process of renewal and innovation' (p. 207). Clearly, such ideas have informed Blair's comments on the NHS and his attempts to reform the education sectors through devices such as audit, appraisal and performance-related pay which were discussed in earlier chapters.

Social science thinking, then, is having a strong influence on how Britain's employment policies are being shaped. Thus it becomes even more crucial that social scientists mount a critical examination of the currently influential myths, exposing their one-sidedness and partiality. We have argued the need for careful empirical research, which collects information on the points of view of all parties involved, to replace unfounded assertion based on the view from the top. We have discussed the need to look carefully at continuities as well as changes and how they shape day-to-day realities. Finally, we consider the kind of conceptual and theoretical work required if our grasp of workplace relations is to proceed beyond the mythical.

Theoretical Implications

Throughout this book we have used a range of theories to make sense of work and its attendant myths, although we have privileged certain theories and criticized others. In this final section we hope to clarify our position with respect to theory. At the outset, however, we feel we must stress that myths at work only become visible and graspable through the application of theory. Without coherent theoretical intervention into workplace studies we will be unable to disentangle myth from reality, speculation from certainty.

Social theory has undergone radical changes in recent years. The arrival of poststructural theory has been slow to permeate sociological studies of work, but there is now a large body of such writing addressing issues of work and employment. There are, of course, a range of poststructural approaches available – indeed, 'poststructural' is a portmanteau term to describe approaches that seek to refute the grand narratives of modernity, and even a cursory inspection of some of these texts will reveal that these approaches are often at odds with each other. However, two notable perspectives – the Foucauldian and the social constructionist – are gaining prominence in the sociology of work.

In many ways this is laudable: such approaches have broken the hegemony of labour process studies and allowed a range of new analytical perspectives to emerge. Grint and Woolgar's social constructionist approach to work, drawing on Latour's actor network theory, reveal the ways in which individuals in workplaces locate themselves within networks of animate and inanimate objects, constructing a world around themselves and others. Casey's Foucauldian attempts at developing a poststructural social psychology includes reference to the uptake and deployment of different forms of workplace discourse in the construction of the self. Du Gay's Foucauldian perspective reveals the ways that managers and workers are involved in a process of continuous identity formation through the use of discursive strategies. These varied approaches tell us that work has changed, and that our analyses of work must change. However, they suffer from a fatal drawback: through focusing so exclusively on the individual and his/her individual situation, they lose sight of wider, structural contexts within which the individual is located. Such rejection of wider contexts leads, we suggest, to fatalism. Theorists who ignore the economic, social, cultural and political contexts external to the workplace lead us to believe that the context cannot be changed or altered – it has become, for them, a given that does its own thing – or they see it as an irrelevance. Thus poststructuralists sometimes take 'capitalism' as a given and fail to explore it in any satisfactory way. Against this, we argue that analysis of context is vital. Bradley, with respect to gender and power, sums up in critique of post-structural studies:

> It would be nice if the social world were no more than a contestation, so that, merely by renaming the world, we could change it. . . . This underestimates the multi-dimensionality of gendered power which has both cultural and material aspects. . . . Our everyday engagement with the process of defining the world takes place within relationships of power which involve differential control of, and access to, a range of resources, material, political, cultural and symbolic, including the utilization of means of force and violence. (Bradley 1996: 9)

Workers are not in a situation where they can pick and choose at will from an infinite range of possible identities or orientations, nor are they in a situation where external structures merely turn them into pawns. Rather, they are constrained by forces and structures external to them and to their workplace, but they also have access to a range of resources that can be utilized in workplace struggles, construction of identity and forms of resistance. Thus we must be wary of the contrary error: merely locating work in wider, structural contexts, with little or no consideration of workers and the ways in which they are actively involved in constructing workplace relationships and identities. This is our primary criticism of what we termed 'traditional' sociology of work approaches (see chapter 9). There is more to work than just the operation of capital.

Our approach differs from those mentioned above by recognizing the diverse factors implicit and explicit in the world of work. We need a theoretical perspective allowing us to make sense of work which fully reflects the ways in which workers themselves are making sense of work, hence our stress on the need for inclusive case studies and representative fieldwork. Allowing the voices of those involved in work to come to the fore is essential, and necessary to counter the propagation of myths by those not involved in the forms of work they are mythologizing. We also stress the need for close and critical analysis of the role of economics and economic structures in society, and the role of government in overseeing these. Capitalist economies are the source of important social divisions in society and in workplaces, shaping the underlying structure of the material conditions of society and those who inhabit it. Theory must be able to identify that there are economic conditions that structure choices and, at least in part, identity.

As we identify such structures in society, we must critically evaluate these. Social structures, such as capitalist economies, are not merely 'given': they are actively constructed through the operation of power and resources that can be identified and questioned. In addition, structures may not be the formal or traditional objects that have been recognized in the past. In this book we have considered science and technology to have a structural dimension, a dimension that is often called upon as a legitimation for technical interventions in workplaces, but we have also shown that the structure of science and technology is determined by social action and external forces. Social structures are not only external to individuals: we are caught up in networks of structures and social actions that each determine the outcome of the other. We must recognize this to avoid producing reductive analyses of the social world – analyses that will explain all social phenomena through, for example, reference only to the economic base or the structure of consciousness.

While avoiding reductive analyses, we need to be able to locate different sites of resistance and dissent, and we must recognise that these can be diverse. We cannot allow ourselves merely to focus on formal structures of resistance – for example, trade unions – at the expense of individual forms of resistance – for example, noncompliance in corporate culture. At the same time, we need a frame of reference that allows us to place these things in relation to each other: not all actors in the workplace have similar access to power and control, and perspectives that suggest that they do are quite simply wrong.

We must also grasp that differences, such as those of gender, age and ethnicity, are built into many social situations, not least workplaces. By recognizing that difference is inbuilt, we can begin to understand workplaces from the perspectives of the different participants involved. But these conceptions of difference must be located in wider contexts: gender, race, sexuality, (dis)ability are, at least in part, social constructs and should not be treated as being essential or immutable.

Our theoretical perspective can be summed up as being a 'critical theory'. It is critical in the sense that it offers a critique of existing approaches and understandings of workplaces, in the ways that it proposes alternatives to existing structures of power and domination, and in the ways that it challenges the orthodoxy and myths surrounding work and workplaces. In addition to providing theoretical insights into work and workplaces, their relation to economic and other social structures and the ways that identities are formed and articulated in workplaces, we recognize the need for a theoretical approach that avoids the fatalism of other contemporary workplace analyses. Without a critical analysis of all the possibilities of change we are doomed to repeat the endless cycle of exploitation and appropriation that characterizes capitalist societies.

Notes

Introduction: Myths at work

1 In Britain in 1998/9 there were 23,393 students of Business and Management Studies in English and Welsh institutions and 78,350 undergraduates studying in these areas (figures supplied by HESA, the Higher Education Statistics Agency).

2 Examples for Britain include Huw Beynon, *Working For Ford*; Theo Nichols and Huw Beynon, *Living with Capitalism*; Anna Pollert, *Girls, Wives, Factory Lives*; Ruth Cavendish, *Women on the Line*; Sally Westwood, *All Day, Every Day*; Cynthia Cockburn, *Brothers*. For America, Eli Chinoy, *Automobile Workers and the American Dream*; Alvin Gouldner, *Wildcat Strike*; Michael Burawoy, *Manufacturing Consent*.

3 Excellent accounts of the influence of the sociological classics on the sociology of work are offered in John Eldridge's *Sociology and Industrial Life* (1971) and Graeme Salaman's *Class and the Corporation* (1981).

4 Full accounts are featured in Rose (1975), Parker et al. (1977) and Grint (1998).

5 There are notable exceptions, for example Garrahan and Stewart's (1992) work on the Nissan factory in Sunderland (though it is significant they were refused permission to interview workers in the plant), the studies carried out in South Wales by Andy Danford (1996), by Rick Delbridge (1998) of workers in Japanized factories and by Milkman (1997) of American autoworkers.

6 As we have indicated, this is not true of Casey or Du Gay but what they choose to tell us about what the employees told them curiously refracts the voicing of concerns offered by managers.

7 Jean-François Lyotard in *The Postmodern Condition* famously defined postmodernism as 'incredulity towards metanarratives' (1984: xxiii).

8 From our own experience we can vouch for the difficulty of gaining access to employees for interviews, especially in a climate of 'lean production' where time is money. In increasingly pressurized and integrated labour processes, withdrawing workers from 'the line' is genuinely problematic for managers. This proved a problem for Harriet Bradley in her case studies, especially in interviewing factory and retail workers where shifts and schedules are tightly organized to cut slack in employment. Mark Erickson's attempts to interview employees in the defence industry were impeded by closures and financial crises in the companies he approached. Political factors are also at play here: Carol Stephenson was forced to interview Nissan workers outside the factory because of the company's unwillingness to allow sociological researchers into the plant. Steve Williams found that political tensions and changes of regimes in some of unions he approached for his North East study made access difficult, while Mark Erickson faced a range of difficulties created by the culture of secrecy – both military and industrial – which surrounds the UK defence industry.

Chapter 1 The myth of globalization

1 Wallerstein considered that from that period onwards the emergence and consolidation of a capitalist 'world system', comprising core states, peripheral and semi-peripheral areas, could be discerned. 'Core' states, principally the most advanced capitalist societies with strong institutions of state governance and forms of national culture, benefited from the exploitative nature of the economic relationships they established with the peripheral and semi-peripheral areas. For the purposes of this chapter, the most important feature of Wallerstein's argument relates to the way in which the nature of the 'world system' is held to be determined not by intra-state factors, but by the relationship between states (Wallerstein 1979).
2 Although Giddens writes of 'time–space distanciation', whereas Harvey appears to identify a contrary trend, 'time-space compression', McGrew (1992) has noted that these two apparently distinctive approaches are easily reconciled since globalization can be seen as involving both greater 'scope (stretching)' and 'intensity (deepening)' in the scale of human interaction.
3 FDI can be defined as the 'ownership of or investment in overseas enterprises in which the investor plays a direct managerial role' (Held et al. 1999: 191).
4 Dicken (1998), who prefers to use the term 'trans-national corporation' (TNC), believing it to reflect more accurately the global character of many companies, defines it as 'a firm which has the power to co-ordinate and control operations in more than one country, even if it does not own them' (p. 177).
5 In the US the growth of labour market inequality has largely manifested itself in falling real incomes and low wages. In the more heavily regulated labour markets of Western Europe high levels of unemployment

have been attributed to the growth of competition from the 'south' (Freeman 1997).

6 With the notable exception of Castells (1996).

7 We take the 'North East' region to encompass the counties of Durham, Northumberland, Cleveland and Tyne & Wear.

8 In 1998, 67.5% of North East employees worked in services (*Regional Trends*, vol. 33, 1998). In classifying regions official statistics use 'North' rather than 'North East' and include the county of Cumbria.

Chapter 2 The myth of lean production

The quotations from Nissan UK workers in this chapter are drawn from interviews conducted by Stephenson between 1989 and 1991 as part of the 'Nissan Enigma' project (Garrahan and Stewart 1992), and more recent interviews with workers from Nissan UK and its supplier plants in 1998 and 2000.

1 The Department of Trade and Industry (DTI) has published a series of advisory documents promoting these ideas and indicating how they can be adopted; in particular, the 1993 document, *Total Quality Management*, which sees these strategies as key ingredients to economic and corporate rejuvenation and effective leadership.

2 Part of a speech to the British Venture Capitalist Association in July 1999, quoted in the *Guardian*, 7 July 1999.

3 In regions such as the North East of England, for example, where coal extraction, steel manufacture and shipbuilding formed the economic base, Fordist techniques were never the primary form of labour process (Hudson 1989).

4 In 1985 Nissan negotiated a highly restrictive, single-union, so-called 'no-strike' agreement with the Amalgamated Engineering and Electrical Union (AEEU) (Stephenson 1988). The union was given the right to recruit, but denied any meaningful role in representing its members. The agreement went as far as to promise union compliance with whatever changes the company wished to introduce, irrespective of implications for members (*Financial Times*, 23 April 1985).

5 Laurie Graham was a participant observer of lean production in the USA-based Subaru-Isuzu plant.

6 New United Motors Manufacturers Inc., based in California, is a joint venture between General Motors and Toyota.

7 'Brownfield' is the term used to describe an established site, while 'greenfield' refers to a new site.

8 A Nissan worker interviewed as part of the Nissan Enigma project said: 'At the interview one manager came out and had his say about what he thought about trade unions. . . . There is a policy at Nissan of telling managers what they want to hear . . . they [managers] make it very clear what they think politically, so everybody makes out they are bluer than blue. . . . I have never said actually Arthur Scargill is my favourite person' (Nissan maintenance worker).

9 Unions within Rover in the UK were prepared to 'embrace' new work strategies, believing negotiation and opposition was futile. By contrast, during the same period, unions at competitors Vauxhall – part of General Motors – 'engaged' with new strategies and were able to negotiate relatively successfully with employers in order to avoid the most damaging effects of lean production (Coyne and Williamson 1991; Stewart and Vass 1998).

Chapter 3 The myth of non-standard employment

The second epigraph is quoted in Bradley (1999: 123).

1 For statistical purposes, part-time employment is officially defined as paid employment of thirty hours a week or less.
2 NATFHE represents staff in FE and HE, particularly those in the 'new', post-1992 universities. The AUT (Association of University Teachers) organizes academics and related staff in 'old' universities.
3 The figures are based on 137 institutions, representing 77 per cent of the HE sector.
4 The Bett report recommended that a common core of minimum conditions of service – covering maternity leave, sick pay and access to grievance procedures, for example – should be applied to all employees, on a pro rata basis if necessary. It criticized the increased reliance on casual employment and argued that employees on fixed-term contracts should be entitled to claim redundancy payments after one year of service. This would reduce the attractiveness of further casualization (Bett 1999: 7, 104).
5 A position strongly contested by Ginn et al. (1996) and Ginn and Sandall (1997).
6 To a limited degree, this will have been reduced by the national minimum wage of £3.60 an hour (implemented in 1999). However, workers aged between eighteen and twenty-one benefit only from a reduced rate and those aged under eighteen do not qualify at all.

Chapter 4 The myth of the female takeover

Epigraphs from the Conservative politician Edwina Currie, interviewed in the *Guardian*, 24 February 1999; from Tom Peters, quoted in Wajcman (1998: 58); and Fay Weldon, quoted in the *Guardian*, 4 March 1999.

1 For a somewhat similar categorization see Humphries and Rubery (1992).
2 There are many ways of measuring unemployment none of which are entirely satisfactory. The analysis of Rubery et al. discussed here involves a variety of measures. This particular figure is based on the ILO measure which counts as unemployed all people without jobs who have sought employment in the past four weeks and are available for work.
3 Those who have taken a part-time job not by preference but because they are unable to find full-time employment.

4 HEFCE statistics, reported in the *Guardian*, 11 March 1999.
5 See the discussion in Bradley 1996, chapter 4.
6 See, among many others, the case studies in Ledwith and Colgan, 1996; Wajcman, 1998; Marshall, 1984; 1995; and McDowell, 1997.

Chapter 5 The myth of technology

1 There are a number of notable exceptions to this general omission: Latour and Woolgar's classic 1979 study *Laboratory Life* does investigate the social production of scientific knowledge inside a scientific workplace, although no mention of key sociology of work concepts, such as the labour process, is made. Harold Garfinkel's study of the discovery of the optical pulsar is another example, although from a different theoretical perspective, of a workplace-based science study (Garfinkel et al. 1981). Dorothy Nelkin and Michael Brown's *Workers at Risk* (1984) uses interviews with workers in laboratories and research institutes to identify the ways in which risk is perceived by those involved in knowledge production and high-tech work environments. Unlike the studies of Latour and Woolgar or Garfinkel, they are concerned to find the connections between the operation of capital and the deployment of science in workplaces. Bruno Latour's *Science in Action* investigates the creation of 'technoscience' and examines the ways in which scientific workplaces (for example, research laboratories) have been taken over by a technoscience that encompasses knowledge, technology and scientific professionalization (Latour 1987).
2 See Grint and Woolgar (1997: 6–38) for a wide-ranging discussion of theories of technology.
3 It is worth pointing out that microprocessors were not released into the non-military world until 1971. These early microprocessors were only found in calculators and it was not until the early 1980s that personal computers became widely available.
4 Braverman subsequently notes that scientific management lacked the character of 'true' science because 'its assumptions reflect nothing more than the outlook of the capitalist with regard to the conditions of production' (Braverman 1974: 86).
5 Flow-forming is a method of extruding metals at high temperature and high pressure to very precise tolerances. At RO Birtley it was mainly used for the production of rocket bodies.
6 When surveying the opinions of the entire BAe defence sector workforce in 1994, BAe's own research team asked employees to assess the statement: 'The company care about their employees.' Ten per cent agreed at Birtley; 16 per cent agreed in the whole BAe defence division.
7 Stephenson's work at Nissan (1994) shows similar results in a 'pure' Japanization regime.
8 Barry Wilkinson points out that there are few ways of distinguishing between the 'objective measures' of efficiency and the 'ideological jus-

tifications' for it, particularly where new technology is concerned (Wilkinson 1983: 82–6).

9 See Ron Sakolsky (1992) for a historical and theoretical review of disciplinary power, panopticism and the workplace.

Chapter 6 The myth of the skills revolution

1 See Kumar (1986) for a critical evaluation of Bell's thesis.

2 Reich also identified the presence of two other categories of employees in the United States: those involved in 'routine production services', including workers in the emerging high technology industries as well as those older manufacturing plants; and those responsible for 'in-person services', such as retail, hotel and catering and care workers (Reich 1991: 171–84).

3 See chapter 8 for a refutation of the argument that adversarial industrial relations have withered away. To be fair, Frenkel et al. (1995) admit that their propositions regarding workplace change require 'testing against empirical evidence' (p. 789).

4 The research findings cited here come from a project jointly undertaken by the Tavistock Institute and Newcastle University's Centre for Urban and Regional Development Studies: 'Work opportunities for women in the information society: call centre teleworking'. They are reported in the *IRS Employment Review*, 675, March 1999, 2.

5 See MSC/DES (1986) and DE/DES (1986) for further details.

6 This case study of the reform of vocational qualifications is based on research which was funded by the Open University's Centre for Educational Policy and Management and the Economic and Social Research Council. See Raggatt and Williams (1999) for a more comprehensive account.

7 See the Qualification and Curriculum Authority's website for further details (http://www.qca.org.uk/).

8 For example, see Beaumont (1996).

9 See Employee Development Bulletin (1999) for an in-depth account of the recent changes.

10 The MSC had been established in 1973 as a non-departmental government body, under the aegis of the then Department of Employment (DE). Its remit included the running of the national network of job centres and the promotion of industrial training. Its tripartite character – employer and trade union representatives sat on the Commission itself – subsequently gave the MSC a significant degree of influence. For further details see Ainley and Corney (1990).

11 See Mansfield and Mitchell (1996) for an in-depth, albeit overly sanguine, look at 'functional analysis' from two of its leading originators.

12 The DfE (Department for Education) from 1992 to 1995. In July 1995 it was merged with the DE to form the Department for Education and Employment (DfEE).

Chapter 7 The myth of the death of class

The second epigraph is taken from an interview with Jimmy Young, Radio 2, 19 August 1999.

1 For example, Collinson and Hearn (1996), McDowell (1997), Wajcman (1999) and Jenkins (1999).
2 Nelson and Smith (1999) make the same point.
3 Reported in the *Guardian*, 19 March 1999; Elliott (1999).
4 Reported in the *Guardian*, 9 September 1998.
5 UNICEF World Development Report, reported in the *Guardian*, 17 October 1998.
6 Reported in the *Guardian*, 15 September 1998.
7 UN Human Development Report, 1998, reported in the *Guardian*, 9 September 1998.
8 See Bradley (1996: ch. 3) for a short introduction to debates on class; Crompton (1998) provides the most comprehensive survey of class analysis.
9 The seven SECs are (1) higher managerial and professional occupations; (2) lower managerial and occupational occupations; (3) intermediate occupations; (4) small employers and own account workers; (5) lower supervisory, craft and related occupations; (6) semi-routine occupations; (7) routine occupations. A lively debate between Rose and O'Reilly and some of their critics can be found in *Work, Employment and Society*, 12 (4).
10 This research is being carried out for a Ph.D by Gail Hebson among union workers, factory workers and women service employees.
11 For example, research into middle-class mobility by Fiona Devine, or work on the long-term unemployed by Robert MacDonald. For useful published work on the middle class see Savage et al. (1992) and Butler and Savage (1995). On the 'underclass' see Morris (1994), Wilson (1993) and Murray (1990).

Chapter 8 The myth of the end of trade unionism

The epigraph from the Chief Executive of Zurich Insurance, a company which de-recognized unions in the early 1990s, is quoted in House of Commons Employment Committee (1994: 342).

1 For a useful analysis, see also the contribution of Crouch (1995: 247–51).
2 Byers was later to enter the Cabinet as Chief Secretary to the Treasury in 1998, before succeeding Peter Mandelson as Secretary of State for Trade and Industry (and becoming ultimately responsible for industrial relations legislation) later that year.
3 For an analysis of the conduct of industrial relations in non-unionized companies, see McLoughlin and Gourlay (1994).

4 Data from the 1998 Workplace Employment Relations Survey (WERS '98) show that 45 per cent of workplaces recognize unions for collective bargaining (DTI 1998b).
5 Drawing on developments in the US, Beaumont (1991) has pointed to some of the elements that make up a distinctive HRM package. These include flexible and well-trained employees, high commitment to business objectives, the importance of individual employee performance, and personnel policies and procedures that complement and support overall business strategy. See Legge (1995) and Storey (1995) for extensive studies of HRM.
6 For a discussion of the differences between the Certification Officer data and those provided by the LFS, see Cully and Woodland (1998). The overall decline in union membership may have bottomed out in 1998. According to the autumn 1998 LFS, it stabilized at just over seven million (*Labour Market Trends*, July 1999).
7 This exemplar is based on the account provided by Paul Stewart (1997).
8 This exemplar has been drawn from contemporary press accounts of the dispute, in particular two pieces written by Seumas Milne in the *Guardian*: 'Jubilee line strike crisis intensifies' (25 November 1998) and 'Jubilee Line climbdown on safety strike' (26 November 1998).
9 But see Darlington (1994) for an analysis of the way in which union organization at Ford's Halewood plant has been 'seriously undermined' since the 1970s. Furthermore, unions have been excluded from Honda's UK operations.
10 See Waddington and Whitston (1995: 170–2) for an analysis of the effect on trade union membership levels of compositional changes in employment.
11 Firms with twenty or fewer employees will be exempt from this procedure.

Chapter 9 The myth of the 'economic worker'

1 Ironically, in management discourse concerning the necessary restructuring of the UK defence industry, the workers have often been charged with being the primary obstacle to diversification or conversion. See Lovering (1990) for a review of such management perspectives.
2 This is despite significant research into the relationship between pay and performance and into motivations and attitudes of employees. Drawing on the work of Diana Coole and Nancy Fraser, Bradley summarizes recent research into the link between demands for redistribution and demands for recognition from women workers. Class and gender politics diverge at times with respect to these two interests, with class politics focusing on redistribution and gender politics looking for recognition, although Fraser argues that gender politics must embrace both. Bradley concludes, in relation to her own research findings, that 'women wished to achieve equal pay with men and gain equal access to top posi-

tions; but they also wanted their distinctive contributions in "women's jobs" to be acknowledged and re-evaluated and not to be considered inferior workers' (Bradley 1999: 208).

3 Although offered to teachers in 1999, the controversy that greeted the package delayed its implementation, but it appeared that Tony Blair was committed to pushing it through.

4 The payment-by-results scheme was scrapped because it led to drilling and rote-learning, with children packed into huge classes, and was seen by progressive educationists as inimical to learning based on real understanding and self-development.

5 Reported in the *Guardian*, 31 March 1999.

6 UCAS (Universities and Colleges Admissions Service) figures for undergraduate applications to degree programmes in primary education in 1999 were down 11 per cent on the previous year. Doug McAvoy, General Secretary of the National Union of Teachers, noted that this showed the failure of the government's short-term bribes to influence young people who recognized the inadequacy of existing pay levels (*Guardian*, 21 July 1999).

7 The survey, carried out by the *Guardian*, revealed that average pay increases for boardroom executives in the past year had been 22 per cent, with top directors in the UK's biggest companies awarding themselves 26 per cent. This compares with average profits increasing by 6.9 per cent, while in the companies listed in the FTSE employees' pay rises averaged 5.02 per cent (*Guardian*, 21 July 1999).

8 Reported in the *Guardian*, 17 July 1999.

9 Alex Brummer in the *Guardian*, 20 July 1999, argued that of the thirty-five or so directors who earned over one million pounds only a handful, such as those at the drug companies SmithKline Beecham and Glaxo Wellcome, could be seen as delivering a world-class product. Brummer, the paper's financial editor, suggested that, given the poor level of trading profits, people who sanctioned such rises deserved to be sacked!

10 Speech to the British Venture Capitalist Association, 6 July 1999.

11 See Bradley (1999) for discussion of this public-service ethos. It was for this reason that occupational groups such as nurses, policemen, teachers and lecturers were, until quite recently, reluctant to go on strike.

Conclusion: Beyond the myths?

The epigraphs are taken from Blair's speech to the British Labour Party Conference, 28 September 1999; and David Blunkett, quoted by Mahony (1998: 40), from the DfEE publication *Excellence in Schools* (1997).

Bibliography

Adkins, L. 1995: *Gendered Work*. Milton Keynes: Open University Press.

Adler, S., Laney, J. and Packer, M. 1993: *Managing Women.* Milton Keynes: Open University Press.

Ainley, P. and Corney, M. 1990: *Training for the Future: the rise and fall of the Manpower Services Commission.* London: Cassell.

Albrow, M. 1996: *The Global Age: state and society beyond modernity.* Cambridge: Polity Press.

Allen, J. 1995: Crossing borders: footloose multinationals? In J. Allen and C. Hammet (eds), *A Shrinking World? Global unevenness and inequality*, Oxford: Oxford University Press, 55–92.

Allen, J. and Hammett, C. 1995: Uneven worlds. In J. Allen and C. Hammet (eds), *A Shrinking World? Global unevenness and inequality*, Oxford: Oxford University Press, 233–54.

Allen, S. 1997: What is work for? The right to work and the right to be idle. In R. Brown (ed.), *The Changing Shape of Work*, London: Macmillan, 54–69.

Amin, A. and Thrift, N. 1997: Globalization, socio-economics, territoriality. In J. Wills and R. Lee (eds), *Geographies of Economies*, London: Arnold, 147–57.

Arber, S. and Ginn, J. 1995: The mirage of gender equality: occupational success in the labour market and within marriage. *British Journal of Sociology*, 46 (1), 21–44.

Arendt, H. 1959: *The Human Condition*. New York, Doubleday.

Armstrong, P. 1988: Labour and monopoly capital. In R. Hyman and W. Streeck (eds), *New Technology and Industrial Relations*, Oxford: Blackwell, 143–59.

Arnetz, B.B. and Wilholm, C. 1997: Technological stress: psychophysiological symptoms in modern offices. *Journal of Psychosomatic Research*, 43 (1), 35–42.

Aronowitz, S. and DiFazio, W. 1994: *The Jobless Future: sci-tech and the dogma of work*. Minnesota, Minnesota University Press.

Ashton, D. and Green, F. 1996: *Education, Training and the Global Economy*. Cheltenham: Edward Elgar.

Atkinson, J. 1984: Manpower strategies for flexible organisations. *Personnel Management*, 16, August, 28–31.

Atkinson, J. 1986: Flexibility planning for an uncertain future. *Manpower Policy and Practice*, Summer, 26.

Atkinson J. and Meager N. 1986a: Is flexibility just a flash in the pan? *Personnel Management*, 18, September, 25–9.

Atkinson, J. and Meager, N. 1986b: *Changing Work Patterns: how companies achieve flexibility to meet new needs*. London: National Economic Development Office.

Bacon, N. and Storey, J. 1996: Individualism and collectivism and the changing role of the trade unions. In P. Ackers, C. Smith and P. Smith (eds), *The New Workplace and Trade Unionism*, London: Routledge, 41–76.

Bailey, R. 1996: Public sector industrial relations. In I. Beardwell (ed.), *Contemporary Industrial Relations: a critical analysis*, Oxford: Oxford University Press, 121–50.

Baldry, C., Bain, P. and Taylor, P. 1998: 'Bright satanic offices': intensification, control and contradiction in the software labour process. In P. Thompson and C. Warhurst (eds), *Workplaces of the Future*, Houndsmill: Macmillan Business, 163–83.

Banham, J. 1992: Taking forward the skills revolution. *Policy Studies*, 13 (1), 5–12.

Banks, J., Dilnot, A. and Lowe, H. 1996: Patterns of financial wealth-holding in the United Kingdom. In J. Hills (ed.), *New Inequalities*, Cambridge: Cambridge University Press, 321–47.

Baritz, L. 1965: *Servants of Power*. New York: Wiley.

Bassett, P. 1986: *Strike Free: new industrial relations in Britain*. London: Macmillan.

Bassett, P. and Cave, A. 1993: *All for One: the future of the unions*. London: Fabian Society.

Bauman, Z. 1998: *Work, Consumerism and the New Poor*. Cambridge, Polity.

Baxter, J. 1999: Moving towards equality? Questions of change and equality in household work patterns. In M. Gatens and A. Mackinnon (ed.), *Gender and Institutions: welfare, work and citizenship*, Cambridge: Cambridge University Press, 55–72.

Bayliss, V. 1998: *Redefining Work*. London: Royal Society of Arts.

Beale, D. 1994: *Driven by Nissan*. London: Lawrence & Wishart.

Beatson, M. 1995: Progress toward a flexible labour market. *Employment Gazette*, 103, 255–65.

Beaumont, G. 1996: *Review of 100 NVQs and SVQs*. London: Department for Education and Employment.

Beaumont, P. 1991: Trade unions and HRM. *Industrial Relations Journal*, 22 (4), 300–8.

Beck, U. 1992: *Risk Society*. London: Sage.

Becker, H. 1970: *Sociological Work*. New Brunswick: Transaction Books.

Bell, D. 1974: *The Coming of Post-industrial Society*. London: Heinemann.

Berger, P. 1963: *Invitation to Sociology*. Harmondsworth: Penguin.

Berggren, C. 1989: New production concepts in final assembly – the Swedish experience. In S. Wood (ed.), *The Transformation of Work*, London: Unwin Hyman, 156–71.

Bett, M. 1999: *Independent Review of Higher Education Pay and Conditions: a review chaired by Sir Michael Bett*. London: Stationery Office.

Beynon, H. 1984: *Working for Ford*. Harmondsworth: Penguin.

Beynon, H. 1997: The changing practices of work. In R. Brown (ed.), *The Changing Shape of Work*, London: Macmillan, 20–54.

Beynon, H. and Austrin, T. 1994: *Masters and Servants: class and patronage in the making of a labour organization*. London: Rivers Oram Press.

Beynon, H., Hudson, R. and Sadler, D. 1994: *A Place called Teesside: a locality in a global economy*. Edinburgh: University of Edinburgh Press.

Birchall, D. and Hammond, V. 1981: *Tomorrow's Office Today: managing technological change*. London: Business Books.

Blackburn, R. 1997: *The Making of New World Slavery: from the baroque to the modern, 1492–1800*. London: Verso.

Blair, T. 1996: *New Britain: my vision of a young country*. London: 4th Estate.

Blauner, R. 1964: *Alienation and Freedom: the factory worker and his industry*. Chicago: University of Chicago Press.

Blyton, P. and Turnbull, P. 1998: *The Dynamics of Employee Relations*. 2nd edn. Basingstoke: Macmillan.

Bourdieu, P. 1998: *Acts of Resistance*. Cambridge: Polity.

Bradley, H. 1989: *Men's Work, Women's Work*. Cambridge: Polity.

Bradley, H. 1994: Divided we fall: unions and their members. *Employee Relations*, 16 (2), 41–52.

Bradley, H. 1996: *Fractured Identities: changing patterns of inequality*. Cambridge: Polity.

Bradley, H. 1999: *Gender and Power in the Workplace: analysing the impact of economic change*. Basingstoke: Macmillan.

Brannen, J. 1998: Employment and family lives: equalities and inequalities. In E. Drew, R. Emerek and E. Mahon (ed.), *Women, Work and the Family in Europe*, London: Routledge, 76–86.

Braverman, H. 1974: *Labor and Monopoly Capital: the degradation of work in the twentieth century*. New York: Monthly Review Press.

Brody, D. 1993: *In Labor's Cause: main themes on the history of the American worker*. Oxford: Oxford University Press.

Brown, P. 1994: Education, training and economic change. *Work, Employment and Society*, 8 (4), 607–21.

Brown, P. and Scase, R. (eds) 1991: *Poor Work: disadvantage and the division of labour*. Milton Keynes: Open University Press.

Brown, R. 1992: *Understanding Industrial Organisations: theoretical perspectives in industrial sociology*. London: Routledge.

Brown, R. 1997: Flexibility and security: contradictions in the contemporary labour market. In R. Brown (ed.), *The Changing Shape of Work*, Basingstoke: Macmillan, 69–86.

Brown, R. (ed.) 1997: *The Changing Shape of Work.* London: Macmillan.

Brown, W. 1993: The contraction of collective bargaining in Britain. *British Journal of Industrial Relations*, 31 (2), 189–200.

Bruegel I. 1996: Whose myths are they anyway? A comment. *British Journal of Sociology*, 47 (1), 175–7.

Bryson, A. and McKay, S. 1997: What about the workers? In R. Jowell, J. Curtice, A. Park, L. Brook, K. Thomson and C. Bryson (eds), *British Social Attitudes: the 14th Report. The end of Conservative values?* Aldershot: Ashgate, 23–48.

Burawoy, M. 1979: *Manufacturing Consent.* Chicago: University of Chicago Press.

Butler, T. and Savage, M. (eds) 1996: *Social Change and the Middle Classes.* London: UCL.

Cairncross, F. 1997: *The Death of Distance.* London: Orion Business Books.

Casey, C. 1995: *Work, Self and Society: after industrialism.* London: Routledge.

Castells, M. 1996: *The Rise of the Network Society*. Oxford: Blackwell.

Castells, M. 1997: *The Power of Identity*. Oxford: Blackwell.

Cavendish, R. 1982: *Women on the Line.* London: Routledge.

Chinoy, E. 1955: *Automobile Workers and the American Dream*. New York: Doubleday.

Clarke, S. 1990: New Utopias for old: Fordist dreams and post-Fordist fantasies. *Capital and Class*, 42, 131–55.

Claydon, T. 1996: Union de-recognition: a re-examination. In I. Beardwell (ed.), *Contemporary Industrial Relations: a critical analysis*, Oxford: Oxford University Press, 151–74.

Cockburn, C. 1983: *Brothers: male dominance and technological change.* London: Pluto.

Cockburn, C. 1985: *Machinery of Dominance: women, men and technical know-how.* London: Pluto.

Cockburn, C. 1991: *In the Way of Women.* London: Macmillan.

Cockburn, C. and Ormrod, S. 1993: *Gender and Technology in the Making.* London: Sage.

Cohen, R.S. 1985: More work for mother: technology and housework in the USA. In L. Levidow and B. Young (eds), *Science, Technology and the Labour Process*, vol. 2, London: Free Association Books, 88–128.

Collinson, D. and Hearn, J. (eds) 1996: *Men as Managers, Managers as Men.* London: Sage.

Confederation of British Industry (CBI) 1989: *Towards a Skills Revolution.* London: Confederation of British Industry.

Conlock, C. 1998: *Homeworking: the hidden workforce.* West Yorkshire: West Yorkshire Homeworking Unit.

Coole, D. 1996: Is class a difference that makes a difference? *Radical Philosophy*, 77, 17–25.

Coward, R. 1992: *Our Treacherous Hearts.* London: Faber & Faber.

Coyne, G. and Williamson, H. 1991: *New Union Strategies.* London: Centre for Alternative Industrial Technology Systems.

Cregan, C. 1999: *Young People in the Workplace.* London: Mansell.

Crompton, R. 1989: Women in banking: continuity and change since the Second World War. *Work, Employment and Society*, 3 (3), 141–56.

Crompton, R. 1997: *Women and Work in Modern Britain*. Oxford: Oxford University Press.

Crompton, R. 1998: *Class and Stratification*. 2nd ed. Cambridge: Polity.

Crompton, R. and Jones, G. 1984: *White Collar Proletariat: deskilling and gender in clerical work*. London: Macmillan.

Crompton, R. and Le Feuvre, N. 1992: Gender and bureaucracy: women in finance in Britain and France. In M. Savage and A. Witz (eds), *Gender and Bureaucracy*, Oxford: Blackwell, 94–123.

Crompton, R. and Sanderson, K. 1990: *Gendered Jobs and Social Change*. London: Unwin Hyman.

Crook, S., Pakulski, J. and Waters, M. 1992: *Postmodernization: change in advanced society*. London: Sage.

Cross, M. 1988: Changes in working practices in UK manufacturing, 1981–1988. *Industrial Relations Review and Report*, 415, 2–10.

Crouch, C. 1995: The state: economic management and incomes policy. In P.K. Edwards (ed.), *Industrial Relations: theory and practice in Britain*, Oxford: Blackwell, 229–54.

Cully, M. and Woodland, S. 1998: Trade union membership and recognition 1996–97: an analysis of data from the Certification Officer and the LFS. *Labour Market Trends*, July, 353–64.

Dahrendorf, R. 1959: *Class and Class Conflict in the Industrial Society*. London: Routledge.

Danford, A. 1996: *Japanese management techniques and British workers*. Ph.D, University of Bristol.

Danford, A. 1997: The 'new industrial relations' and class struggle in the 1990s. *Capital and Class*, 61, 107–41.

Darlington, R. 1994: Shop stewards' organisation in Ford Halewood: from Beynon to today. *Industrial Relations Journal*, 25 (2), 136–49.

Davies, P. and Freedland, M. 1993: *Labour Legislation and Public Policy*. Oxford: Oxford University Press.

Defence Analytical Services Agency (DASA) 1993: *UK Defence Statistics*. London: HMSO.

Delbridge, R. 1998: *Life on the Line in Contemporary Manufacturing*. Oxford: Oxford University Press.

Delsen, L. 1998: When do men work part-time? In J. O'Reilly and C. Fagan (eds), *Part-time Prospects*, London: Routledge, 57–76.

Department for Education and Employment (DfEE) 1996: *NCVQ Quinquennial Review: Stage Two Report*. London: DfEE.

Department for Education and Employment (DfEE) 1997: *Labour Market and Skill Trends 1997/1998*. London: DfEE.

Department for Education and Employment (DfEE) 1998: *Education and Training Statistics for the United Kingdom*. London: Stationery Office.

Department of Employment/Department of Education and Science (DE/DES) 1986: *Working Together: education and training*. London: HMSO.

Department of Trade and Industry (DTI) 1993: *Total Quality Management and Effective Leadership: a strategic overview*. London: HMSO.
Department of Trade and Industry (DTI) 1998a: *Fairness at Work*. London: DTI.
Department of Trade and Industry (DTI) 1998b: *First Findings from the 1998 Workplace Employment Relations Survey*. London: DTI.
Department of Trade and Industry (DTI) 1998c: *The 1998 Competitiveness White Paper: building the knowledge driven economy*. London: DTI.
Devine, F. 1997: *Social Class in Britain and America*. Edinburgh: Edinburgh University Press.
Dex, S. and McCulloch, A. 1997: *Flexible Employment*. Basingstoke: Macmillan.
Dicken, P. 1998: *Global Shift: transforming the world economy*. London: Paul Chapman.
Dicken, P., Peck, J. and Tickell, A. 1997: Unpacking the global. In J. Wills and R. Lee (eds), *Geographies of Economies*, London: Arnold, 158–66.
Dickens, L. 1994: Wasted resources? Equal opportunities in employment. In K. Sisson (ed.), *Personnel Management: a comprehensive guide to theory and practice in Britain*, Oxford: Blackwell, 253–96.
Dickens, L. and Hall, M. 1995: The state: labour law and industrial relations. In P.K. Edwards (ed.), *Industrial Relations: theory and practice in Britain*, Oxford: Blackwell, 255–303.
Drew, E. 1998: Re-conceptualising families. In E. Drew, R. Emerek and E. Mahon (eds), *Women, Work and the Family in Europe*, London: Routledge, 11–26.
Drew, E. and Emerek, R. 1998: Employment, flexibility and gender. In E. Drew, R. Emerek and E. Mahon (eds), *Women, Work and the Family in Europe*, London: Routledge, 89–99.
Drew, E., Emerek, R. and Mahon, E. (eds) 1998: *Women, Work and the Family in Europe*. London: Routledge.
Drucker, P.F. 1970: *Technology, Management and Society*. London: Heinemann.
Drucker, P.F. 1993: *Post-capitalist Society*. London: Butterworth-Heinemann.
Du Gay, P. 1996: *Consumption and Identity at Work*. London: Sage.
Dundon, T. 1998: Post-privatised shop steward organisation and union renewal at Girobank. *Industrial Relations Journal*, 29 (2), 126–36.
Dunn, S. and Metcalf, D. 1996: Trade union law since 1979. In I. Beardwell (ed.), *Contemporary Industrial Relations: a critical analysis*, Oxford: Oxford University Press, 66–98.
Eder, K. 1993: *The New Politics of Class*. London: Sage.
Edwards, P. 1995: Assessment: markets and managerialism. In P. Edwards (ed.), *Industrial Relations: theory and practice in Britain*, Oxford: Blackwell, 599–613.
Edwards, R. 1979: *The Contested Terrain*. London: Heinemann.
Eldridge, J.E.T. 1971: *Sociology and Industrial Life*. London: Michael Joseph.
Elger, T. 1979: Valorisation and deskilling: a critique of Braverman. *Capital and Class*, 7, 58–99.

Elger, T. 1990: Technical innovation and work reorganization in British manufacturing in the 1980s: continuity, intensification or transformation? *Work, Employment and Society*, special issue, May, 67–101.

Elliott, L. 1999: 50 per cent of children are poor. *Guardian*, 29 March.

Emerek, R. 1998: Atypical working time: examples from Denmark. In E. Drew, R. Emerek and E. Mahon (eds), *Women, Work and the Family in Europe*, London: Routledge, 131–9.

Employee Development Bulletin 1999: NVQs and SVQs mean business. *Employee Development Bulletin*, 109, 6–14.

Esping-Andersen, G. 1990. *The Three Worlds of Welfare Capitalism*. Cambridge: Polity.

Esping-Andersen, G. (ed.) 1993: *Changing Classes.* London: Sage.

Eveline, J. 1999: Heavy, dirty and limp stories: male advantage at work. In M. Gatens and A. Mackinnon (eds), *Gender and Institutions: welfare, work and citizenship*, Cambridge: Cambridge University Press, 90–106.

Fabian Society 1996: *Changing Work.* London: Fabian Society.

Fairbrother, P. 1994: Privatization and local trade unionism. *Work, Employment and Society*, 8 (3), 339–56.

Fairbrother, P. 1996: Workplace trade unionism in the state sector. In P. Ackers, C. Smith and P. Smith (eds), *The New Workplace and Trade Unionism*, London: Routledge, 110–48.

Faludi, S. 1992: *Backlash*. London: Chatto & Windus.

Farnham, D. 1996: New Labour, the new unions and the new labour market. *Parliamentary Affairs*, 49 (4), 584–98.

Felstead, A. 1994: Funding government training schemes: mechanisms and consequences. *British Journal of Education and Work*, 7 (3), 21–42.

Felstead, A. 1997: Unequal shares for women: qualitative gaps in the national targets for education and training. In H. Metcalf (ed.), *Half Our Future: women, skill development and training*, London: Policy Studies Institute, 7–41.

Fevre R. 1991: Emerging 'alternatives' to full-time and permanent employment. In P. Brown and R. Scase (eds), *Poor Work: disadvantage and the division of labour*, Milton Keynes: Open University Press, 56–71.

Findlay, P. and Newton, T. 1998: Re-framing Foucault: the case of perfomance appraisal. In A. McKinlay and K. Starkey (eds), *Foucault, Management and Organization Theory: from panopticon to technologies of the self*, London: Sage, 211–29.

Finegold, D. and Soskice, D. 1988: The failure of training in Britain: analysis and prescription. *Oxford Review of Economic Policy*, 4 (3), 21–53.

Finn, D. 1987: *Training without Jobs.* London, Macmillan.

Fitzgerald, N. 1997: Harnessing the potential of globalization for the consumer and citizen. *International Affairs*, 73 (4), 739–46.

Folbre, N. 1994: *Who Pays for the Kids?* London: Routledge.

Foucault, M. 1979: *Discipline and Punish: the birth of the prison.* Harmondsworth: Peregrine.

Foucault, M. 1980: *Power/Knowledge.* Brighton: Harvester.

Francis, A. 1986: *New Technology at Work*. Oxford: Clarendon Press.

Fraser, N. 1995: From redistribution to recognition? Dilemmas of justice in the post-socialist age. *New Left Review*, 212, 68–93.

Freeman, R. 1997: Does globalization threaten low-skilled western workers? In J. Philpott (ed.), *Working for Full Employment*, Basingstoke: Macmillan, 132–50.

Frenkel, S., Korczynski, M., Donoghue, L. and Shire K. 1995: Re-constituting work: trends towards knowledge work and info-normative control. *Work, Employment and Society*, 9 (4), 773–96.

Fuller, S. 1997: *Science*. Buckingham: Open University Press.

Gabriel, Y. 1988: *Working Lives in Catering*. London: Routledge.

Gall, G. 1997: Developments in trade unionism in the financial sector in Britain. *Work, Employment and Society*, 11 (2), 219–35.

Gall, G. and McKay, S. 1994: Trade union derecognition in Britain, 1988–1994. *British Journal of Industrial Relations*, 32 (3), 433–48.

Gallie, D. 1994: Patterns of skill change: upskilling, deskilling or polarization? In R. Penn, M. Rose and J. Rubery (eds), *Skill and Occupational Change*. Oxford: Oxford University Press, 41–76.

Gallie, D. 1998: The flexible workforce? The employment conditions of part-time and temporary workers. Paper presented at ESRC Social Stratification Workshop, Essex University, January 1998.

Gallie, D., Penn, R. and Rose, M. (eds) 1996: *Trade Unionism in Recession*. Oxford: Oxford University Press.

Garfinkel, H., Lynch, M. and Livingston, E. 1981: The work of a discovering science construed with materials from the optically discovered pulsar. *Philosophy of the Social Sciences*, 11, 131–58.

Garrahan, P. and Stewart, P. 1992: *The Nissan Enigma*. London: Mansell.

Geary, J. 1995: Work practices: the structure of work. In P.K. Edwards (ed.), *Industrial Relations: theory and practice in Britain*, Oxford: Blackwell, 368–96.

Gergen, K. 1991: *The Saturated Self*. New York: Basic Books.

Giddens, A. 1990: *The Consequences of Modernity*. Cambridge: Polity.

Giddens, A. 1994: *Beyond Left and Right*. Cambridge: Polity.

Giddens, A. 1998: *The Third Way*. Cambridge: Polity.

Giddens, A. 1999: *Runaway World*. BBC Reith Lectures, http://news.bbc.co.uk/hi/english/static/events/reith_99/default.htm (accessed 8 June 1999).

Ginn, J. and Arber, S. 1998: How does part-time work lead to low pension income? In J. O'Reilly and C. Fagan (eds), *Part-time Prospects*, London: Routledge, 156–73.

Ginn, J. and Sandall, J. 1997: Balancing home and employment: stress reported by social services staff. *Work, Employment and Society*, 11 (3), 413–34.

Ginn, J., Arber, S., Brannen, J., Dale, A., Dex, S., Elias, P., Moss, P., Pahl, J., Roberts, C. and Rubery, J. 1996: Feminist Fallacies: a reply to Hakim on women's employment. *British Journal of Sociology*, 47 (1), 167–74.

Glucksmann, M. 1995: Why 'work'? Gender and the 'total social organization of labour'. *Gender, Work and Organization*, 2 (2) 63–75.

Goldthorpe, J. 1982: On the service class, its formation and its future. In A. Giddens and G. Mackenzie (eds), *Social Class and the Division of Labour:*

essays in honour of Ilya Neustadt, Cambridge: Cambridge University Press, 162–85.

Goldthorpe, J., Llewellyn, C. and Payne, C. 1980: *Social Mobility and Class Structure in Modern Britain.* Oxford: Clarendon Press.

Goldthorpe, J., Lockwood, D., Bechhofer, F. and Platt, J. 1969: *The Affluent Worker in the Class Structure*. Cambridge: Cambridge University Press.

Gorz, A. 1980: *Ecology and Politics*. Boston: South End Press.

Gorz, A. 1982: *Farewell to the Working Class*. London: Pluto.

Gosling, A., Machin, S. and Meghir, C. 1996: What has happened to the wages of men since 1996? In J. Hills (eds.), *New Inequalities*, Cambridge: Cambridge University Press, 135–57.

Gouldner, A. 1965: *Wildcat Strike*. New York: Harper & Row.

Graham, L. 1995: *On the Line at Subaru-Isuzu: the Japanese model and the American worker*. Ithaca: Cornell University Press.

Gray, J. 1998: *False Dawn: the delusions of global capitalism*. London: Granta Books.

Green, F. 1994: Training: inequality and inefficiency. In A. Glyn and D. Miliband (eds), *Paying for Inequality: the economic cost of social injustice,* London: River Oram Press, 65–79.

Greenbaum, J. 1998a: From Chaplin to Dilbert: the origins of computer concepts. In S. Aronowitz and J. Cutler (eds), *Post-work: the wages of cybernation*, New York: Routledge, 167–84.

Greenbaum, J. 1998b: The times they are a' changing: dividing and recombining labour through computer systems. In P. Thompson and C. Warhurst (eds), *Workplaces of the Future*, Houndsmill: Macmillan Business, 124–41.

Gregg, P. and Wadsworth, J. 1996: More work in fewer households? In J. Hills (ed.), *New Inequalities*, Cambridge: Cambridge University Press, 181–207.

Gregson, N. and Lowe, M. 1994: *Servicing the Middle Classes*. London: Routledge.

Grint, K. 1998: *The Sociology of Work*. 2nd edn. Cambridge: Polity.

Grint, K. and Woolgar, S. 1997: *The Machine at Work*. Cambridge: Polity.

Guest, D. 1989: Human resource management: its implications for industrial relations and trade unions. In J. Storey (ed.), *New Perspectives on Human Resource Management*, London: Routledge, 39–55.

Guest, D. 1995: Human resource management, trade unions and industrial relations. In J. Storey (ed.), *Human Resource Management: a critical text*, London: Routledge, 110–41.

Habermas, J. 1971: *Toward a Rational Society: student protest, science, politics.* Boston: Beacon Press.

Habermas, J. 1984: *The Theory of Communicative Action*, vol. 1: *Reason and the Rationalization of Society*. Boston: Beacon Press.

Habermas, J. 1987: *The Theory of Communicative Action*, vol. 2: *Lifeworld and System.* Cambridge: Polity Press.

Haddon, L. and Silverstone, R. 1993: *Teleworking in the 1990s: a view from the home.* Science Policy Research Unit Report Series, No. 10.

Hakim, C. 1979: *Occupational Segregation by Sex* (Research Paper No. 9). Department of Employment. London: HMSO.

Hakim, C. 1991: Grateful slaves and self-made women: fact and fantasy in women's work orientations. *European Sociological Review*, 7 (2), 101–21.

Hakim, C. 1995: Five feminist myths about women's employment. *British Journal of Sociology*, 46 (3), 429–55.

Hakim, C. 1996: *Issues in Women's Work.* London: Athlone Press.

Halford, S., Savage, M. and Witz, A. 1995: *Gender, Careers and Organization.* London: Macmillan.

Hammer, M. 1996: *Beyond Re-engineering.* London: HarperCollins.

Handy, C. 1994: *The Empty Raincoat.* London: Hutchinson.

Handy, C. 1984: *The Future of Work.* Oxford: Blackwell.

Harkness, S., Machin, S. and Waldfogel, J. 1996: Women's pay and family incomes in Britain 1979–91. In J. Hills (ed.), *New Inequalities*, Cambridge: Cambridge University Press, 158–80.

Harkness, S., Machin, S. and Waldfogel, J. 1998: Female employment and changes in the share of women's earnings in total family income in Great Britain. In P. Lawless, R. Martin and S. Hardy (eds), *Unemployment and Social Exclusion*, London: Jessica Kingsley, 182–200.

Harrop, J. and Moss, P. 1995: Trends in parental employment. *Work, Employment and Society*, 7 (1), 97–120.

Harvey, D. 1989: *The Condition of Postmodernity*. Oxford: Basil Blackwell.

Haslam, C., Williams, K., Johal, S. and Williams, J. 1996: A fallen idol? Japanese management in the 1990s. In P. Stewart (ed.), *Beyond Japanese Management*, Trowbridge: Frank Cass, 21–44.

Healy, G. and Kraithman, D. 1996: Different careers – equal professionals: women in teaching. In S. Ledwith and F. Colgan (eds), *Women in Organisations: challenging gender politics*, London: Macmillan, 186–211.

Heery, E. 1996: The new new unionism. In I. Beardwell (ed.), *Contemporary Industrial Relations: a critical analysis*, Oxford: Oxford University Press, 175–202.

Heery, E. 1998a: Campaigning for part-time workers. *Work, Employment and Society*, 12 (2), 351–66.

Heery, E. 1998b: The relaunch of the Trades Union Congress. *British Journal of Industrial Relations*, 36 (3), 339–60.

Heery, E. and Kelly, J. 1994: Professional, participative and managerial unionism: an interpretation of change in trade unions. *Work, Employment and Society*, 8 (1), 1–22.

Held, D., McGrew, A., Goldblatt, D. and Perraton, J. 1999: *Global Transformations*. Cambridge: Polity.

Hetherington, P. 1998: Workers count the cost of Fujitsu factory closure. *Guardian*, 5 September.

Hewitt, P. 1993: *About Time: the revolution in work and family life.* London: Rivers Oram Press.

Hills, J. (ed.) 1996: *New Inequalities*. Cambridge: Cambridge University Press.

Hinvers, J. 1988: Editorial. *Target Magazine*. February, 25–35.

Hirst, P. 1997: The global economy – myths and realities. *International Affairs*, 73 (3), 409–25.

Hirst, P. and Thompson, G. 1995: Globalization and the future of the nation state. *Economy and Society*, 24 (3), 408–42.
Hirst, P. and Thompson, G. 1996: *Globalization in Question*. Cambridge, Polity Press.
Hobsbawm, E. 1979: The development of the world economy. *Cambridge Journal of Economics*, 3, 305–10.
Hochschild, A. 1983: *The Managed Heart*. Berkeley: University of California Press.
Hochschild, A. 1989: *The Second Shift*. New York: Viking.
Hochschild, A. 1997: *The Time Bind*. New York: Metropolitan Books.
Hollinshead, G., Nicholls, P. and Tailby, S. 1999: *Employee Relations*. London: Financial Times Management.
Holloway, J. 1987: The Great Bear, Post-Fordism and class struggle: a comment on Bonefeld and Jessop. *Capital and Class*, 32, 93–104.
House of Commons Education and Employment Committee 1999: *Part-time Work*, vol. 2: Minutes of Evidence and Appendices. London: HMSO.
House of Commons Employment Committee 1994: *The Future of the Unions*. Minutes of Evidence. London: HMSO.
House of Commons Employment Committee 1996: *The Work of TECs*. Minutes of Evidence. London: HMSO.
Hudson, R. 1989: *Wrecking the Region: state policies, party politics and regional change in the North East of England*. London: Pion.
Humphries, J. 1983: The emancipation of women in the 1970s and 1980s. *Capital and Class*, 20, 6–27.
Humphries, J. and Rubery, J. 1992: The legacy for women's employment: integration, differentiation and polarisation. In J. Michie (ed.), *The Economic Legacy, 1979–1992*, London: Academic Press, 236–54.
Hutton, W. 1995: *The State We're In*. London: Vintage.
Huws, U. 1994: *Home Truths: key results from a national survey of homeworkers*. Batley: National Group on Homeworking.
Huws, U., Jagger, N. and O'Regan, S. 1999: *Teleworking and Globalization*. Brighton: Institute of Employment Studies.
Hyland, T. 1994: *Competence, Education and NVQs: dissenting perspectives*. London: Cassell.
Hyman, R. 1989: *The Political Economy of Industrial Relations*. Basingstoke: Macmillan.
Hyman, R. 1991: European unions: towards 2000. *Work, Employment and Society*, 5 (4), 621–39.
Hyman, R. 1992: Trade unions and the disaggregation of the working class. In M. Regini (ed.), *The Future of Labour Movements*, London: Sage, 150–68.
Hyman, R. 1997: The future of employee representation. *British Journal of Industrial Relations*, 35 (3), 309–36.
Industrial Relations Services (IRS) 1997: Organising the unorganised. *IRS Employment Treads*, 644, 4–10.
International Labour Organization (ILO) 1996: *World Employment 1996/97: national policies in a global context*. Geneva: ILO.

International Labour Organization (ILO) 1998: *World Employment Report 1998–99*. Geneva: ILO.

Jahoda, M., Lazarsfeld, P. and Zeisel, H. 1972: *Marienthal*. London: Tavistock.

Jenkins, S. 1999: *Gendering Workplace Change: an analysis of women in organisations*. Ph.D, University of Northumbria.

Jenson, J., Hagen, E. and Reddy, C. (eds) 1988: *Feminization of the Labour Force*. Polity: Cambridge.

Jessup, G. 1991: *Outcomes, NVQs and the Emerging Model of Education and Training*. London: Falmer Press.

Jones S. 1986: *Policewomen and Equality: formal policy v. informal practice*. Basingstoke: Macmillan.

Jones, M. 1999: *New Institutional Spaces: TECs and the remarking of economic governance*. London: Jessica Kingsley.

Kahn-Freund, O. 1964: Legal framework. In A. Flanders and H. A. Clegg (eds), *The System of Industrial Relations in Great Britain*, Oxford: Basil Blackwell, 42–127.

Keep, E. 1999: Missing links. *People Management*, 28 January 35.

Keep, E. and Mayhew, K. 1996: Evaluating the assumptions that underlie training policy. In A. Booth and D. Snower (eds), *Acquiring Skills: market failures, their symptoms and policy responses*, Cambridge: Cambridge University Press, 305–34.

Kelly, J. 1990: British trade unionism 1979–89: change, continuity and contradictions. *Work, Employment and Society*, special issue, May, 29–65.

Kelly, J. 1996: Union militancy and social partnership. In P. Ackers, C. Smith and P. Smith (eds), *The New Workplace and Trade Unionism*, London: Routledge, 77–109.

Kelly, J. 1998: *Rethinking Industrial Relations*. London: Routledge.

Kelly, J. and Waddington, J. 1995: New prospects for British labour. *Organization*, 2 (3/4), 425–6.

Kenney, M. and Florida, R. 1988: Beyond mass production: production and the labour process in Japan. *Politics and Society*, 16 (1), 121–58.

Kerr, C., Dunlop, J., Harbison, F. and Myers, C. 1960: *Industrialism and Industrial Man*. London: Heinemann.

Kirby, M. 1999a: New approaches to social inequality. *Sociology Review*, 8 (3), 17–21.

Kirby, M. 1999b: *Stratification and Differentiation*. London: Macmillan.

Knights, D., Wilmott, H. and Collinson, D. 1985: (eds), *Job Redesign: critical perspectives on the labour process*. London: Gower.

Kochan, T., Katz, H. and McKersie, R. 1986: *The Transformation of American Industrial Relations*. New York: Basic Books.

Kozul-Wright, R. 1995: Transnational corporations and the nation state. In J. Michie and J. Grieve-Smith (eds), *Managing the Global Economy*, Oxford: Oxford University Press, 135–71.

Kumar, K. 1986: *Prophecy and Progress: the sociology of industrial and post-industrial society*. Harmondsworth: Penguin.

Kumar, K. 1995: *From Post-industrial to Post-modern Society: new theories of the contemporary world*. Oxford: Blackwell.

Labour Market Trends 1999. London: HMSO.

Labour Research Department 1998: Organise, activate and motivate. *Labour Research*, 87 (6), 13–15.

Labour Research Department 1999: Part-time workforce continues grow and part-timers gain new employment rights. Labour Research Department press release, 1 March.

Land, H. 1994: The demise of the male breadwinner. In S. Baldwin and J. Falkingham (eds), *Social Security and Social Change*, London: Harvester Wheatsheaf, 100–5.

Lash, S. and Urry, J. 1987: *The End of Organized Capitalism*. Cambridge: Polity.

Latour, B. 1987: *Science in Action*. Cambridge, MA: Harvard University Press.

Latour, B. and Woolgar, S. 1979: *Laboratory Life: the social construction of scientific facts*. London: Sage.

Lawless, P., Martin, M. and Hardy, S. 1996: *Unemployment and Social Exclusion*. London: Jessica Kingsley.

Leadbeater, C. 1999: *Living on Thin Air*. London: Viking.

Ledwith, S. and Colgan, F. 1996: *Women in Organisations: challenging gender politics*. London: Macmillan.

Lee, D. 1989: The transformation of training and the transformation of work in Britain. In S. Wood (ed.), *The Transformation of Work*, London: Unwin Hyman, 156–70.

Legge, K. 1995: *Human Resource Management: rhetoric and realities*. London: Macmillan.

Levitas, R. 1998: *The Inclusive Society*. London: Macmillan.

Lewchuk W. and Robertson, D. 1996: Working conditions under lean production: a worker-based benchmarking study. In P. Stewart (ed.), *Beyond Japanese Management: the end of modern times?* London: Frank Cass, 60–82.

Lewontin, R. C. 1993: *Biology as Ideology: the doctrine of DNA*. New York: HarperPerennial.

Leyshon, A. 1995: Annihilating space? The speed-up of communications. In J. Allen and C. Hammett (eds), *A Shrinking World? Global unevenness and inequality*, Oxford: Oxford University Press, 11–46.

Lister, R. 1994: 'She has other duties' – women, citizenship and social security. In S. Baldwin and J. Falkingham (eds), *Social Security and Social Change*, London: Harvester Wheatsheaf, 31–44.

Lloyd, C. 1996: Skill shortages in the clothing industry: an endemic problem? *Work, Employment and Society*, 10 (4), 717–36.

Lodge, D. 1989: *Nice Work*. London: Penguin.

Lovering, J. 1990: *High-Fliers and Hostages: scientists and engineers in the defence industry*. Bristol: School of Advanced Urban Studies.

Lyotard, J.-F. 1984: *The Postmodern Condition: a report on knowledge*. Manchester: Manchester University Press.

Macaulay, I. and Wood, R. 1992: Hotel and catering employees' attitudes towards trade unions. *Employee Relations*, 14 (3), 20–7.

MacDonald, R. 1997: Informal working, survival strategies and the idea of an underclass. In R. Brown (ed.), *The Changing Shape of Work*, London: Macmillan, 103–25.

MacDonald, R. and Coffield, F. 1991: *Risky Business? Youth and enterprise culture*. Basingstoke: Falmer Press.

Machin, S. and Wilkinson, D. 1995: *Employee Training: unequal access and economic performance*. London: Institute of Public Policy Research.

Macran, S., Joshi, H. and Dex, S. 1996: Employment after childbearing: a survival analysis. *Work, Employment and Society*, 10 (2), 273–96.

Mahony, P. 1998: Girls will be girls and boys will be first. In D. Epstein, J. Elwood, V. Hey and J. Maw, *Failing Boys*, Buckingham: Open University Press, 37–55.

Mahony, P. and Zmroczek, C. (eds) 1997: *Class Matters: 'working-class' women's perspectives on class*. London: Taylor & Francis.

Manpower Services Commission/Department of Education and Science (MSC/DES) 1986: *Review of Vocational Qualifications in England and Wales*. London: HMSO.

Mansfield, B. and Mitchell, L. 1996: *Towards a Competent Workforce*. Aldershot: Gower.

Marcuse, H. 1964: *One Dimensional Man*. Harmondsworth: Penguin.

Marshall, G. 1997: *Repositioning Class: social inequality in industrial societies*. London: Sage.

Marshall, G., Rose, D., Newby, H. and Vogler, C. 1988: *Social Class in Modern Britain*. London: Unwin Hyman.

Marshall, J. 1984: *Women Managers: travellers in a male world*. Chichester: Wiley.

Marshall, J. 1995: *Women Managers Moving on*. London: Routledge.

Martin, R., Sunley, P. and Wills, J. 1993: The geography of trade union decline: spatial dispersal or regional resilience? *Transactions of the Institute of British Geographers*, 18, 36–62.

Martin, R., Smith, P., Fosh, P., Morris, H. and Undy, R. 1995: The legislative reform of union government 1979–94. *Industrial Relations Journal*, 26 (2), 146–55.

Marx, K. 1975: *Early Writings*. Harmondsworth: Penguin.

McDowell, L. 1997: *Capital Culture*. Oxford: Blackwell.

McGrew, A. 1992: A global society? In S. Hall, D. Held and A. McGrew (eds), *Modernity and Its Futures*, Cambridge: Polity, 61–102.

McIlroy, J. 1995: *Trade Unions in Britain Today*. Manchester: Manchester University Press.

McIlroy, J. 1998: The enduring alliance? Trade unions and the making of New Labour. *British Journal of Industrial Relations*, 36 (4), 537–64.

McKinstry, L. 1996: *Fit to Govern?* London: Bantam Press.

McIntosh, M. 1992: Defence Procurement Policy: the way ahead. *RUSI Journal*, October, 71–5.

McLoughlin, S. and Gourlay, S. 1994: *Enterprise without Unions*. Buckingham: Open University Press.

McLuhan, M. 1964: *Understanding Media: the extensions of man*. London: Routledge & Kegan Paul.

McRae, S. 1991: Occupational change over childbirth. *Sociology*, 25 (4), 589–605.

McRae, S. 1993: Returning to work after childbirth: opportunities and inequalities. *European Sociological Review*, 9, 125–38.

Meadows, P. 1999: *The Flexible Labour Market: implications for pension provision*. London: National Association of Pension Funds.

Mellor, M. 1992: *Breaking the Boundaries: toward a feminist green socialism*. London: Virago Press.

Middlemas, K. 1979: *Politics in Industrial Society*. London: Andre Deutsch.

Milkman, R. 1992: The impact of foreign investment on US industrial relations: the case of California's Japanese-owned plants. *Economic and Industrial Democracy*, 13, 151–82.

Milkman, R. 1997: *Farewell to the Factory: autoworkers in the late 20th century*. Berkeley: University of California Press.

Millward, N. 1994: *The New Industrial Relations?* Poole: Policy Studies Institute.

Millward, N., Stevens, D., Smart, N. and Hawes, W. 1992: *Workplace Industrial Relations in Transition*. Aldershot: Dartmouth.

Minkin, L. 1991: *The Contentious Alliance: trade unions and the Labour Party*. Edinburgh: Edinburgh University Press.

Modood, T., Berthoud, R., Lakey, J., Nazroo, J., Smith, P., Virdee, S. and Beishon, S. (eds) 1997: *Ethnic Minorities in Britain; diversity and disadvantage*. London: Policy Studies Institute.

Moody, K. 1997: *Workers in a Lean World: unions in the international economy*. London: Verso.

Morris, L. 1994: *Dangerous Classes*. London: Routledge.

Murray, C. 1990: *The Emerging British Underclass*. London: Institute of Economic Affairs.

National Association of Teachers in Further and Higher Education 1998: *Evidence to the Inquiry into Part-time Working by the Employment Sub-Committee of the House of Commons Select Committee on Education and Employment*. London: NATFHE.

National Audit Office (NAO) 1993: *Ministry of Defence: the award of the contract for the landing platform for helicopters. Report by the Comptroller and Auditor General*. London: HMSO.

Nelkin, D. and Brown, M. S. 1984: *Workers at Risk: voices from the workplace*. Chicago: University of Chicago Press.

Nelson, M. and Smith, J. 1999: *Working Hard and Making Do*. Berkeley: University of California Press.

Nichols, T. and Beynon, H. 1977: *Living with Capitalism: class relations and the modern factory*. London: Routledge & Kegan Paul.

Noon, M. and Blyton, P. 1997: *The Realities of Work*. Basingstoke: Macmillan.

O'Reilly, J. and Fagan, C. (eds) 1998: *Part-time Prospects*. London: Routledge.

O'Reilly, K. and Rose, D. 1998: Changing employment relations: plus ça change, plus c'est la même chose? Reflections arising from the ESRC review of government social classification. *Work, Employment and Society*, 12 (4), 713–33.

Ohmae, K. 1994: *The Borderless World: power and strategy in the global market place*. London: HarperCollins.
Oliver, N. and Wilkinson, B. 1988: *The Japanization of British Industry* Oxford: Blackwell.
Oliver, N. and Wilkinson, B. 1990: Contemporary industrial change: the implications of the Japanization of Britain. In P. Stewart, P. Garrahan and S. Crowther (eds), *Restructuring for Economic Flexibility*, Aldershot: Avebury, 9–53.
Outhwaite, W. 1994: *Habermas: a critical introduction*. Cambridge: Polity Press.
Oz, E., Glass, R. and Behling, R. 1999: Electronic workplace monitoring: what employees think. *International Journal of Management Science*, 27 (2), 167–77.
Pahl, R. 1995: *After Success*. Cambridge: Polity.
Pakulski, J., and Waters, M. 1996: *The Death of Class*. London: Sage.
Panitch, L. 1994: Globalisation and the state. In R. Miliband and L. Panitch (eds), *Socialist Register 1994: between globalism and nationalism*, London: Merlin, 60–93.
Parker, M. and Slaughter, J. 1988: *Choosing Sides: unions and the team concept*. Boston, MA: Labor Notes.
Parker, S., Brown, R.K., Child, J. and Smith, M.A. 1977: *The Sociology of Industry*. London: George Allen & Unwin.
Pateman, C. 1988: *The Sexual Contract*. Oxford: Polity.
Peck, F. and Stone, I. 1992: *New Inward Investment and the Northern Region Labour Market*. Research Series No. 6. Sheffield: Employment Department.
Perraton, J., Goldblatt, D., Held, D. and McGrew, A. 1997: The globalisation of economic activity. *New Political Economy*, 2 (2), 257–77.
Perrons, D. 1998: Gender as a form of social exclusion. In P. Lawless, R. Martin and S. Hardy (eds), *Unemployment and Social Exclusion*. London: Jessica Kingsley, 154–81.
Peters, T. 1992: *Liberation Management: necessary disorganization for the nano-second nineties*. London: Macmillan.
Phelps Brown, H. 1990: The counter-revolution of our time. *Industrial Relations*, 29 (1), 1–14.
Phillips, A. and Taylor, B. 1986: Sex and skill. In *Feminist Review* (ed.), *Waged Work: a reader*, London: Virago, 54–66.
Pilcher, J. 1998: *Women of Their Time: generation, gender issues and feminism*. London: Ashgate.
Piore, M.J. 1986: Perspectives on labour market flexibility. *Industrial Relations Journal*, 2 (2), 146–66.
Piore, M.J. and Sabel, C. 1984: *The Second Industrial Divide*. New York: Basic Books.
Pollert, A. 1981: *Girls, Wives, Factory Lives*. London: Macmillan.
Pollert, A. 1988a: The flexible firm: fixation or fact? *Work, Employment and Society*, 2 (3), 281–316.
Pollert, A. 1988b: Dismantling flexibility. *Capital and Class*, 34, 42–75.

Prais, S. 1989: How Europe would see the new British initiative for standardizing vocational qualifications. *National Institute Economic Review*, August, 52–4.

Price, L. and Price, R. 1994: Change and continuity in the status divide. In K. Sisson (ed.), *Personnel Management: a comprehensive guide to theory and practice in Britain*, Oxford: Blackwell, 527–61.

Price, R. 1983: White-collar unions: growth, character and attitudes in the 1970s. In R. Hyman and R. Price (eds), *The New Working Class? White-collar workers and their organizations*, Basingstoke: Macmillan, 147–83.

Procter, I., and Padfield, M. 1998: *Young Adult Women, Work and Family: living a contradiction*. London: Mansell.

Procter, S. and Ackroyd, S. 1998: Against Japanization: understanding the reorganisation of British manufacturing. *Employee Relations*, 20 (3), 237–48.

Purcell, K., Hogarth, T. and Simm, C. 1999: *Whose flexibility? The costs and benefits of non-standard working arrangements and contractual relations*. York: Joseph Rowntree Foundation.

Raggatt, P. and Williams, S. 1999: *Government, Markets and Vocational Qualifications: an anatomy of policy*. London: Falmer.

Regional Trends 1998. London: HMSO.

Reich, R. 1991: *The Work of Nations: preparing ourselves for 21st century capitalism*. London: Simon & Schuster.

Rifkin, J. 1995: *The End of Work*. New York: Jeremy Tarcher/Putnam.

Ritzer, G. 1998: *The McDonaldization Thesis*. London: Sage.

Robertson, J. 1985: *Future Work: jobs, self-employment and leisure after the industrial age*. London: Gower/Maurice Temple Smith.

Robinson, F. 1988: *Post-industrial Tyneside: an economic and social survey of Tyneside in the 1980s*. Newcastle: Newcastle City Arts and Libraries.

Robinson, O. 1988: The changing labour market: growth of part-time employment and labour market segregation in Britain. In S. Walby (ed.), *Gender Segregation at Work*, Milton Keynes: Open University Press, 114–34.

Robinson, P. 1996: *Rhetoric and Reality: Britain's new vocational qualifications*. London: Centre for Economic Performance.

Roper, I., Prabhu, V. and Van Zwanenberg, N. 1997: (Only) just-in-time: Japanization and the 'non-learning' firm. *Work, Employment and Society*, 11 (1), 27–46.

Rorty, R. 1998: *Achieving our Country*. Cambridge, MA: Harvard University Press.

Rose, M. 1975: *Industrial Behaviour*. Harmondsworth: Penguin.

Rosener, J. 1990: Ways women lead. *Harvard Business Review*, October, 199–225.

Rowbotham, S. 1998: Weapons of the weak: homeworkers' networking in Europe. *European Journal of Women's Studies*, 5, 453–63.

Roy, D. 1960: 'Banana Time': job satisfaction and informal interaction. *Human Organization*, 18 (4), 158–68.

Rubery, J. 1998: Part-time work: a threat to labour standards. In J. O'Reilly and C. Fagan (eds), *Part-time Prospects*, London: Routledge, 137–55.

Rubery, J., Smith, M., Fagan, C. and Grimshaw, D. 1998: *Women and European Employment*. London: Routledge.

Sakolsky, R. 1992: 'Disciplinary power' and the labour process. In A. Sturdy, D. Knights and H. Willmott (eds), *Skill and Consent: contemporary studies in the labour process*, London: Routledge, 235–54.

Salaman, G. 1981: *Class and the Corporation*. London: Fontana.

Saunders, P. 1990: *Social Class and Stratification*. London: Routledge.

Savage, M., Barlow, J., Dickens, A. and Fielding, T. 1992: *Property, Bureaucracy and Culture: middle class formation in contemporary Britain*. London: Routledge.

Sayer, A. 1986: New developments in manufacturing: the just in time system. *Capital and Class*, 30, 43–72.

Sawbridge, D., Bright, D. and Smith, R. 1984: Industrial relations in north-east England. *Employee Relations*, 6 (4), 3–32.

Scott, A. 1994: *Willing Slaves? British workers under Human Resource Management*. Cambridge: Cambridge University Press.

Scott, A.M. (ed.) 1994: *Gender Segregation and Social Change*. Oxford: Oxford University Press.

Sennett, R. 1998: *The Corrosion of Character: the personal consequences of work in the new capitalism*. London: W. W. Norton.

Shaw, K. 1994: Continuity and change in urban governance: urban regeneration initiatives in the North East of England. In P. Garrahan and P. Stewart (eds), *Urban Change and Renewal: the politics of place*, Aldershot: Avebury, 49–65.

Simpson, R. 1998: Presenteeism, power and organisational change. *British Journal of Management*, 9, 37–50.

Sisson, K. 1993: In search of HRM. *British Journal of Industrial Relations*, 32 (2), 201–10.

Skeggs, B. 1997: *Formations of Class and Gender*. London: Sage.

Sly, F. 1993: Women in the labour market. *Employment Gazette*, November, 482–92.

Smith, P. and Morton, G. 1993: Union exclusion and the decollectivization of industrial relations in contemporary Britain. *British Journal of Industrial Relations*, 31 (1), 97–114.

Smithers, A. 1993: *All Our Futures: Britain's education revolution*. London: Channel Four.

Spender, D. and Sarah, E. 1980: *Learning to Lose*. London: Women's Press.

Spilsbury, M., Moralee, J. and Evans, C. 1995: *Employer's Use of the NVQ System*. Institute of Employment Studies Report 293. Brighton: Institute of Employment Studies.

Steedman, H. and Hawkins, J. 1994: Shifting foundations: the impact of NVQs on youth training for the building trades. *National Institute Economic Review*, 149, 93–102.

Stephenson, C. 1988: *Nissan and Single Union Agreements: the road forward or a dead end?* Newcastle upon Tyne: Tyne and Wear County Association of Trades Councils.

Stephenson, C. 1994: *Worker Consent to Lean, Flexible Production in a Depressed Regional Economy: a case study examination of two companies operating JIT*. Ph.D, University of Sunderland.

Stewart, P. 1997: Striking smarter and harder at Vauxhall: the new industrial relations of lean production? *Capital and Class*, 61, 1–7.

Stewart, P. and Vass, V. 1998: From 'embrace and change' to 'engage and change': trade union renewal and new management strategies in the UK automotive industry. *New Technology, Work and Employment*, 13 (2), 77–93.

Stewart, P., Garrahan, P. and Crowther S. (eds) 1990: *Restructuring for Economic Flexibility*, Aldershot: Avebury.

Stone, I. and Peck, F. 1992: *Defending the North: diversification of defence industries in Tyne & Wear*. Newcastle: University of Northumbria at Newcastle.

Storey, J. 1992: *Developments in the Management of Human Resources*. Oxford: Blackwell.

Storey, J. (ed.) 1995: *Human Resource Management: a critical text*. London: Routledge.

Storey, J. and Sisson, K. 1993: *Managing Human Resources and Industrial Relations*. Milton Keynes: Open University Press.

Strange, S. 1996: *The Retreat of the State: the diffusion of power in the world economy*. Cambridge: Cambridge University Press.

Stredwick, J. and Ellis, S. 1998: *Flexible Working Practices: techniques and innovations*. London: Institute of Personnel and Development.

Taylor, R. 1993: *The Trade Union Question in British Politics*. Oxford: Blackwell.

Tenner, E. 1996: *Why Things Bite Back: predicting the problems of progress*. London: Fourth Estate.

Terry, M. 1982: Organising a fragmented workforce: shop stewards in local government. *British Journal of Industrial Relations*, 20 (1), 1–19.

Terry, M. 1983: Shop steward development and managerial strategies. In G. Bain (ed.), *Industrial Relations in Britain*, Oxford: Blackwell, 67–91.

Thompson, P. and Ackroyd, S. 1995: All quiet on the workplace front? A critique of recent trends in British industrial sociology. *Sociology*, 29 (4), 615–33.

Thompson, P. and Warhurst, C. 1998: Hands, hearts and minds: changing work and workers at the end of the century. In P. Thompson and C. Warhurst (eds), *Workplaces of the Future*, Basingstoke: Macmillan, 1–24.

Thornley, C. 1996: Segmentation and inequality in the nursing workforce: re-evaluating the evaluation of skills. In R. Crompton, D. Gallie and K. Purcell (eds), *Changing Forms of Employment: organisation, skills and gender*, London: Routledge, 160–81.

Thornley, C., Contrepois, S. and Jeffreys, S. 1997: Trade unions, restructuring and individualization in French and British banks. *European Journal of Industrial Relations*, 3 (1), 83–105.

Thrift, N. 1999: Capitalism's cultural turn. In L. Ray and A. Sayer, *Culture and Economy after the Cultural Turn*, London: Sage, 135–61.
Tilly, C. 1996: *Half a Job: bad and good part-time jobs in a changing labour market*. Philadelphia: Temple University Press.
Touraine, A. 1986: Unionism as a social movement. In S. Lipset (ed.), *Unions in Transition*, San Francisco: ICS, 151–73.
Towers, B. 1997: *The Representation Gap: change and reform in the British and American workplace*. Oxford: Oxford University Press.
Trades Union Congress (TUC) 1999: Second generation academy trainees get organised. TUC press release, 5 February.
Transport and General Workers Union (TGWU) 1993: *One Union*. London: TGWU.
Trickey, H., Kellard, K., Walker, R., Ashworth, K. and Smith, A. 1998: *Unemployment and Jobseeking: two years on: a report of research carried out*. Leeds: Corporate Document Series (No. 87).
UNISON 1993: Newcastle City Works questionnaire for part-time workers in cleaning and catering. UNISON, Newcastle upon Tyne.
Vandenbroucke, F. 1998: *Globalisation, Inequality and Social Democracy*. London: Institute for Public Policy Research.
Veenis, E. 1998: Working parents: experience from the Netherlands. In E. Drew, R. Emerek and E. Mahon (eds), *Women, Work and the Family in Europe*, London: Routledge, 182–90.
Waddington, J. and Whitston, C. 1995: Trade unions: growth, structure, policy. In P.K. Edwards (ed.), *Industrial Relations: theory and practice in Britain*, Oxford: Blackwell, 151–202.
Waddington, J. and Whitston, C. 1997: Why do people join unions in a period of membership decline? *British Journal of Industrial Relations*, 35 (4), 515–46.
Wajcman, J. 1998: *Managing Like a Man*. Cambridge: Polity.
Walby, S. 1990: *Theorizing Patriarchy*. Cambridge: Polity.
Walby, S. 1997: *Gender Transformations*. London: Routledge.
Wallerstein, I. 1979: *The Capitalist World Economy*. Cambridge: Cambridge University Press.
Warde, A. 1992: Industrial discipline: factory regime and politics in Lancaster. In A. Sturdy, D. Knights and H. Willmott (eds), *Skill and Consent: contemporary studies in the labour process*, London: Routledge. 97–114.
Waters, M. 1995: *Globalization*. London: Routledge.
Weber, M. 1938: *The Protestant Ethic and the Spirit of Capitalism*. London: Unwin.
Weber, M. 1978: *Economy and Society*, vol. 1. Berkeley: University of California Press.
Webster, F. 1995: *Theories of the Information Society*. London: Routledge.
Weiss, L. 1997: Globalization and the myth of the powerless state. *New Left Review*, 225, 3–27.
Westwood, S. 1984: *All Day, Every Day*. London: Pluto.
Wickens, P. 1987: *The Road to Nissan*. London: Macmillan.
Wickens, P. 1993: Lean production and beyond: the system, its critics and its future. Paper to University of Sunderland, 29 January.

Wilkinson, A., Redman, T., Snape, E. and Marchington, M. 1997: *Managing with Total Quality Management*. Basingstoke: Macmillan.

Wilkinson, B. 1983: *The Shopfloor Politics of New Technology*. London: Heinemann Educational Books.

Williams, K., Haslam, C., Adcroft, A. and Roos, D. 1992: Against lean production. *Economy and society*, 12 (2), 321–54.

Williams, S. 1998: The Management of Employment Policy and Employment Relations in English Further Education Colleges. Unpublished paper, Milton Keynes: Centre for Education Policy and Management: The Open University.

Willis, P. Jones, S., Canaan, J. and Hurd, G. 1990: *Common Culture*. Milton Keynes: Open University Press.

Wilson, W. J. (ed.) 1993: *The Ghetto Underclass*. London: Sage.

Womack, J. P., Jones, D. T. and Roos, D. 1990: *The Machine that Changed the World*. New York: Maxwell Macmillan International.

Womack, J. and Jones, D. 1996: *Lean Thinking*. New York: Simon & Schuster.

Wood, A. 1994: *North–South Trade, Employment and Inequality: changing fortunes in a skill-driven world*. Oxford: Clarendon Press.

Wood, S. 1989: The transformation of work? In S. Wood (ed.), *the Transformation of Work*, London: Unwin Hyman, 1–43.

Wood, S. (ed.) 1982: *The Degradation of Work?* London: Hutchinson.

Wood, S. (ed.) 1989: *The Transformation of Work*. London: Unwin Hyman.

Wray, D. 1996: Paternalism and its discontents: a case study. *Work, Employment and Society*, 10 (4), 701–15.

Wright, E. O. 1976: Class boundaries in advanced capitalist societies. *New Left Review*, 98, 3–41.

Wright, E. O. 1985: *Classes*. London: Verso.

Wyatt, S. and Langridge, C. 1996: Getting to the top in the National Health Service. In S. Ledwith and F. Colgan (eds), *Women in Organisations: challenging gender politics*, London: Macmillan, 212–44.

Yorkshire and Humberside Low Pay Unit 1999: *Pay Inequalities in Britain: 1998/1999 information pack*. Batley: YHLPU.

Young, I. M. 1990: *Justice and the Politics of Difference*. Princeton NJ: Princeton University Press.

Younge, G. 1999: Called to account. *Guardian*, 30 August.

Index